Meeting God
in the
Silent Places
365 Daily Devotions

William W. Moore

James E. Cornwell Co.

435 E. Walnut Street

Springfield, Missouri 65806

(417) 619-4939

Copyright © 2015 by William W. Moore

ISBN: 978-0-9898137-5-4

LCCN: 2015953196

Author: William W. Moore

Cover Design: Harold Scherler

Prepared for Publication: JE Cornwell

Printed in USA

All rights reserved.

This publication; *Meeting God in the Silent Places, 365 Daily Devotions*, its content and cover are the property of William W. Moore. This book, or parts thereof, may not be reproduced in any form without permission from the author or publisher, exceptions are made for printed reviews, advertising, and marketing excerpts.

Introduction

This book is an attempt to make Christians think about the important things of our faith, and world. In thinking deeply about such things, it is hoped that we will grow in our knowledge and relationship with Jesus Christ and our sisters and brothers who share this planet with us.

The title: "Meeting God in the Silent Places" lifts up a much neglected aspect of our spirituality: the practice of silence. With cell phones, busy schedules, and countless things demanding our immediate, and constant attention there is little room for silence. Interspersed throughout these devotions are challenges to enter in to Silence where God is found.

Before Creation there was nothing but God and silence!

When the Hebrew people were fleeing the Pharaoh and arrived at the sea – with no way out – Moses declared: "fear not!... the Lord will fight for you, and you have only to be still!" (Exodus 14:13-14)

When Elijah fled for his life from the evil Jezebel, he hid in a cave where he met God in the silence of the "still – small – Voice." (I Kings 19:12b)

The Psalmist tells us that the Lord "leads (us) beside the still waters...(and there) He restores (our) souls..." (Psalm 23:2 & 3a)

God calls us through the Psalmist to "be still and know that I am God!" (Psalm 46:10) How do we know God to be God – by being still!

Isaiah says: "In quietness and trust shall be your strength." (Isaiah 30:15) And again on finding strength: "They who wait on the Lord shall renew their strength..." (Isaiah 40:31) NOT through endless chatter, but calmly, and quietly waiting upon the Lord!

Then our Lord speaks to the tumult of the sea: "Peace be still!" (Mark 4:39) THERE—He—is!

Paul writing to the church in Rome speaks of how "the Spirit intercedes for us with sighs too deep for words." (Romans 8:26b) That is wordless prayer. . . initiated by God while we wait in silence.

I hope that these pages will call you, among other things, to be still in God's Presence that you might KNOW your Creator God!

William Wilder Moore

March 14, 2015

Day 1

Genesis 1:1-2:3

Some scientists believe that the human race is here by happenstance. They think that carbon, oxygen, and other elements combined to create what became the first humans. That after millions of years human beings arrived in the evolutionary chain.

Did we get here by chance or by choice?

If by chance, then life has no meaning; no real worth – in fact we are alone in the vast indifferent night!

If by choice, then we can affirm: "in the beginning God created …" Now life has meaning, purpose, and worth!

We have a tradition at our house that each Fourth of July we celebrate our twin sons' birthday by my wife fixing a red velvet cake. When I look at the cake, I think: "There has to be a cook!" It didn't just happen! No amount of time can explain the simple concoction of this wonderful cake!

And when I look at the world with all its complexities, I think: "There has to be a Creator!" It couldn't have just happened! There has to be an adequate causal agent, and time alone is not such an adequate agent!

Science does not contradict the faith story! It just reveals more and more of the wonders and mysteries of creation! Genesis 1 is not a scientific treatise, but an affirmation that God is the Creator.

A grandfather took his grandson fishing. As they sat on the dock watching the sunset on the horizon, the lad said, "Grandpa, can you see God?" Grandpa smiled, then answered, "Son, sometimes I can hardly see anything else!"

Prayer: "O Lord, our Lord, when I consider the heavens which You have made …." I am overwhelmed with wonder and awe! Your handiwork is everywhere! (See Psalm 8:3-4)

Day 2

Acts 2:1-21

"When the day of Pentecost had come, they were all together in one place."

Can you recall a place where you encountered God?

I remember the old First Methodist Church in Lebanon, Missouri where I grew up. There were massive stained glass windows opposite each other on the sides of the sanctuary. They were made in Italy in the 1870's. I would study those windows, and then when the preacher began his sermon, I would lay over in my mother's lap and take a nap! One depicted Jesus in the Garden agonizing in prayer. The other showed him as the good shepherd holding a lamb with the mother ewe looking up with a sense of pride and peace. I felt a nearness to the One who suffered in love for me! "When the day of Pentecost has come, they were all together in one place."

"All these with one accord devoted themselves to prayer". (Acts 1:14). If we, in our spiritual walk, are to go further we must go deeper – deeper in prayer! We must return again and again to the quarry from which we were hewn – <u>back to prayer!</u>

Those gathered in the Upper Room in Jerusalem prayed for <u>10 days</u> before the spirit of God – the Spirit of the Risen Christ - was poured out upon them, and the Church was born!

A few moments before, they had been hiding out in fear. Fear that what happened to their Master would happen to them. Now they fearlessly went out into the streets and began to proclaim the Good News of Jesus Christ!

Why are we not more courageous in our walk? Because we have neglected <u>the discipline of prayer!</u>

Prayer: Lord! There are so many foes lurking in the darkness! Help me to lean this day on your everlasting arms that I may know the peace of your first followers! Amen.

Day 3

Luke 24:49; Acts 1:8

There has been much debate over the years about what happened at Pentecost (Acts 2:1ff). Jesus said that the first Christians, who were there that day, were to receive the Power of God! (Acts 1:8a) That is, those who waited in prayer, as noted in yesterday's devotion, would receive Power when the Holy Spirit came upon them. Those frightened souls, who were hiding out in prayer in Jerusalem, would receive a Power that would enable them – in spite of their fears – to face the enemy with courage!

John Wesley, and the early Methodists, understood this to be "assurance." Assurance is confidence in the face of death. That is, when they "received the Holy Spirit," these early Methodists became so aware of the Presence of the Risen Christ, that they realized if they died tonight they would go to be with God in Heaven! They came to know that He who had died and arose was now with them! In that is an awesome peace!

The Acts Christians received this Power, and went out to face the powers of evil and death with confidence!

Where is Nero? Where is the tyrannical Caligula? Where is all the insurmountable power of the Roman Empire? Yet, the Church of Jesus Christ lives on!

You face some awesome foes today! It is part of the human condition! Thus, the Lord speaks to you: "Wait – Pray – Receive Power!"

To put it another way: "Ask …seek…knock…" and He will "give the Holy Spirit to those who ask." (Luke 11:9-13) He alone gives you peace amid the storm! (See Matthew 8:24)

Prayer: Lord, I do not ask today for things that money can buy….I only ask to know your Presence for that is all I need! Amen.

Day 4

Romans 8:26-39

There comes a time in the Christian's life when "we do not know how to pray as we ought." (v.26a)

My father died in 1980 after a two year battle with emphysema. Daily he struggled to breathe, and many times it looked like he wasn't going to get his breath at all!

It was hard to know how to pray! I would have liked a miracle, but I knew that was not likely. I sometimes prayed that he could just die and go to be with the Lord!

Other times I would sit by his side in silence – "the Spirit himself [interceding] for [me] with sighs too deep for words." (v.26b)

Over the years I have found that that is my "best" praying!

"Private prayers" often become "ask-its."

The "Saturday Review" many years ago had a cartoon by William Hoest. It depicted a pajama clad youngster going off to bed, then turning toward his parents, and calling out, "I'm going to say my prayers. Anyone want anything?"

Sad, if the only times we heard from our children was when they wanted something!

We can do without wealth. We can do without health. We can do without family and friends, but we cannot do without God! How beautiful to spend some time in the Presence of the Lord, in silence: letting the Spirit do the "praying!"

Is this not the deepest form of prayer? "Too deep for words!" (v.26b)

Prayer: Spend five minutes in silence basking in the Light of God's Presence. To quiet your mind you will find it helpful to repeat the name of Jesus, or the 23rd Psalm. Imagine you are a sheep, Jesus the Shepherd. Otherwise, our mind easily turns to our "to do" list or "worry list."

Day 5

Genesis 32:22-31

If I were to name a biblical character that I most identify with it would be Jacob, for Jacob wrestled with God!

Jacob steals his brother, Esau's, birthright as the eldest son. Esau is mad enough to kill him, so Jacob flees to go live with his uncle in the valley of the Tigris and Euphrates rivers. There he marries and settles down.

In time Jacob's conniving ways get him in trouble with his uncle! So, he realizes it is time to run! Like the prodigal son of Jesus' parable, he decides to return home. As he arrives one evening at the Jabbok River, word comes that his brother, Esau, is coming with 400 men!

He sends his wives and flocks on across the river, and Jacob beds down alone. It is a frightening time! He does not know what tomorrow will bring. As you can imagine, Jacob spent a restless night on the river bank! He describes it as wrestling with a man all night!

The Man/God, Jesus, wrestled with God on the cross when the He cried: "My God, my God, why have you forsaken me?"

The apostle Paul wrestled with God when he announced he was ready to die! "The time for my departure has come!" II Timothy 4:6 "Better for me to go to the Lord, but for your sake...." Philippians 1:22-23.

The Psalmist often wrestled with God: "Even though I walk through the valley of the shadow of death..." -- a frightening time! Don't rush on to the great conclusion of this Psalm, as we are prone to do, or you will miss what is SO important here: wrestling with God!

Jacob was very close to God, you can't be far away and wrestle! In the morning light God blessed Jacob – yet left him with a limp, so he would remember the night. Every dark night for the soul is followed by the morning light. When we realize it was God – it IS God who was with us!

Prayer: Lord, I don't always understand "why?" but I do know "Who!" For it is YOU who are with me in my struggles holding in your hand a special blessing. Thank you, Lord! Amen.

Day 6

Matthew 14:22-33

Jesus made his disciples get into a boat (v.22). He remained behind and dismissed the crowd.

A storm arose on Lake Galilee. The wind blew! The waves broke into the boat! The disciples were terrified! Then Jesus came to them – walking on the water! (v.25)

How often He comes amid life's tempests!

Yet, the disciples did not recognize Him – thinking: If the storm isn't enough, now we have a ghost coming toward us!

Peter cries in hope mixed with despair: "Lord! IF it is you, let me come to you on the water!" (v.28). Jesus called him to come.

As he slid over the side of the boat he wondered how this was going to work out! But buoyed by a little bit of faith, he started walking - like a baby taking his/her first steps – with hands outstretched. With fear, excitement, and wonder in each step!

Almost to the Lord, he looked at the waves and felt the strong wind, and became afraid, and began to sink! (v.30). He cried out: "Lord, save me!" Jesus reaches down and lifts him out of his watery grave! (v.31).

Often God invites us to get out of the boat – out of our safety net – out of our familiar surroundings – and do the impossible: for GOD!

Prayer: Lord! Help me to remember that there is NO foe greater than You! Help me to come to You on life's stormy sea. Help me to step out in faith – that I might glorify your name! Amen.

Day 7

Genesis 45:1-7

What is the most difficult task to face the Christian? It is to forgive those who do us great harm!

A couple went to a Prayer Meeting at the church. It was the custom for the pastor to ask for prayer concerns. One elderly woman rose to share her need. At the same time her husband dozed off in the pew beside her. At the climax to her sharing she shouted: "I fight old Satan all week long!" Her words woke her husband. Not knowing what all she had shared, he protested: "But Pastor! I can't help it! She's just hard to get along with!"

You have some persons in your life who are difficult to get along with - difficult to forgive! We all do!

In our Scripture for today Joseph must have struggled with forgiving his older brothers. They were jealous of young Joseph, for he was his father's favorite son. So when he came carrying water to them in the heat of the day, they began to plot against him. One suggested they kill him! But finally they agreed to throw him in an old cistern until they could decide what to do. With Joseph in the dark pit pondering what was going to happen next, a caravan came by headed south to Egypt to sell their wares. The brothers flagged them down, and sold Joseph as a slave.

Joseph's future was now a hopeless one! He had lost all worldly possessions – all family and friends – all freedom to do as he pleased. He was at the mercy of his owners!

But God began to gradually work a miracle! (Most of God's miracles happen slowly.)

In time this Joseph caught the attention of the Pharaoh through his gift of seeing the future through dreams. He rose through the ranks of the Pharaoh's associates. Finally, he was appointed Secretary of Agriculture! He predicted a famine of seven years, and in the meantime directed that as much grain as could be grown – should be grown. He ordered that silos be built to hold the grain.

Sure enough the famine came, and amazingly Egypt was ready! But back home in Palestine his family was in dire straits! There Jacob heard of the abundance of grain in Egypt, and so he sends his sons to purchase grain there.

They arrive in Egypt and are directed to the Agriculture Department. Yes, they were ushered in before their brother, Joseph! But they didn't recognize him. Joseph could easily have had them arrested and killed! But, instead, he ordered his subordinates to leave the room. Joseph weeps as he tells them who he is. His brothers fall on their knees before him. But Joseph steps forward and embraces each of them through many tears. Then sends them home with wagons loaded with grain – free of charge!

Resentment is the poison we drink to kill our enemy! It destroys us physically, emotionally, and spiritually! (See Job 4:7-8.)

Thus, "pray for your enemies" that you may receive the love from God that enables you to forgive them as God forgives you. (Matthew 6:12).

Prayer: Lord, you prayed from the Cross: "Father, forgive them…" That included ME! Help me to forgive _____ _____. Amen.

Day 8

Romans 12:1-8

"To be or not to be?" are words made famous by Shakespeare's Hamlet. They are the challenge to us Christians today!

The world says: "It is OK to take advantage of the poor as long as you make a profit!" "It is all right to, like a vulture, feed on your sister or brother's mishaps – sharing the carrion with those who are a part of your flock." "It is fine to step on others for your political gain or personal success." "Sex outside of marriage is good – as long as you 'luv' one another, who needs commitment?!"

The list of sins is endless – not because they are in "the Book," but because of the harm they do to you and/or others!

Thomas Merton wrote: "We may spend our whole life climbing the ladder of success only to find our ladder is leaning against the wrong wall."

"To be or not to be?" is the question we ask ourselves today and every day.

We do not answer the question once when we are baptized, but millions of times throughout our lives! "To be or not to be?"

Prayer: Lord, help me to stand while all around me fall! Help me to not look down on anyone today, but to live simply as a beggar who tells another beggar where he/she received the bread. Amen..

Day 9

Exodus 3:1-15

We live in stressful times! It seems that danger lurks at every turn: danger from disease, danger from terrorist attack, danger from accident, dangers!

Moses faced uncertain days! He saw an Egyptian beating a Hebrew and he ran to his aid and killed the Egyptian. He became a "man on the run!" He ran northeast and crossed over into the desert wasteland of the Sinai Peninsula. Where could he go?! How could he survive?! The dangers were everywhere!

He finally came across some nomads and landed a job herding sheep – a most lowly job!

But, through watching over a flock of sheep in the desert, he learned, in time, that God was preparing him to lead the Hebrew people through that same desert to the Promised Land.

One day he saw a bush afire, but yet it was not being consumed! He thought: "this is strange! I shall go see what is going on!" So he drew near to the bush. Suddenly a Voice called out from amidst the bush: "Moses, Moses...take off your shoes...for you are standing on holy ground." (vs. 2-5).

It was then God called Moses to go lead his people out of slavery in Egypt to the Promised Land. Back to Egypt where there was a price on his head?! You've got to be kidding, God! He was to convince the pharaoh to give up the free labor that he and his people enjoyed?! You really got to be kidding now!

Could there be "burning bushes" that we pass by every day because we are too busy?

Two persons sitting in the same pew – a successful businesswoman and a tenant farmer – one leaves saying: "The organist hit a sour note today!" The other leaves saying: "The Mighty God spoke to me through that preacher! I must go and tackle impossible foes in the service of the Lord!"

Elizabeth Barrett Browning wrote:

"Earth's crammed with heaven,

And every common bush afire with God,

And only he who sees takes off his shoes,

The rest sit around and pick blackberries."

May you seek to "see" – with your very soul – the burning bushes by your path today, and "hear" the Mighty God speak to you out of the flames!

Prayer: Lord, I have missed some burning bushes along the way. I was so consumed with my duties – overwhelmed by the foes within and without! Lord, today I will seek your voice, and lean on your Everlasting Arms. Amen.

After thought: It is amazing what God can do through one person – WHOLLY surrendered to the Him!

Day 10

Exodus 14: 15-16 and 21-22

The Hebrew people, after being set free from slavery, came upon the Sea of Reeds blocking their path! If that weren't enough, Word comes that the Pharaoh had changed his mind, and had sent the cavalry (chariots) after them. Moses saw that their options were few or none!

Moses falls on his knees in earnest prayer. But God answered: "Why do you cry to me. Tell the people to go forward!"

Have you ever faced a roadblock? You HAD to go forward, but there was an insurmountable barrier in your way!

There comes a time, after much prayer, when we must stop praying and simply step out in faith!

My version of the story goes like this: Moses gives the order: "Forward!!" The mass of humanity begins to move. But as they did they murmured: "Has Moses lost it? He's got to be insane! That's the sea down there!" But the alternative was to go back into slavery, so they kept plodding.

They stepped into the sea (my version). They waded up to their waists – then to their chins! Only when they were sputtering in sea water did God act! He parted the sea, and made the ground beneath the sea dry, so that they were able to cross without getting mud on their shoes.

When I was eight years old God began calling me to the ministry. I didn't hear with my ears the Voice – it was rather a deep hunch in my soul.

As a teenager when I went to church camp in the summer – when I stopped long enough to listen – there was that Voice. "But!" I complained, "Lord you know I'm too shy to ever preach a sermon!" ("Tell the people to go forward.")

After I graduated from high school, and was preparing to go off to college, our pastor invited the Reverend Billy Fullerton from England to preach for three nights. He was touring the country preaching at various churches. Our family had him for a meal on his second day.

On the third night he asked, those who felt led to do so, to come forward for prayer. Suddenly the "Voice" said: "Bill, if you want to know whether I want you to go into the ministry – go forward for prayer." Many were going forward which gave me the courage to join in.

I went – then made my way to the far end of the chancel rail and knelt (I didn't want any preacher laying hands on me!)

Hardly had I knelt when he came – past a couple of dozen others – to me, and laid hands on my head and prayed: "Lord, call Bill into the ministry."

This call was later confirmed when I was at the little Sleeper Methodist Church. I will tell about that subsequently.

The first sermon was a terrifying experience for this very shy young man! I was hoping no one would come. But soon I was wishing more could hear the Good News!

In what aspect of your life is God calling you to step out in faith?

Prayer: Lord, give me courage today to step forward into the frightening future. I thank you that you are greater than all my foes I face. Amen.

Day 11

Matthew 20:1-16

Jesus tells a story: It was 6 a.m. when the owner of the vineyard went to town to hire workers for the day. Several were standing at the curb when he drove up. He said "Need a job?" They replied: "Yes!" so, they climbed on board. He told them he was paying $10 a day – a goodly amount for those days!

About 9 a.m. the owner of the vineyard saw, that with the abundance of the crop, he was going to need more workers. He went to town, and hired six workers – telling them I'll pay you whatever is right. They went with him and began picking the grapes.

Again about 3 p.m. he again goes to town and hires more. Then again at 5 p.m. At 6 p.m. the work for the day was done. It was the custom in Jesus' day for those hired last to be paid first. So, the owner asked the men to line up in order in which they were hired. He pulled out a wad of bills and gave those who had worked only an hour $10! The rest thought: "Wow! He is going to pay us a lot more than he said."

But when he came to the next group, he gave them $10 each – as he had promised. Grumbling began to spread through the crowd: "This isn't fair!!" Then he continued until he reached those he had hired at 6 a.m. giving them each $10.

The issue this parable raises is: Isn't God JUST?! The answer is, thank God He is not "just," for if the Lord was just we would be in trouble! We, and Jesus' hearers that day, must thank God that he is merciful! For we stand with those who received more than they deserved!

Jesus told the story to let us know that God's grace is limitless! We can't earn it, or be entitled to it, it is a free gift for all who turn in sorrow from their sins, and ask forgiveness.

Prayer: Lord, thank you for NOT giving us what we deserve, but for taking the punishment for our sin upon yourself so that we can be forgiven! Amen.

Day 12

Philippians 4:4-7

After several Sundays of study of the letter to the Philippians, a youngster commented to the teacher: "I like Paul's letter to the Filipinos." I like that!

"Do not worry about anything!" he writes. (v.6a) We are prone to say: "If only Paul knew about my troubles he couldn't be so positive!"

But Paul was in prison facing the very real possibility of execution! If that were not enough – he could be worried about the fledgling churches that he had established whose future was in question. His life was completely out of his control! Yet he could write: "Do not worry about anything."

"How?!" we ask.

Paul answers: "But in everything by prayer and supplication with thanksgiving let your requests be made known to God." (v.6b)

That is by telling God what worries us (i.e. "prayer and supplication"), and rehearsing all the ways God has been faithful in the past (i.e. "with thanksgiving") we are set free from worries.

Rehearsal theology - i.e. counting our blessings - builds our faith – our confidence – the assurance that all is well! In that is peace of mind!

In the days of sailing ships a man was on board a schooner transporting him from England to the colonies. On the third day out the ship was caught in a horrendous storm. The winds blew, the waves billowed high, and began to crash across the deck. The vessel shuddered at their impact! It appeared to the passengers below the deck that the ship would be torn asunder, and they would go down into a watery grave!

Suddenly the hatch opened, and the captain came down into the hold. A confident seaman, who had endured many such storms. He began to speak reassuringly, and as he spoke the passengers looked up into his face, and sensed that all is well.

Prayer: Lord, help us this day to look into your face that we too may know that all is well. Amen.

Day 13

Colossians 1:19; John 1:1, 14

Several years ago two devout Jehovah's Witnesses came knocking at our door. I knew they, along with a number of misguided persons of faith of other denominations, believe that Jesus is God's Boy. Not the "Son" as in the physical Presence of the Mighty God. So, I asked the two young men at my door how they interpreted John 1:1b: "...The Word was God?" They replied: "Oh, our Bible says He was 'A God.'" (But that is not what the original Greek says!)

Why does it make any difference?

If God the Father sent His boy into the world to suffer on the cross while he sat in Heaven – we would consider Him the penultimate child abuser!

But because the New Testament repeatedly declares, in various ways, that "God was in Christ reconciling the world to Himself." (II Corinthians 5:9) That tells us: God loves us so much that He came Himself to save us from guilt, and death! (See also: Colossians 1:19, & 2:9)

Share this Good News with your circle of friends today! GOD loves them too!

Prayer: Lord, thank you for coming to us in the Man/God of Galilee! Help me to have the courage to share this Good News with those in my circle of influence this day. Amen.

Day 14

Luke 17: 11-19

While we were living in Liberty, MO I picked up the Kansas City Star on the day before Thanksgiving. A headline read: "Giving Thanks is Out of Fashion Perhaps, But Life is Good."

As Christians do we have more petition days than we do thanksgiving days? That is, do we spend as much time asking God as we do thanking Him?

I am convinced that the measure of our joy in life is in direct proportion to the time we spend in thanksgiving.

In the Scripture lesson for today, Jesus heals the ten lepers, but only one comes back to thank Him. Jesus asks: "Where are the nine?" He did not need their thanks, but they needed to give thanks!

Life lived on the plain of ingratitude has no room for God! It is a life that cries: "Look what I have done!"

The leper who returned to thank the Lord received all Jesus intended to give the ten – not just healing of his body, but far more important: the healing of his soul in the gift of the grateful heart.

Prayer: Lord, give me a heart that overflows with gratitude that I may know this day the Joy of life in You! (Spend five minutes naming your blessings) Amen.

BLESSINGS
- CHRIST LIVING W/IN ME & THE HOLY SPIRIT
- I AM A CHILD OF GOD.
- SCHWEITZER - MY HOME CHURCH
- CHRISTIAN FRIENDS
- GARY BE ABLE TO LIVE AT HOME
- OUR HOME
- BOOMER
- LOVE OF NATURE
- CREATIVE TALENTS

Day 15

Romans 8:12-17; II Timothy 1:12b RSV

Wouldn't it be nice if we could KNOW God?! Think of it: if we knew God we would not worry about the world situation. Our personal woes would all but vanish. Death would no longer be something we dread or fear. Life would have meaning and purpose, for we would no longer be the accidental conglomeration of the cosmos – our lives would have eternal worth!

The New Testament Church, and countless sages through the centuries, cries out to us: "You CAN know!"

What else could explain the leaders of the New Testament Church moving from hiding in fear in Jerusalem (John 20:19) to coming out in the street to claim and name the Risen Christ as their Savior? (Acts 2:5-11) They had come to know the Christ that they at first only believed in. (II Timothy 1:12b)

How is this possible? We only get to know persons that we fellowship with – talk to – listen to – and walk the valleys together! Thus, to know God is to spend considerable time in quietness – walking and talking – traversing some trials together, and climbing some mountain tops with each other.

The early Christians devoted 10 days to prayer before the Spirit descended on them.

Prayer: Lord, teach me the blessed life that comes in the stillness. Teach me to pray. Teach me to listen. Teach me to know your Presence and power for the living of these days. Amen.

Day 16

Ephesians 2:1-10

English poet W.H. Auden visited a night club in New York City. Sitting at a table in the corner he studied the faces of the customers. Sensing their feelings of futility and boredom, he wrote on a napkin: "Faces along the bar cling to their average day. The lights must never go out; the music must always play, lest we should see who we are, lost in a haunted wood, children afraid of the night who have never been happy or good."

Most of us know what it is to be "lost in a haunted wood," but thanks be to God we also know that it is "by grace [we] have been saved through faith, ….this is not our own doing, it is a gift of God – not because of works lest anyone should boast." (Ephesians 2:8-9 RSV)

Paul goes on to write we are "created in Christ Jesus for good works". (v.10b)

O may we reach out today to the "faces along the bar," who are in our circle of influence, as "one beggar telling another beggar where he got the bread." (D.T. Niles)

Prayer: Lord, you have saved us from emptiness and fear to the victorious life that is in you. Help me to love another toward your Kingdom today. Amen.

GOD MADE US ALIVE IN CHRIST.
BY GRACE YOU HAVE BEEN SAVED.
THE GIFT OF GOD

Day 17

Hosea 11:1-9

Did you realize that the Apostle Paul was a parent? In I Corinthians 13:11b he writes how he "put away childish things" (KJV) i.e. toys in the floor, little clothes on the bed....

We ALL have children: our biological children, or children of the Community of Faith. Thus, we all have a God-given task to raise them in the faith!

Hosea gives us what I would call a kite-model to guide us in raising our children to be followers of Christ.

Children – like kites – must be led (Hosea 11:4). A study revealed that if Mother and Father actively worshipped God 72% of their children would follow their example. If Dad only attended – 55% of children would do likewise. If Mother was the one who worshiped the Lord on a weekly basis – 15% of the children in that family would follow in her footsteps. If neither parent worshiped weekly – only 6% would do the same.

This tells us how important the role of fathers is in rearing children in the faith.

Like kites, children must be limited. Hosea writes: "I led them with cords of compassion – bands of love". (v.4b)

Back in the 1950s when I was growing up we children could play outside – even after dark – until our Mother came to the door, called our name, and then we knew it was time to go home. But one of our playmates was never called home. How sad!

Children know we love them when we have guidelines for them to live by.

Third, children need to be lifted!

A kite does not get airborne until we lift it high and run into the prevailing wind.

Life has an abundance of critics, but only a few encouragers! Many persons would do well to count the true encouragers on both hands! Yet how vital they are!

Like a kite our children need to be loosed! The kite is not doing what it was made to do if it remains at arm's length.

Thus, we need to gradually give greater and greater freedom to our children. If we give freedom too quickly they will take a nose-dive, and we must quickly pull back on the "cord" and then begin all over releasing them to soar to greater heights. Until they are ready for college or career and we can just be there for them and watch them soar!

Prayer: Lord, help me to parent the children, grandchildren you have given me today. Amen.

Day 18

Genesis 22:1-14

Have you ever lost someone very near and dear to you? Even though we know they have gone to a "better place," the loss is still horrific! <u>Great love brings great pain</u>! The one left behind is the one who pays this price for the love shared over the years.

Abraham – the Father of the Judaeo-Christian and Islamic faiths – knew great pain. He and Sarah had no children. In the patriarchal society of his day it was expected that a man have a son.

When Abraham was 100 and Sarah 90, the Lord spoke to Abraham telling him that he and Sarah would have a son and would name him Isaac. (Who thinks God doesn't have a sense of humor!) Imagine Sarah going to worship, and when the joys and concerns were called for, she raised her hand, and with a voice cracking and creaking with age, she says: "I have some very good news! Abe and I are expecting a boy!" The place would explode with uncontrollable laughter, and joy!

<u>Isaac, whose name means laughter in Hebrew,</u> is born. Sarah and Abraham are overjoyed with this precious gift from God!!

But when the lad is five or six years old God speaks to Abraham: "Abraham! Abraham!" "Yes, Lord!" "Abraham, I want you to take Isaac up that mountain over there and sacrifice him to me."

They go. Together they gather the wood. Isaac asks: "Daddy! Where is our offering that we are going to sacrifice?" With tears streaming down his cheeks, he turns away from his son and answers: "God will provide a lamb."

Before the deed is done, God calls out: "Abraham! Abraham! Do not harm the boy! There is a lamb caught in the briars over there. Get it. Sacrifice it instead!"

Imagine the relief! Father and son embrace with many tears! Abraham pleads forgiveness of his boy, and the youngster says: "I understand, Dad! Your God – our God - must always be <u>our first love in life!</u>"

I must confess something. When we retired in 2007 after forty years of ministry my wife, Ginya, was diagnosed with a rare, and very aggressive uterine cancer. I was crushed! She was calmer – believing that whatever happened – it was going to be all right!

Suddenly I realized: I loved my Ginny as much as I loved God! And now in retirement my life now was more centered in her! God had lovingly taken me out behind the woodshed! And I got the message. "Take your first love, Ginny, up that mountain and sacrifice her up to Me!"

It was the most difficult thing I have ever done! And I knew it was going to take a lot more praying – a lot more delving into the Word – if I was to climb this mountain! This book is a part of the result of the journey.

Well, God provided a lamb! Ginny's cancer was caught early before it had spread, and now five years later there has been no recurrence – and more than this: as she would remind me – the Lord is once again: "King of Kings and Lord of Lords" in my life!

Prayer: Lord! Help me to see any other loves and loyalties that have crept on to the throne of my life – no matter how good and worthy they are - and help me establish you as Lord of all! Amen.

• SEEK THE TRUTH IN CHILDL
CHILDLIKE FAITH. -HI
RECEIVE THE TRUTH OF G
ONLY GOD HOLDS ALL THE
• "KNOW" MEANS MORE THA
AN INTIMATE RELATIO

THE REST THAT JESUS PROMISES IS LOVE, HEALING & PEACE W/GOD.

Day 19

Matthew 11:16-19, 25-30

The people of pre-Columbus days were right. The earth DOES have edges! For the Creator has placed certain limits on us. If we go beyond the limits we will pay a price!

We can go just a few minutes without air, some say 180 days without food, but only a few hours without water. We need potassium, magnesium, and salt in constant supply -- along with hope.

We can ignore these laws and get away with it for awhile – but only for awhile! We do not break God's laws – but break ourselves upon them! If I live against the grain of the universe I will get splinters: i.e. worries, fears galore!

Through all of this the Lord calls shouts: "Come to me all who labor and are heavy laden, and I will give you rest." (v.28)

As a lad of about 9, I heard my dog, Shep, barking ferociously in the back-yard. I thought he had probably treed an opossum, so I got my flashlight and went out to see. As I stepped into the blackness of the night, I heard chains rattling in the barn about fifty yards behind the house.

I raced back into the house – leaving the dog to fend for himself! I hurriedly told Dad that someone in chains was walking around the barn! He smiled. Took my hand, and together we went out into the darkness. I had never before noticed how calloused – how strong – my father's hand felt!

When we got to the barn, Dad shone the light into the open shed on the end of the barn revealing three cows – one of which was butting her head against some tire chains hanging from a nail on the barn wall. All was well!

How often we borrow trouble by running ahead of God – by imagining things that never come to fruition. Such times are calls to go to the Lord in prayer, and then go with Him from there.

Prayer: Lord! Forgive me for trying to play God! Enable me this day to reach up, and grasp your strong hand – and find rest for my soul. Amen.

Day 20

Matthew 13:1-9; 18-23

Have you ever felt like much of your efforts are in vain?

> A school teacher strives to instill learning and insight amid discipline problems – little appreciation and meager pay – and will often wait years before she/he sees any real results.

Every church has a roll with a number of persons who began the race, then gave up, drifted away. As one woman said to me, "I'm a Christian! But I'm just not practicing it at present!"

The imagery of the Sower in Jesus' parable is one that we all experience at one time or another!

As Christians our job is not to force the little seeds to grow. I have tried – believe me it doesn't work! That is God's job! Our task is to sow the seeds of love, and then <u>wait</u> – <u>pray</u> – and <u>wait</u> some more!

Saint Augustine had a mother, Monica, who prayed for him through his teen years ….through his twenties….through his thirties….and into his forties. Through all those years he rebelled against the God of her faith! It seemed as though her prayers would never be answered!

Then there came that day when Augustine stopped running. The seed that Monica had sown over the years came to fruition! Her beloved son came to Christ – gave his life to Him! In time Saint Augustine, as he would later be called, became Bishop of Hippo and one of the greatest theologians of the church!

Prayer: Lord, give me the patience to pray when it seems it is in vain. Teach me persistence in my prayer life, and in my witness of love, that I may daily walk a little closer to You. Amen.

A miracle of God's Holy Spirit as He uses your words to lead others to Him.
Root in faith.

9 - He who has ears, let him hear • Spiritual hearing.
    A deeper listening.
    Spiritual truth.

Day 21

Luke 10:25-37

An attorney tries to trap Jesus with this question: "What must I do to inherit eternal life?" Will He, as a good rabbi, lift up the Law as the sole answer to his question? No, Jesus points ultimately to the importance of loving "the Lord your God... and your neighbor as yourself."

The attorney comes back with another question: "Who is my neighbor?"

Jesus answers with the Parable of the Good Samaritan. In that parable it looks like Jesus is saying that the one left beaten and robbed is the neighbor. But, look again. Jesus is saying it is the Samaritan who is our neighbor - the hated Samaritan. The attorney, and all the rest of the Lord's hearers would be shocked that the Jesus would have the Samaritan be the hero of the story! Thus Jesus was calling them to look again at the Samaritan as one for whom good deeds were possible.

Who are we prejudiced against? Who must we allow to be neighbor to us? This is not just semantics, it falls at the root of what it means to be a Christian! Wow!

To love the Lord our God with all our heart is to love ALL His children - as our neighbor!

Prayer: Lord, forgive me of my biases against others. Instill within me a desire to be a neighbor to those persons too, and to allow them to be a neighbor to me. For your sake and the Gospel's. Amen

LOVE THY NEIGHBOR.
• ACTING TO MEET THE PERSON'S NEED.

Day 22

Luke 2:41-51

When Jesus was twelve years old His parents took Him to Jerusalem for the feast of the Passover. As they were returning they finally realize they had forgotten Jesus! "Supposing Him to be in the company" of the travelers who were with them.

Have you ever forgotten Jesus for a day – a week – or more?

They simply walked away! Isaiah says: "All we like sheep have gone astray." (Isaiah 53:6) Sheep don't have any evil intent. When they go astray, they simply feed away from the shepherd. But that is the way they get into trouble! For out there are wolves and coyotes that can devour them!

Joseph and Mary found Jesus when they retraced their steps back to Jerusalem – to the Temple.

Years ago I took a group of youth in the church van to a district event in another town. I was not familiar with where we were going, and missed a turn. Finally I realized I had made a mistake! We didn't get back on track until we retraced our steps back to the intersection, and went the right direction.

We can leave Jesus behind when we – without evil intent – simply wander away. It is not until we retrace our steps back to the neglected prayer life – back to worship and service – that we begin to find our way once again.

Prayer: Lord, we are prone to wander away from you. Help me to be aware as soon as I stray, so that it doesn't become so difficult to find my way back. Amen.

ASPIRE TO BE AS MUCH LIKE CHRIST AS POSSIBLE.
DEVOTED TO GOD'S DESIRES RATHER THAN OUR OWN

Day 23

Matthew 5:38-48, especially v.48

A woman wrote "Dear Abby," the advice columnist, "Dear Abby, I am single, 40 years of age, and would like to find a man about the same age who has no bad habits." Abby responded: "So would I!"

In our youth we may well have imagined a person of the opposite sex who would make that perfect wife/husband. But such a person does not exist – unless, as one woman put it, "The only perfect person was my husband's mother!"

Yet, Jesus said: "YOU must be perfect, as your heavenly Father is perfect." (v.48)

If you note the discussion concerning love leading up to this, you realize Jesus is talking of being perfect in love!

If you are not planning to attain perfection in love, then how much less than that are you willing to accept? That opens us up to all kinds of compromises with lovelessness in our lives.

In January 1968, while attending the Candler School of Theology in Atlanta, I was asked by a fellow student to take over his church down near Warm Springs, Georgia. He was graduating from seminary, and the district superintendent told him to look for a student to take over.

I went to "try out" with the congregation, very much aware of the rampant racism across our country and of its presence in there in "old south" of the 1960s. So as I preached, I said: "The 11:00 hour on Sunday morning is the most racially segregated hour of the week!"

After the service the people were most gracious to us! But no one said a word about whether I passed or failed. On Monday, the phone rang and the patriarch on the other end of the line said: "Bill, we would like for you to come again Sunday – to try out." I went back and preached a sermon realizing I had been too bold in splashing cold water in the faces of strangers! I needed to get to know them. Love them. THEN challenge them on any lovelessness present among them. I had been prophetic – but not loving under the circumstances. Those people taught me a LOT about the Love of God, and paradoxically, because they were followers of the Master, they came to see and accept that all was not well in their own lives.

Prayer: Lord, help me to often pause in your Word and Presence that I might become more loving in every way. Amen.

Day 24

Mark 9:2-9

One of the strangest stories in the Bible is recorded in Mark 9. Our Lord had been very busy, and as a result He was tired! So, He takes Peter, James, and John and leads them up a high mountain to have some "down time" as we would say.

Then it happened! There appeared to them Elijah and Moses! - Hold it! They have been dead for centuries, and yet they are there with them on the mountain!

Hebrew 12:1 declares: "We are surrounded by so great a cloud of witnesses!" That is: those who die in the Lord and go on before are not off in some distant Heaven – they are here -surrounding us like a cloud.

In the great Doxology that the Church has sung for centuries, we sing: "Praise God from whom all blessings flow. Praise Him all creatures here below. Praise Him above ye heavenly host. Praise Father, Son and Holy Ghost."

I imagine a great conductor leading the massive choir, when it comes time for those of us "here below" to come in, she gestures toward us with the baton. Then, the "heavenly host" - she looks up to the saints above, and points for their moment to chime in.

In worship we are especially near to the heavenly host as were the four on the mountain long ago. Then when we share in Holy Communion, the tradition passed down was for the clergy person to cry: "Therefore with angels and archangels and all the company of Heaven we laud and magnify Your name!" Again in the hymn:

"The Church's One Foundation", we sing of "mystic sweet communion with those whose rest is won."

Some Sundays when I stand to preach I sense their presence in a powerful way! In so doing I feel encouraged – cheered, and emboldened to not let them or our Lord down!

Prayer: Lord, thank you for the possibility of communion with you and the saints! Help me to run the race today in such a way that I don't let them, or you down. Amen.

GOD-CENTERED

Day 25

Matthew 6:1-6, 16-21

Jesus taught that there should be a secret life for every Christian.

It should involve three things: fasting, praying, and giving. Each of these should remain secret in that we should not use them to boast – like the Pharisees did. Because selfish pride is cancer for the soul.

Jesus says: "WHEN you fast …" (v.16). Our Lord does not say: "IF" you fast – as though it is optional – but "when" i.e. it is expected!

Christians have practiced fasting in differing ways down through the centuries: total fast – abstaining from all food and drink: which needs be limited for health–sake. More commonly, Christians have abstained from food for a period of time – not to lose weight – but for spiritual benefit.

What is the spiritual benefit? We cannot give God a life that is running out of control! We first have to get a hold of the reins – bring the wild steed under control – and then hand it over to the Master.

Fasting helps develop spiritual muscle, by bringing under control a basic appetite – in this case: for food – that we might be better disciplined in other areas of our Christian walk: prayer…. loving…. serving…

Second, Jesus says: "WHEN you pray… you should go into your closet and shut the door…" lest you pray to the wrong audience! (Preachers, beware!)

Prayer, I believe, is best described as friendship with God. What do friends do? They talk AND listen. They enjoy quiet moments – when neither speaks or listens. It is a time when He speaks for us: "prays" for us: "With sighs too deep for words" (Acts 8:26b).

Third, Jesus says: "WHEN you give…" not "IF you give!" Jesus taught us that the tithe or tenth of our take-home-pay is a minimal offering. For many of us, our offering should be over-and-above the tithe.

In light of the gift of God in Christ, how can I claim to be a follower of the Crucified One without a sacrificial gift of my money?!

Prayer: Lord, guide me in my fasting, praying, and giving that I might reflect your Presence in my daily life. Amen.

Day 26

Jeremiah 31:31-34

There are times in each of our lives when we do things, or fail to act and cause others pain. We would love to strike the "delete button," and erase it from our lives! In about 600 B.C., God said to the prophet Jeremiah concerning the sins of the people of Israel: "I will forgive their iniquity, and remember their sin no more!" (v.34b)

Think of it, for this is Good News: All of the sins and missteps of our past can be erased by God - forgiven!

God says that not only does He forgive our sins, but remembers them no more! That is: when God forgives, He forgets it – forever!

I don't know about you, but after I ask for and receive God's forgiveness, I still remember the sin clearly. I still feel guilty! So, again I go to God and pray: "Lord forgive me!" And God answers: "Bill! Forgive you of what?!" For He has forgotten it!

Thus, our guilt is imagined guilt! It is just as painful as real guilt. Thus, we need to do some self-talk! "Bill, I know you still feel guilty, but God has forgiven you. Forgive yourself! Quit beating up on yourself. God loves you - love yourself a little more!"

Prayer: Lord, help me to love myself as you love me. Help me to accept your forgiveness, and live this day thanking you for your wondrous grace. Amen.

WHEN WE TURN OUR LIVES OVER TO GOD, HE, BY HIS HOLY SPIRIT, BUILDS INTO US THE DESIRE TO OBEY, HIM.

Day 27

Mark 8:31-38

I have often worked with surviving spouses in their grief. I have also painfully witnessed other Christians who did not understand their grief. "Does he not know that his wife is in Heaven?!" "She is better off than we are." Or: "It must be God's will." All this is our effort to squelch the grief process - it is our way of saying: "Stop grieving in front of me, I can't stand the pain!"

It is NOT that the grieving one doesn't believe, but that they miss the loved one now! And the more he loved her the greater the pain! Could it be that as Christians ours is a greater pain, because of the love Christ has instilled within us? Thus, as Christians we must not add to another's pain by questioning their faith!

At Lazarus' death the scripture says: "Jesus wept." (John 11:35) The people standing around declared: "How He must have loved him!" (John 11:35)

Survivors pay the price for a love shared. I have found that some find consolation in knowing that the pain they feel is suffered on their loved one's behalf, who would have had to suffer this pain if they had been the survivor. So he/she can say: "I am enduring this pain for them!"

Prayer: Lord, help me be sensitive to those I meet who are grieving, that I might not add to their grief with platitudes – but listen and hurt with them. Help me in grief to be comforted in the thought that I am grieving on my loved one's behalf. Amen.

Day 28

John 20:1-18

Have you ever asked: "WHY did Mary Magdalene not recognize the Lord after he arose?"

(v.14) She knew Him well, but still didn't realize that this One standing before her was the Lord!

Oliver Wendell Holmes went walking one day back in the days of innocence. Several blocks down the street a young girl came out of her yard and walked with him. Suddenly she announced: "I must go home." The famous jurist said: "Well, when you get home tell your mother that you have been walking with Oliver Wendall Holmes!"

Unimpressed she said: "Well, when you get home tell your wife you have been walking with Mary Susanna Brown."

Why didn't Mary Magdalene recognize the King of Kings? There are several possibilities. First she may not have recognized Him because – though He arose bodily – His resurrection body was different from His earthly body. Second, it could be – and at least partially was – that she had seen Him die, and you don't expect a day after the funeral to see the person walking around in the cemetery. Third, it could be the tears in her eyes blurred her vision.

Whatever the reason or reasons, how often do you and I meet Him, and not recognize Him?! Life teaches us to see gardeners – but not God - human possibilities, but not divine!

Jean Millett, the French artist, tells of an experience he had as a boy. Late one afternoon he went for a walk with his father. Finally the sun began to set with its most glorious hues of gold, orange, and red. His father turned, took off his cap, and studied the beauty for a long time. Finally he spoke: "Son, it – is – God!"

Mary said, "I have seen the Lord!" (v.18)

Prayer: Lord help me to see you today in the flower's bloom – the baby bird in the nest – the child's laughter at play. Help me to be – still – and know you are God! Amen.

Day 29

John 20: 24-28

I thank God for Thomas! For everyone, whose faith doesn't come cheaply, has a special relationship with the Lord.

God is like a mother. We yet to be born babes cannot see her face. No matter what direction we reach out – there is darkness! We may not yet believe in Her, but that does not matter to Her, the love she feels toward us – the constant care and nurture she gives us - abides nevertheless!

One day we shall see Her face, and in that moment of birth we will cry with Thomas of old: "My Lord, and my God!" (v.28)

THEN we will be ready to face the storms of life! THEN life will have meaning and eternal purpose! THEN we shall cry: "Was ever love like this?!" THEN we will have peace beyond understanding! (Philippians 4:7)

A young man, who was fitting me for a suit, asked: "What do you do?" (The answer brings horror or affirmation! If horror – the person is afraid I'm going to take up an offering, pin them to the floor until they affirm faith, or do something religious.) I answered: "I am a pastor." He responded: "I am an atheist!" God put a response in my mouth that I would never have thought of, I responded: "That's all right, God believes in you!" Stillness swept over us, as the young man pondered the possibility of a God THAT BIG!

Prayer: Lord, help me to speak when I need to speak – and be quiet when I need to step back – not mess things up – and simply trust you! Amen.

Day 30

Psalm 23

Read again Psalm 23. Read it slowly…prayerfully…realizing you are one of the sheep and Jesus is the Shepherd. (Spend several minutes doing this.)

What did the Shepherd do – toward you? Did He speak to you? What did He say? Does this encounter with God's Word cause you to view the issues you are facing today differently? (Do this kind of reading/praying of the scripture stories often. God will speak more – and – more to you as you practice this discipline.)

My father was a shepherd – for one month. In the 1920s he went to Wyoming. He worked for some time on the LAK Ranch in eastern Wyoming outside Newcastle. Dad was good at lassoing! Once he caught a steer with what turned out to be a figure-eight loop around its hind feet – stopping it with his horse just as its head went through a barbed wire fence!

A sheep rancher asked him to shepherd some of his sheep. Dad agreed. He was taken out in the rolling, arid hills "fifty miles from nowhere." He was given enough food and water for a month and a shepherd's wagon and told that the rancher would be back in 30 days.

My father was not a Christian at the time.

After three weeks he was running very low on water! In spite of rationing what he had left, he ran out with five days to go! He said, "In a region where it never rained in the summer, he realized he could be dead by the time the rancher returned!" The next day a single, small, dark cloud appeared. It moved over his wagon, and started pouring! Dad jumped into his wagon, and got pots and pans which he placed around the wagon to catch the rain as it rolled off the canvas. He got more than enough to drink, cook with, and even bathe in for those last few days!

"The Lord is my Shepherd – I shall not want!" (23:1) -- Even when you don't know the Shepherd!

Prayer: Lord! How often you have provided for me when I wasn't aware it was from You! Forgive me, Lord! Give me this day a grateful heart that my heart may sing your praise, and be mindful of Your sufficiency and care. Amen.

Day 31

Romans 8:12-17

Back in the 1970s there was a popular movie called "Close Encounters of a Third Kind". The movie centered around encounters with UFOs and the little green men that are supposed to go with them. The movie's title came from the three levels of encounter with these foreign visitors to earth.

The first level of encounter is hearing about them. The second is believing that they exist. And the third level of encounter is seeing them – knowing they exist!

Well, my preacher mind jumped on this ready-made sermon! For if you substitute God for the green men – every person on the earth has had the first level of encounter. Many the second, and a few the third.

The apostle Paul goes to considerable length to affirm his third level of experience with God, when he writes: "I know whom I have believed." (II Timothy 1:12b) Once he had only heard about God. On another level he had believed in Him. And finally he had come to know God!

John and Charles Wesley, and the great evangelical revival that gave birth to Methodism, had a heavy emphasis on assurance: i.e. knowing personally the Lord! New Christians were asked to "pray through." That is, pray until they received assurance, and then they would WANT to go out and share it with others.

Prayer: Lord, thank you for seeking me all my days! Give me a sense of your Presence in my walk this day – that I may come to

"know you more fully, and love you more dearly day-by-day-by day." Amen

BEING LED BY THE SPIRIT.

Day 32

I John 4:7-21

Many well-meaning Christians – without thought – cross the line into hate! Often you hear it said, "I love the sinner, I just hate their sin!" There is a razor thin line that most of us are not able to maintain: "I love … but hate…"

You know the issues that provoke these comments. The problem is the line runs right down the middle of each of us! The examples are endless!

In 1553 noted churchman and theologian John Calvin stood on the outskirts of Geneva and supervised the burning at the stake of Servetus – all because Servetus did not affirm the orthodox understanding of the Trinity!

John Wesley, the founder of Methodism, said: "[We] can be as orthodox as the devil – and as wicked!"

Do we still believe in love? Do we really believe in its Power – God's Power – to redeem lives?

A man hanging on a Cross is not our idea of a model to replicate, and certainly not any demonstration of Power! Yet we know that the cross reminds us of an empty tomb, and the resurrection Power of God to redeem lives!

Scores of times the New Testament reminds us that humble, self-sacrificing, love is the hallmark of what it means to be a Christian!

Prayer: Lord, I wish your Word didn't teach that! For to abide by it is impossible! I guess that is why I must abide in You. Help me, Lord, to do that today. Amen.

21: WHOEVER LOVES GOD MUST ALSO LOVE HIS BROTHER.

Day 33

Psalm 18:28

The Psalmist writes: "You light my lamp" (Psalm 18:28).

Every child, every spouse, every person has a lamp. For every good trait – skill realized ... we can point back to a person who encouraged us – who lit the lamp in our lives.

Poet Robert Burns was eating in a Scottish Inn with some friends. The young waiter bringing the tray of food and drinks tripped and fell. Broken goblets scattered across the floor along with the plates of food.

The irate innkeeper came running, grabbed the lad and shook him, and amidst a shower of curses fired him on the spot!

As the dejected young man walked out, Robert Burns followed him. Caught up with him, and putting his arm around the lad's shoulders said: "Remember, you have a bright future!"

Sir Walter Scott never forgot that! Later, while he was writing "Lady of the Lake" and "Ivanhoe" he said: "the greatest lift I ever got was when Bobbie Burns told me I could be somebody."

A lamp was lit in a young man's life that transformed it! You will meet persons today who desperately need such an encouraging word!

Prayer: Lord, help me be a lamplighter today to those you send my way, that they may realize all you have instilled in them to be. Amen.

Day 34

I Samuel 3:1-20

"The word of the Lord was rare in those days." (v.1b) There are dry times – when rain from heaven does not fall – when spirits wilt.

In Samuel Beckett's play: "Waiting for Godot", two men sit under a dead tree in the middle of the stage, and wait! They are waiting for Godot – God that is – to come and rescue them. Throughout the whole play they wait, and Godot never comes! The play ends with the two of them still sitting – waiting beneath the dead tree.

If that isn't depressing enough what is?! Each of us experience the dry times when it seems that God is asleep – not moving – not speaking.

Imagine the shock of the young Samuel – while serving under the priest, Eli - when God called: "Samuel – Samuel!" (v.4) Samuel is sure that it is Eli who is calling, so he goes and checks on his priest. Three times the Lord calls, and three times he runs to Eli asking what he wants.

How often we understand too soon! We think what we "hear" is a human voice – and maybe it is! But in the midst of it all we fail to hear – to realize it is the Mighty God who is speaking – calling our name in the middle of our night! "Samuel! Samuel!"

Finally, Samuel answered: "Speak, Lord, for you servant hears." And God called Samuel to be His prophet. (v.20)

God calls the most unlikely persons – even a young boy – at unlikely times – to do unbelievable tasks!

Today, He calls your name!

Prayer: Lord, help me to hear – to go – to do your work in our time. Amen.

Day 35

II Corinthians 4:5-12

The world does not need a course on good behavior – it needs Christ who changes us from the inside out!

But the only Christ the world will see or hear is YOU! If you're with me on this one, you are probably saying: "The world is in trouble then, because I'm not a Christ!" Yet, is that not the calling of every Christian: i.e. to be a "little Christ" – as Martin Luther said. (See Romans 13:14, I Corinthians 2:16, Philippians 1:2)

"But!" we protest with Paul, "We are only the earthenware jars!" Cracked jars! Broken jars! Imperfect jars! Paul says, Yes that is right! – common – clay – pots! "To prove that such an overwhelming power belongs to God – not us!" (v.7b) It was the same power that transformed Paul the murderer into Paul the apostle of Jesus Christ, and has kept the faith thriving through lions' dens and tyrants' power ever since!

AND – you –and I – have the privilege of carrying this Treasure: i.e. Christ, to a lost and dying world! So that when one comes to Christ, we have to give God all the credit!

Prayer: Lord, we thank you that you are able to use us broken vessels to enable the world to see your light. Help us not to excuse ourselves by our inadequacies, but rather claim Your adequacy to use even us. Amen.

6. FOR GOD, WHO SAID, "LET LIGHT SHINE OUT OF DARKNESS," MADE HIS LIGHT SHINE IN OUR HEARTS to GIVE US THE LIGHT OF THE KNOWLEDGE OF GOD'S GLORY DISPLAYED IN THE FACE OF CHRIST

Day 36

Judges 7:1-21

Back in the early 1960s we learned to sing: "We shall overcome – someday … God is on our side…" Of course the song was the anthem of the Civil Rights Movement. Dr. Martin Luther King, Jr. was the most noted representative of the cause. He was a reluctant leader! Persons who had witnessed his charisma and great speaking ability saw in him the potentiality of an outstanding leader. But he had to be talked into doing "just one" protest, and the rest is history – for God was there!

Gideon was another instrument of God. He had a little army of 32,000 men. The Midianites who stood against him and his men numbered in the tens of thousands: like locusts in the valley – too many to count!

God spoke to Gideon: "Gideon, you have too many men! Tell everyone who is afraid to go home!" (Who said God doesn't have a sense of humor!) The result: 22,000 packed up and left! Now Gideon has 10,000 soldiers against impossible odds!

God speaks again: "Gideon" "What is it Lord?" "Take your soldiers down to the stream and let them drink." (Their tongues were sticking to the roofs of their mouths! Have you ever been that nervous?!) "Those who lap the water like a dog will qualify for your army. The rest send home." Only 300 lapped – like dogs! "With these, I will deliver the enemy into your hand."

Gideon takes his little band. Surrounds the enemy, and with torches blazing and trumpets blaring GOD delivered the Midianites into their hands!

Often – should I say ALWAYS – when God has a great work to do, He calls upon the committed few, so that He may be glorified!

Prayer: Lord, help me to see that there is no foe too great – no task too large – but what you and I can take it on – and conquer! Amen.

Post thought: For you preachers and teachers this story can be outlined: Committed to a cause/ Dedicated to a discipline/ Surrounded by support/ Provided with Power!

Day 37

Mark 4:35-41

Many of you have read the story of the Storm at Sea, so you have seen the "movie" before – you know how it comes out. Thus, this is one of those scriptures that is harder to deal with – to mine from it something new!

Note that the disciples were doing the Lord's will when they got in trouble! Jesus asks them to go across the Sea of Galilee to get away – to rest – when the storm strikes.

When Rembrandt painted "The Storm at Sea" he included not 12 disciples and the Lord, but 13! When you look close, Rembrandt is in the boat too!

Storms come to every life! Even – we might say – especially to Christians! To keep us close. To keep us leaning on the Lord. Often God does not save us from the storms of life, but in the storms of life!

Sometimes we even cry out: "[Lord] do you not care that we perish?!" For God is often slow, in human terms. But we sailors also know how he often does speak …. and there [is] "a great calm". (v.39)

Prayer: Lord, I don't like the uncertainties! But again I know that you are with me, and in your own time will speak peace – the greatest gift of all! Amen.

Day 38

Matthew 6:9-13

Forgive me, Lord, in the same way I forgive others. That is what Jesus was saying here in verse 12.

We all have known persons who were very difficult to forgive. It was difficult for me to forgive the doctor and staff who could see that our son, Wesley, was purple with lack of oxygen at birth, but did not seek to give him emergency care. Instead the nurse carried him out of the delivery room, and walked to the nursery some seventy-five feet away. That left him mentally challenged.

Forgiving those who do us great harm is actually impossible for us alone!

In August 1992, we went to England. One day we visited the ruins of Coventry Cathedral which had been destroyed by German fire bombs during World War II. The parishioners left the walls of their once majestic cathedral standing with the insides gone - as a reminder of the evils of war. Where once the altar stood, they placed two charred beams in the form of a cross. Beneath it I read: "Father forgive!" NOT: "Father forgive THEM," for they were giving testimony to the fact that we are ALL sinners – saved by grace!

Thus, we find power to forgive as we pause often before the Cross, and remember the price the Christ made to forgive us.

We will never find peace until we forgive! We never know the love of God outside the Cross!

Prayer: Lord, help me to forgive _____ as you have forgiven me. Amen.

Day 39

Matthew 6:9-13

Two men were walking in a field when they spotted an angry bull charging toward them! They climbed a small tree nearby, and as soon as they were about 8 feet off the ground, the bull arrived, and began to butt the tree. It swayed back and forth, and the men knew their moments to hang on were limited! In panic, the one called out to the other; "Pray for us!" "I don't know any prayers", came the reply. "Well, say something!" Remembering hearing his father pray when he was a child, he cried: "Lord, for what we are about to receive – make us truly grateful!"

Have you ever doubted that God was going to provide for you what you needed? In verse 11 of our lesson for today Jesus taught us to pray with confidence: "Give us this day our daily bread". Or: "Give us today our basic needs".

Remember in Exodus 16 how God provided for the Israelites – in the barren desert of the Sinai – manna and drink each day!

We have each experienced God's sufficiency! Recalling those blessings fills our hearts with gratitude, increases our faith for tomorrow, and gives us peace and joy!

Prayer: Lord, let my heart flow forth in gratitude, that my life may sing your praises.

(Spend two minutes recalling what you have to be thankful for.) Amen.

Day 40

Romans 5:12-17

Years ago noted psychiatrist Dr. Karl Menninger wrote a book entitled: "Whatever Became of Sin?" The idea he developed was: No culprit – No cure! If the doctor cannot determine the cause of the malady, he or she will not be able to come up with a cure!

The problem in the last couple of decades is we have largely ruled out sin as a reality. Thus, society's ills are now to be fixed by resolutions to do better – education about harmful behavior – or threats from the justice system. But all these have utterly failed to save us from the breakdown of the family, violent crime, addiction to drugs, wars and rumors of wars, meaningless living…

Paul writing to the Church at Rome asks: "Wretched man that I am – who can save me from this body of sin and death?" Then he concludes: "Thanks be to God through our Lord Jesus Christ!" (Romans 7:24-25)

Our problem is sin: i.e. a broken relationship with our Maker, that leads us to commit destructive acts. For over 2000 years Christian people have affirmed the problem, and have known that Christ is the answer. For when we encounter a Love like is seen in the Lord, persons take on worth. We begin to respect each other. Further, we want to live a life that is pleasing to our Creator.

The hymn, "When I Survey the Wondrous Cross," states it well: "Love so amazing, so divine, demands my soul, my life, my all!"

We know the culprit, and we know the Cure - and His name is Jesus!

Prayer: Lord, help me to daily confess my sins, and to live today a life of love that draws all persons to you. Amen.

Day 41

Romans 16:1-16

Homiletics professors tell us, when planning a sermon, "Stay out of the lists!" A list of names, like our scripture lesson can be like quicksand! You can easily slip beneath its ambiguity and "die!"

But we each have a list! I would dare say that the persons who we would name are persons who over the years – encouraged us – believed in us even when we did not believe in ourselves! They are those who – through all our years – stood with us in trial. Their names would be on our list!

Our dear friend, Dr. Nancy Curry, has a niece who is blind. Nancy is very close to her. When she heard that her niece had a chance to go skiing in Colorado with other blind youth, she paid her way so she could go too! The trip was a glorious experience!

After she returned, she wrote Nancy a thank you. She concluded with: "God said, 'Let there be light' ... and there was none. God said, 'Let there be light!'... and there was none. God said, 'Let there be light!!'... and there was none. So God sent me Nancy." You can hear the angels sing as you sink into that!

Paul's lists were persons who had been little Christ's to him – standing by him – supporting him – saving him endless times. Ponder your list with reverence!

Prayer: Lord thank you for my list, few in number, but great in the difference they have made in my life! Help me to be added to someone else's list, that they may sing your praises! Amen.

Day 42

I Thessalonians 4:13-18

"I would not have you ignorant brothers concerning those who are asleep that you don't grieve as those who have no hope!" (v.13)

- Paul was not afraid to say it like he believed!
- Did Jesus suffer and die to offer another flavor of religion? (See Acts 4:12)
- Did the early Christians sacrifice life and limb for the sake of pluralism?
- Did Martin Luther, Susannah Wesley, John and Charles Wesley and countless others into the modern day suffer abuse because they thought it was a nicer way than other faiths – No!

The Church today has lost its way! The major denominations are not just declining – they are dying! We need an evangelical awakening – NOT to save the church – but because faithfulness to the Christ demands it! Further, the world desperately needs His Love!!

But let me add! The risen Christ is not dependent upon me taking him (like an infant in my arms) to others! He is already there! Moving by His Holy Spirit among ALL peoples! All I need to do is name Him – but more, to live Him before all people! I am not as worried about persons saying the right words: "Lord, Lord" (Matthew 7:21) as I am their living for Christ –through humble love! Only the risen Christ can make this possible!

Thus, I see Christ alive in Mahatma Ghandi, Rosa Parks, and countless others who I may not know what religion – if any – they may profess! Christ does not need me to save Him – but to so live that He might take up flesh in me!

Prayer: Lord! Help me to be filled with your Spirit today. Help me to walk in humble love before and among all peoples – that they may see You, and come to love YOU as I do! Amen.

Day 43

James 1:17-27

James lifts up three things that are vital to every marriage, and every parent-child relationship.

First he teaches us: "Be quick to listen" (v.19c). Political reformer Lincoln Steffens was 45 when his wife died. In her diary he read of loneliness and pain he didn't know existed! He couldn't help but wonder if things would have been different had he been a better listener! We all can improve in this regard!

How often are we like two ships passing in the night?! We can live in the same house, and even sleep in the same bed, and never really "touch" – know - understand - care.

Second, James instructs us to "be slow to speak." (v.19b) Someone has said that we are each either buzzards or bees. Buzzards spend their day looking for some prey that made a mistake, faced great difficulty – then they swoop down and share all the little tidbits! Gossip is a terrible evil that can destroy lives!

Bees, on the other hand, look for the beautiful, the sweet, the good! We have each known such persons. They were slow to join in when others were tearing apart some poor soul! But often could be heard pointing out the good and beautiful in the world around them, and in the persons they have met: i.e. encouraging them – helping them see the good – the potential in themselves.

Finally, James teaches us to be slow to anger. In the days when a swat on the behind was appropriate by the principal of the school for the misbehaving lad, Jimmy was in the principal's office for the third time in a month. Exasperated, the principal grabbed him up to eye level and said: "Jimmy! I think the Devil has a hold of you!" Jimmy responded: "I do too, sir!"

There are times when we should be angry! When little children are seen starving on our television screens – when injustices are committed toward the "down–and–out". This is righteous anger! It is seen in M.A.D.D – Mothers Against Drunk Driving.

Thus James says: Be angry as love moves you, but be "slow to anger" lest you are just seeking retribution.

Prayer: Lord, Help me for I am too often slow to listen, quick to speak, and quick to become angry. Instill your patience and quiet calm within my spirit today. Amen.

Day 44

Mark 10:17-31

We like "user friendly" religion! One that demands little – a God that we can say our prayers to under the locked door of our hearts. This religion was very popular in churches for a couple of decades, and its remnants still remain.

There is nothing wrong with friendly churches! We need more of that! But selling our faith cheaply to the lowest bidder is an affront to the Gospel of Jesus Christ. We are followers of the Crucified – thus we should expect to sacrifice – put God first – and follow Him! That is neither popular nor easy – especially in our time!

A preacher was preaching a revival in a small church. He later commented on the services: "Well, on Monday we had 120 persons present. But by Friday I had them preached down to 28!" We laugh at such! But if it wasn't because he was such a poor preacher that the people couldn't stand to listen to him, he may well have been simply preaching the true Gospel of Jesus Christ!

Our Lord drew throngs of people up until he began speaking of a Cross in His path. Then the crowds began to melt away!

"Sell all, give to the poor – then come follow and you will have treasure in heaven", Jesus said. The rich man went away sorrowing, because his possessions were many! (Mk.10:21-22)

The rich young man could not follow the Lord – but where could he go?!

Prayer: Lord, there is a chunk of that young man in each of us, for we are addicted to things – to self – to self-made security. Help me this day to wholly lean on you! Help me to know the Peace of being wholly surrendered to you! Amen.

Day 45

Matthew 6:24-34

"Don't worry." For most – if not all of humanity, worry is as natural as breathing, if not as frequent! It saps our energy. It makes us crotchety. It takes the joy out of living! Thus, our Lord says in several different ways: "Do not be anxious" (v.25) "Why are you anxious?" (v.28) "do not be anxious" (v.31) and again in verse 34.

Why does the Lord ask us to do something impossible for us to do?!

"But how can I stop worrying?" we ask. You may not cease from all worry – but you can know a much more peace–filled life!

Jesus says first of all that our problem is having the wrong master! (v.24) If money, popularity, success…are your gods, then you will be an anxious person! But if Christ is your God these worry-producers will cease to exist!

Second He says: "Look at the birds…" (v.26). "Consider the lilies…" (v.28b) God provides for these, and will also provide for you – maybe not what you want, but always what you need!

Rather, He says: "Seek FIRST [the] kingdom [of God] and His righteousness, and all these things will be yours as well!" (v.33).

Prayer: Lord, help me to trust you more, and my own resources less, that my life will give witness to your power and peace! Amen.

Day 46

John 1:1-18, especially verse 14; Hebrews 1:1-2

Back in 1988, when I was a District Superintendent working with Bishop W.T. Handy, we worked out the appointment of the first African American appointed to an all white church in the Missouri West Conference, at Smithville, Missouri. I was very much aware that the Ku Klux Klan was active in the area. They had left their leaflets under the windshield wipers of the cars in the parking lot at Platte Woods United Methodist Church nearby on a recent Sunday morning.

I had asked all the churches in Kansas City North District, if they would accept a cross-racial appointment if the bishop and I felt the person was the most suitable for that church. For the two years that I asked at the annual Church Conferences, it was unanimous that the churches would.

The bishop made the appointment, and it was a wonderful success with the pastor and people working together to make Christ visible in their community. And there was no trouble from the Klan.

"The Word [had once again become] flesh and dwelt among us, full of grace and truth!"

Prayer: Lord, help me to Love as you have loved me – with a holy, humble Love. Help me to love those I find unlovely, that you may truly live in me this day and forever. Amen.

Day 47

I Corinthians 13:1-13

Years ago Burt Bacharach wrote the lyrics to what became a popular song: "What the world needs now is love sweet love".

I don't know how "sweet" love is, for it is often expressed in righteous anger. Yet, Burt's idea was "right on!" The world desperately needs Love – I would add, Christ-like Love!

Paul concludes his most famous love chapter with the three pillars of New Testament teaching: "Faith, Hope, and Love and the greatest of these" – and all the angels of Heaven leaned forward to see what the apostle would write next – "is LOVE!" Greater than faith – which is essential for salvation? YES! Greater than hope that is vital for life? YES! The greatest of all is Love!

Someone has said that we should give the word "love" a rest. It is SO abused in our world today! "I'll luv you for a weekend…" is an example of how superficial it can be. That same person suggested that we instead substitute the word "commitment". For love is commitment to another, and without such it is lacking its most basic ingredient. (That is why I often capitalize the "L" in love in these pages, because Christian Love is so different from the love we encounter in the world!)

Does that mean that I must stay in an abusive relationship? No! For no one person can make a marriage work! It takes two committed, loving persons for it to be fulfilling, and for it to be what God intended.

But we must not hide in the exceptions from real love that is commitment: to friends… to a spouse… to children... to God!

Prayer: Lord, I find it difficult to Love. Too often I seek the easy way out. Too often I am not willing to pay the price of caring. Make me more committed to you and to all those you call me to Love this day. Amen.

Day 48

James 5:13-20

Healing is a work met with suspicion, especially when we speak of "faith healing." Yet, NOT FAITH healing, but GOD healing is repeatedly present in the biblical story!

We should never feel guilty because we are not healed of some disease, because for the Apostle

Paul healing did not come. (II Corinthians 12: 7-9). So, we should always make it clear even great persons of faith – great people of God – are not always healed! For we all will die! Yet Paul saw how his continuing malady was not a detriment to his mission for Christ, but an asset! For who has the greater witness the bedridden soul who declares: "God has been so good to me", or the man in his easy chair who declares: "God is good!" The former of course!

Healing in the Bible comes in three ways:

1. Naturally. Think of it: hundreds – if not thousands of times each day – our bodies fight off germs, viruses, even cancer cells that would make us ill if not die! How many times each year do we get sick, wounded, and then the systems God has placed within us fight off the invader, and we regain our health. God through nature heals us much more than we realize!

2. God heals us miraculously! James 5:14 says: "If any among you is sick [he/she] should...pray over them, anointing them with oil in the name of the Lord. The prayer of faith will save the sick." Some extraordinary healings happen gradually. Others suddenly, but both are cause for thanksgiving!

3. God heals all ultimately! I had an old saint lying in the hospital dying from a leaking aneurysm of the aorta. Surgery was not an option. As I stood by Fred's bedside he told me what was going on, then smiled and told me a joke!

"Bill, have you heard of the man whose wife had him eat oat bran most of the mornings of their married life? His wife preceded him in death. Finally he died. He walked the streets of his new heavenly home taking in its beauty, love, and peace. Finally he ran onto his wife. "Honey!" he cried, "If you hadn't had me eat all that oat bran, I could have been here a whole lot sooner!"

Soon, Fred went home, now fully healed!

Prayer: Lord, pour out your healing Power on me – even now. Help me to value my relationship with you more than life itself! Help me to realize that I am a sojourner. Help me to cling above all to You. Amen.

Day 49

Genesis 45:1-11 & 15; 50:21 & Jeremiah 31:31-34

On "Prime Time Live" back in 1994, presidential candidate, George McGovern, shared how his daughter battled alcoholism. Finally, one night, she was found dead in a snowdrift outside a tavern.

In her diary she shared her frustration with her father for spending so much time with his political career, and so little time with her, and McGovern broke down and sobbed!

We have all "sinned and fallen short" of what God wanted for us. Your sin, whether of omission or commission, may haunt you!

God declares through Jeremiah: "I will forgive their iniquity, and remember their sin no more!" (v.34)

In I John 1:9, John declares: "If we confess our sins, he is faithful and just and will forgive our sins and cleanse us from all unrighteousness".

God is "faithful and just", but praise God He is also merciful! (Exodus 34:6; James 5:11b) In fact – think of it! – God says to you: "I will forgive YOUR iniquity and remember YOUR sin no more!" (Jeremiah 31:34)

That is the Good News of our lesson for today, and you can count on it!

Prayer: Thank you Lord for your gracious, forgiving love! Help me to accept your forgiveness that I may live in joy and peace. Amen.

Day 50

Luke 15:1-7

The late Bishop Monk Bryan told when his son, Jim, was in seminary he and his wife, Carol, and their four year old son, Andy, were in a serious automobile accident. Andy, who moments before was a rambunctious little boy, was now confined to a hospital bed. He mended faster than his parents but, because he had to endure a body cast, he would now have to learn to walk again.

After Andy was out of the body cast, Monk took his grandson by the hand, and helped him take a few steps, then more, and finally Andy was able to walk by himself.

Monk asked us: "When was the last time you held someone by the hand, and helped them learn to walk again?"

Children ... grandchildren ... friends ... business associates – your circle of influence – when?

They need desperately to learn to walk in the steps of the Master that leads to life and that eternally! Will we help them?

Prayer: Lord, place on my heart persons I need to pray for, encourage, and point to you this day. Grant me wisdom and courage as I help this person walk. Amen.

Day 51

Isaiah 55:1-9

Back in the 1920s my step-grandfather was driving an early touring car with the top down in Joplin, MO. My father, who was 12 years old, was riding beside his stepdad. They were on an errand to get a dozen eggs. Eggs were sold, and then put in a brown paper sack in those days. It was my Dad's responsibility to hold the eggs in his lap on the ride home.

They came to the street car track where Granddad looked, then pulled out on the tracks. Suddenly he saw the street car coming. Being a new driver, at first he pulled forward, then – for some reason - thought his best escape was backing up! Hardly had he gotten it in reverse when they were hit broadside, and spun into the side of the street car. Dad heard a scream – looked up to see a horrified woman leaning out a window above, looking down at him! He looked down at himself, and saw a dozen eggs smashed all over his chest and stomach. It looked as though he had burst!

Granddad's actions make no sense to us! Sometimes life doesn't make sense. Tragedy strikes and we cry, "Why?" Then, after our period of grief, we see God hanging on a tree, and we begin to understand. Somehow God's redemption of a lost world comes through suffering – most often innocent suffering!

God said to Isaiah: "My thoughts are not your thoughts, neither are your ways my ways." (v.8)

Prayer: Lord, Help me in those times when I don't understand, to count on what I do understand, and above all to lean – to lean – on your everlasting arms. Amen.

Day 52

Philippians 3:8-14

A soldier back from Vietnam told of an experience he had there. He was riding in a troop convoy. Lining the road were refugees, and they were hungry. Suddenly a soldier threw an empty rations can into the crowd. The people fought and tore at each other until one man finally held up the empty can.

Much of life in this world is spent tearing at each other to attain things that are in essence empty!

We arrive at the pinnacle of our dreams to discover it is not what we thought it was going to be! It is often lonely, and leaves us hungering for that which lasts.

"Indeed I count everything as loss because of the surpassing worth of knowing Christ Jesus my Lord ... that I may know the power of his resurrection ..." Paul writes. (vs. 8a & 10a)

Late one afternoon the Reverend George Mann walked through the sanctuary. The setting sun cast its bright glow through the gloriously tinted window depicting the Good Shepherd holding a lamb close to his breast.

There in the dimming light of the sanctuary, a stranger was seated. "He was not looking at the window, but gazing off in the distance at something," George said, "That I could not see. He was dressed in a clerical garb. When I introduced myself, he told me he was a priest in the Coptic Church of Egypt, one of the oldest Christian bodies in the world. There was something timeless about him. We visited briefly, then I left him seated there – still looking at something I could not see!"

Prayer: O God, help me to fully know Christ Jesus and to see what others may not see – that I may know Him who alone satisfies! Amen.

Day 53

Philippians 2:5-13, especially verse 12b

We all have a "sickness unto death" as Soren Kierkegaard coined the phrase. Each of us is terminally ill! The doctor has not told us how long we have, but God knows.

If all life here is a journey to the cemetery, then it lacks all meaning and purpose! We are left to "whistle through the cemetery" to distract ourselves from ultimate realities lest they cause us to freeze in our tracks – like a rabbit in the crosshairs of the hunter's gun.

The apostle Paul writing to the church at Phillipi declares: "Work out your own salvation with fear and trembling." (v.12b)

In light of our mortality, Paul is saying, this thing of salvation is of the utmost importance! It should make us shudder at the thought that we might get it wrong – choose the wrong savior!

"But I thought," you say, "that salvation is a free gift of God." Yes, like the physical life that we receive through our parents, it is a gift! But is that the end of the story? No! It is just the beginning! We must now work to keep the gift (v.12b). We must feed, exercise, and generally care for these spiritual bodies lest they wither and die!

So, salvation is a gift – pure and simple! But we must pray, witness, serve and above all love – lest we lose the life we have been given! Thus, we must "work out your own salvation with fear and trembling".

Prayer: Lord God, we praise you for the gift of salvation! Help us to care for this gift with great earnestness and attentiveness that we may daily grow to be more like you. Amen.

Day 54

Mark 16: 1-8

Why did the three women go to the grave of our Lord knowing that they could not roll the stone off of the opening? (v.3) They were planning to do the work of embalming the body – since there was not enough time on Friday, and Saturday was the Sabbath when no work was to be done.

They were on a mission impossible! But God loves missions impossible!

So, even though the three women hadn't thought it all through, they were thinking someone – somehow would provide.

Have you ever had a stone in your path? Most of us have! Large stones – huge stones – stones impossible for us to move – get around – get over ... "Who will move the stone?!"

When I stood to preach each time that first year or so, a voice within would whisper: "You can't do it!" I shook with deep anxiety each time, but each time God provided!

When my precious wife, Ginya, was diagnosed with a rare and aggressive cancer, my very soul cried: "Who will move this stone for us?" God did!

If you love – really love – you will have more "stones" in you path! For love always comes with a price!

"And looking up ..." "And looking UP ..." (It is vital that we look up unto Him who comes to us in trial!) "They saw that the stone had been rolled away!"

When we least expect it.

When we are at the end of OUR rope!

God comes – in Power – to provide what our souls most need!

When you go expecting a DEAD Jesus, a living Lord comes to you!

Prayer: O Risen Christ come! Come to me now! Help me to give over control to you – and trust – yes trust in your everlasting arms! Amen.

Day 55

Isaiah 43: 1-7

We have all heard that there are two certainties in life: taxes and death, but God tells Isaiah of a third: trials. "When you pass through deep waters…" NOT: "IF" but "when," for we all face "deep waters" in our lives!

W. H. Maltby once said that, in the Sermon on the Mount, Jesus promised His followers three things: "they would be entirely fearless; they would be absurdly happy; AND they would get into trouble!"

"When you pass through deep waters…" "I will be with you!" (v.2a TEV) Like a Mother who is moved to rush to her child's side when she/he cries out in pain, so God draws nearest to you when you face difficulties!

As I mentioned earlier, Rembrandt in his "Storm at Sea," depicts himself in the boat as the disciples are about to be swamped by the raging waters – for he too realized we ALL face the deep waters! But there also is the Master who calms the sea!

Sometimes He calms the seas about us. Sometimes He calms the storm within us, but ALWAYS He comes to us in the storms of life!

Prayer: Lord, what a wondrous mystery I feel in those times I find peace amid the storm. Help me, even now, to know that "peace that passes all understanding".* Amen

*Philippians 4:7; John 14: 27; Romans 15:33; Ephesians 2:14

Day 56

Romans 8:15-17, especially verse 16 (William Beck translation)

Is it possible to KNOW God?

- Not to know about Him.
- Not to just believe in Him.
- But to know God better than a dear friend!

We see our hunger to know God in:

- Our attempt to gather things that last.
- Our desire to have eternal fellowship with those we love.
- Our efforts to live meaningful/purposeful lives.
- Our attempts to read the signs of the End of Time – to prove to ourselves there is a God, and a God who is in charge.

William Beck translates verse 16: "This Spirit assures our spirit [saying] we are children of God." That is to say, the Lord speaks to our spirit saying: "Fear not, you are my child!" To "hear" that Voice is to KNOW God!

At Pentecost those, who had prayed for 10 days, received this assurance! Thus, they were given courage to face even death, and a sense that they were loved – by God!

Prayer: Lord enable me to SO spend time with you, that I too may come to know you as God – my God. Amen.

Day 57

Mark 6:30-45

Jesus was on vacation! And if Jesus – the God/Man needed rest, think of how important it is for you and me!

There are so many things to stress us: finances, children, job, the world situation ... "Come away to a deserted place by yourselves, and rest a while," Jesus says (v.31). Mark adds: "For many were coming and going, and they had no leisure even to eat." (Mark 6:31) You probably know the feeling!

A study of nurses made back in the 1980s discovered that those most committed to caring burned out quickest! And, I believe, it is true of all vocations that deal with people!

The more you care, the more you need times of rest!

Dr. Paul Tournier, psychiatrist/author, said all of nature observes the law of the three rests: daily rest (for most this comes in the night), weekly rest (i.e. Sabbath rest), and annual rest when the trees drop their leaves – bears go into hibernation – and much of nature rests.

Tournier adds our vacations are – by nature – more refreshing if taken in the winter when a lot of nature takes a respite. Something to ponder.

"Come away .... and rest".

Prayer: Lord, too often I feel it is up to me to "fix it" – to change the world. Help me to realize the tiredness of body and spirit are you calling me to rest. Lord, teach me today the silence of eternity – the withdrawal of trust – that I may be renewed in your Spirit. Amen.

Day 58

I Kings 18:20-21; 30-39

Daily the "prophets of Baal" challenge us! In the popular media it is OK to mock and make fun of our Judeo-Christian heritage, just as the prophets of Baal mocked the faith of Elijah.

But Elijah did not sit idly by and watch. He challenged the false prophets to a dual! Elijah asked the prophets of Baal to build an altar to their gods. Then he built one to Jehovah. Each was given a chance to call down fire from heaven and ignite the sacrifice on the altar.

The Baal prophets danced about their altar chanting – praying. While Elijah taunted them and made fun of them (not a very Christ like behavior). Nothing happened!

Then Elijah called for fire from heaven, and like a great bolt of lightning, fire split the heavens, and consumed the sacrifice, the wood, and even the stones of the altar! Jehovah was established as God of all!

We aren't in a dual to call down fire from heaven, but we are in a dual to prove to the world that God is Love – as shown in Jesus Christ. For the faith we affirm is uniquely one of love. We show the world Jesus and His Power by living the Christ–changed life of love.

Prayer: Lord, help me to so love today that others will see you in me, and the Power of your resurrection. Amen.

Day 59

I Kings 19:9-21

A grandmother told me how her eleven year old grandson was terrified of storms! One night he was staying with her when a thunderstorm came rolling in. The lightning flashed and the thunder shook the house!

"Grandmother, are you afraid?" he asked. "Yes, storms make me nervous too" – but seeing a teaching moment she added: "But I just pray: Lord, watch over me in this storm. The Lord has always done that." Unimpressed he nodded, and went back to what he was doing.

Suddenly, a huge bolt of lightning struck nearby with a great pop followed by earthshaking thunder! The grandson slid over against his grandmother and said: "How did that prayer go?"

Is your god sufficient when the storm clouds come?

Elijah, after defeating the prophets of Baal (as we saw yesterday), got Jezebel, the queen, livid with rage and ready to kill him. He ran scared, feeling all alone!

Isn't it interesting how we can see God's protective care innumerable times, then comes trouble and we are terrified! Yet, God's sufficiency is only made evident in our inadequacy.

As Elijah is holed up in a cave, God speaks to him. Not in the strong wind that began to blow ... Not in the earthquake that shook him to his very core ... Not in the fire that belched forth out of the mountain ... but in "still small voice." (I Kings 19:12) In that small voice of the silence of eternity God called Elijah forth from the hole of his hiding. -- God provided!

Prayer: Lord, help me to rely on your sufficiency when my inadequacy threatens to overwhelm me. Amen.

Spend five minutes in silence before God. You may want to repeat the name of Jesus to keep you centered, and freer from wandering thoughts.

Day 60

II Kings 5:1-14

In 850 B.C. Naaman was the leader of the Syrian Army. But there was a problem. Naaman had leprosy! The disease was beginning to take its toll! Naaman developed splotchy places on his skin. A couple of fingers on one hand wasted away! He was in bad shape!

A little slave girl, working for Naaman's wife, tells her mistress: "Madame, there is a prophet in Israel who can heal your husband!"

Desperate, they are ready to try anything – even a doctor with questionable credentials, down in the punk country of Israel. So, Naaman loads up 750 lbs of silver, 150 lbs of gold – remember Naaman was used to paying his own way!

Along with a large entourage, Naaman pulls up in front of Elisha's house. Elisha doesn't even come out to welcome the general, but sends his maid. She says: "The prophet sends word for you to go down to the Jordan River and wash 7 times – and you will be cleansed of your leprosy."

Naaman is furious! He has been treated with disrespect! Been asked to bathe in a little muddy creek! How dare this preacher try to humiliate him!

No, not the prophet, but God was trying to humble him. For he needed humility before God worse than healing from a dreaded disease! For he had a worse malady than he realized: selfish pride – which destroys the soul! And what were his choices? To dip or to die. At least – just maybe – he could be healed – LIVE! Finally, he reluctantly chooses to dip himself in the stream.

He goes down to the Jordan. Wades out into its waters, and according to the prophet's instructions, dips himself seven times. He comes out clean as a baby! The leprosy is gone!

Skin – healed, but most importantly, his soul was healed to!

Prayer: Lord, make me humble. For I realize all your blessings start right there. Heal my soul. Make me clean. Help me to praise and serve you all my days. Amen

Day 61

Luke 12:49 Jerusalem Bible

Have you ever fought a grass fire?

Our first parsonage was a brand new house in Mound City, Missouri. One morning I went out to burn the trash. I dumped the papers into the incinerator, lit them, but before I could get the wire lid in place, a piece of burning paper blew out. It lit in the dry brown grass and immediately began to spread! I tried to stomp it out, but it was growing ever bigger. So I raced to the house and grabbed the garden hose, and extinguished the flames – just short of the neighbor's garage up the hill!

Jesus said: "I have come to bring fire to the earth, and how I wish it were blazing already."

(Lk. 12:49)

Our Lord was saying he had come to bring the fire of God's love, and how he wished that it were blazing in the hearts and lives of persons everywhere!

Before a fire can spread though, it must be kindled. In this case: kindled in the hearts of women and men, boys and girls. Then it will spread to those in close proximity to the "flame."

Prayer: Lord, send the fire! Kindle the flame in my heart. Make of it a roaring blaze that consumes me, and ignites others with your grace. Amen.

Day 62

Galatians 6:7-10; Luke 6:38

We don't like to think about it, but we often get in life what we have coming. Jesus said: "... Give and it will be given to you, good measure, pressed down, shaken together, running over will be put in your lap. For the measure you give will be the measure you get back." (Luke.6:38)

Again, Paul writes in Galatians 6:7b: "God is not mocked, for whatever a man sows, that will he also reap."

I have seen this truth experienced in the lives of thousands of persons over my 45 years in the ministry - both within the church and beyond it.

Those who sowed happiness in the lives of others through their encouragement and good deeds, reaped joy in return.

Others lived courageously in the face of trials. They reaped the admiration and respect of those around them.

Our Lord's words are borne out daily both good and bad: "The "measure you give is the measure you get." (Luke 6:38)

Yet there are exceptions! The "little Christs" of our world who suffer innocently – as did our Lord! They receive pain for nothing that they did themselves! On the positive side, blessings come to the undeserving folks too - including all of us!

Still the truth remains, that in many instances, life gives us what we put into it both positively and negatively.

Prayer: Lord, give me a grateful heart for all your mercies: earned and unearned. Help me to see that every good and perfect gift comes from you. Help me to strive to use the gifts you have given me to glorify your name. Amen.

Day 63

Acts 16:9-15

In our lesson, Lydia responds to Paul's message, "she and her whole household" are baptized. (v.15) She made her faith decision for herself and her family as well! Most parents do!

But how can we do all we can to see our children come into a saving relationship with God in Christ?

First, we as parents need to believe in having fun!

In Acts 2:15 the early Christians were accused of being drunk! They were having such a good time together! They weren't drunk! They were just having a raucous good time laughing! If you didn't know, you would think they had to be drunk to be having such a high old time amidst a world of pain and suffering.

A contagious faith is one that knows how to laugh often!

You can have all the right beliefs, and not have a contagious faith if there is little room for fun!

Second, our children need to know that we believe in them – because we tell them often!

Think of four or five persons who have had the greatest impact on your life for good, and you will discover what they all had in common was that they believed in you – even when you didn't – and made this known to you.

Finally, and most obviously, to have a contagious faith we need to have a firm faith in Christ!

It is not enough to believe in Christ like you believe there is a Statue of Liberty. Even: "I believe he lived, died, and rose again," is not enough. Biblical belief involves surrender to – allowing Christ to be central to your daily values and life. Those closest to you know who your real God is – may it be the Christ!

Prayer: Lord, we all fall short. We fail the ones we love the most. We have to ask their forgiveness as we ask your forgiveness, but that teaches them what grace is all about. I pray for persons you have placed in my circle of influence. Help me be a little Christ to them. Amen.

Day 64

Galatians 6:7-10

When I was a youngster soda pop came in glass bottles. On the bottles you would read: "No Deposit – No Return." That meant, you would have to bring the bottles back if you wanted to get your deposit on the bottles back.

God's salvation in Christ is a gift, but as John Wesley taught, we avail ourselves to much of what God offers through the Holy Habits of prayer, good deeds, and worship. Through our participation in these, we receive back.

In worship, when we have come prepared by prayer, and are attentive to the service, we are inspired. If we give ourselves to singing the hymns and choruses with gusto, we will be blessed. Preaching involves us as listeners as much as it involves the one who delivers the message, and again we are blessed accordingly. In spite of the missteps of the preacher, or the choir, or the liturgist - we receive as we give.

Yes, "No deposit - No return!"

We have experienced it in our prayer lives! When we began we were like newborn infants: we hardly knew how to form our words. We had trouble focusing on our Mother's face. But oh the BLESSINGS when we have grown in our experience with Her, and come to "see" her face-to-face!

Prayer: Lord, help me be more disciplined in the Holy Habits that I might know you, and the joy you hold for me. Amen.

Day 65

Psalm 121

Oh the mountains majesty! Jutting their stone buttresses toward the heavens – from whence they were made. Dressed in pine and spruce, and crowned with snow and granite's splendor!

I love the mountains!

Biblical folks looked to the hills, for they felt they were closer to God when they went up the hill or mountain, and we can experience a closeness to our Maker there too.

Yet those same hills and mountains were created in great chaos and upheaval! Thrust skyward by mighty earthquakes over aeons of time. They are like the Cross - a symbol of suffering and pain, and yet great good and Love!

Out of chaos – beauty? Out of cataclysmic change – a sense of the majesty and greatness of God? How can this be? Yet, to each of our lives has come this very experience, when we lean on the Almighty - "from whence [our] help comes!"

"Oh Lord, our Lord, how majestic is your name in all the earth!"

Prayer: Lord, teach me the lessons of eternity. Help me to frequent the silent places, to *"Be still my soul and know that [you] are God." Lord teach me to walk the quiet path amid a noisy world; to commune: your Spirit and my spirit. Amen.

*Psalm 46:10

Day 66

Luke 1:26-33

A peasant girl – Mother of God?!

Mary was a hillbilly – we would say – from the hill country of Nazareth. What could be a greater paradox?! The mighty God picks a "nobody" to do the greatest work God planned to do – bring a Savior to the world! Yet, for His greatest works God always picks the most unlikely!

- Moses, was a lowly shepherd, yet he led God's people from bondage.
- He chose Sarah to be the mother of Isaac.
- The twelve – mostly fishermen – common laborers, to give birth to His Church.
- Saul, one determined to stamp out the Church, becomes the Apostle Paul, the greatest missionary evangelist in the history of Christendom!
- The list is endless …

Yet, why is it that Mary, who was chosen by God to be the sole bearer of the Body of Christ to the world in the first century, should not be welcome to bear His Body in the Holy Sacrament of Communion in some arms of the Church today?

Ponder this, and pray for His Church. Pray for all of us, for we all fall short!

Prayer: Lord, how glorious is your Name! To think how you have used the least – the last – the lost to do your greatest work. Help us to see the potential in all persons, and give you all the praise. Renew us in a Christ-like spirit toward others. In your name we pray. Amen.

Day 67

Luke 11:1-13

We have all known a saint: mother, father, grandparent – some elderly person ...

I have known scores of such persons over my forty-five years in the ministry. As I have studied them, I have noted two factors that stand out in the vast majority of their lives. First, they were/are persons of great sufferings, and second, persons of a deep prayer life.

Life usually takes care of the suffering part of it, but if we are to escape self-pity it is up to us to develop and maintain the meaningful prayer life.

Once Jesus was praying, and after He finished – observing all prayer had meant to the Lord – the disciples asked: "Lord, teach us to pray."

Our text – and His life – teaches us this about prayer: We need a place for prayer. That is, a place in our busy schedules, but also a certain place where we go – free of distractions – for prayer. (See: Acts 2:1)

Noted theologian, and professor at Yale University, from the 1930's through the 1960's, H. Richard Niebuhr, was once asked by a student: "Dr. Niebuhr what is your theology of prayer?" The great intellectual giant responded simply: "I don't have a theology of prayer. Prayer is not something you talk about. Prayer is something you DO. It is not the result of theological thought – it is the basis for all theological thought!" The young man sauntered away realizing he had just met something much bigger than himself!

Does prayer have a central place in my daily life?

Prayer: Lord, teach me to pray. Help me to find a place daily for prayer, that I might know its Power through your Presence. Amen.

Day 68

Jeremiah 18:1-11

"So I went down to the potter's shop." There Jeremiah experienced a living parable, as he watched the potter at work at his wheel - a parable that would speak to his very soul!

Have you ever been to the Potter's Shop? Have you gone back to the moment of your birth, and pondered what that meant in God's Plan?

- We have been wondrously made!
- But we have all "messed up!"
- So, lovingly – tenderly – God takes us in His hands, and re-makes us – using all of our brokenness – making us into a a beautiful mosaic - that uses all the pieces!

The old hymn, "Have Thine Own Way," is a wonderful prayer:

"Have thine own way, Lord;

    Have thine own way.

You are the Potter,

    I am the clay.

Mold me and make me

    After Thy will

While I am waiting

    Yielded and still." Amen.

Prayer: Lord, take me now as a lump of clay, and shape me more-and-more into the person you would have me to be. Make me a little Christ, Lord. Amen.

Day 69

Isaiah 43:1-3

Notice how many times God says: "When you pass through ..."

- "When you pass through the waters ..."
- "When you pass through the rivers ..."
- "When you walk through the fire..."
- "When you pass through" God promises, "I will be with you" – giving you victory – a "way out"

Your trials are not terminals, but doorways to greater things.

Remember Moses – after being raised in the Pharaoh's palace – in the wilderness herding sheep. Yet God was preparing him to lead the "people of Israel through that same wilderness!"

God is shouting from the heavens: "Trials are temporary!" "Trial is tempered to make your 'iron' into steel – God knows your load capacity!"

Finally, God is saying: "I will be with you – carrying the heavy end of the load – protecting you – seeing you through". Our God is Triumphant!

Prayer: Lord, help me to remember that my trials don't have the last word! Help me to learn to lean on you. Amen.

Day 70

Hebrews 12:1-2

"Let us run... the race that is set before us, looking to Jesus the pioneer..."

A popular motion picture made the idea of a "bucket list" familiar and popular. In the movie, two older men, realizing that they may live but a decade or two more before they "kick the bucket," decide to list the things they want to do before they die. The film then shows them engaging in these activities – with a lot of humor thrown in.

I am not suggesting that you have a bucket list, but scripture challenges us to "run the race that is set before us looking to Jesus, the pioneer and perfecter of the faith ..."

"Looking to Jesus"

- When trials come...
- When decisions are to be made...
- When the poor meet me at my gate...
- When blessings are bestowed...
- When joy overflows...

Looking to Jesus who is able to carry us across the finish line!

Prayer: Lord, I do not know how long my life will be, but I do know in Whose steps I follow – right on in to Heaven's gate! Amen.

Day 71

Luke 12:22-31

In Philip Keller's book, "Lessons from a Sheep Dog", the author focuses on lessons the Master of the dog teaches us, rather than lessons the dog teaches. For the next several days I want us to look at the lessons a dog can teach us about life - about our relationships with others and our Creator.

I have a part Boxer, part Australian Shepherd, and part clown! She is a "rescue dog" – saved from a plastic bag thrown into someone's yard. She was named Daisy Duke. She is all that name implies and more! She has reminded me often of what is important in life, and in my relationship with God.

When I arrive home I am always greeted with the warmest of welcomes! With tail meeting nose she wiggles with glee her welcome! She again–and–again reminds me that the greatest gift is simply being with those you love - being with God!

Prayer: Lord, amid a long list of wants, help me to learn the lesson: the greatest Gift is simply being with you! Help me remember that today. Amen.

Day 72

I John 1:5-9

There are times when my dog, Daisy, misbehaves, and I yell at her, and she slinks away with her tail between her legs. Then I realize that my reaction was greater than the crime that was committed. So, I apologize, and she is ecstatic, for she cannot stand for us to have a break in our relationship!

On other occasions, I get after her then realize she didn't break the glass – I just sat it too close to the edge of the counter and it fell off! (At least I think that is the way it happened!) So, I apologize to my little buddy, and she instantly responds with glee – as our relationship is mended! She considers it over - forgotten - as though nothing has happened!

Forgiveness is wonderful! It is often easier to give than it is to receive! I sometimes feel bad for my misdeeds in regard to my beloved pet, but then she reminds me that her love is like her Creator's. When she forgives – she forgets it – forever! (Jeremiah 31:34)

I regularly learn of God's forgiving love – from my Daisy!

Prayer: Lord, help me to accept your forgiveness – as I must also accept the forgiveness of those around me. Help me to also forgive _____, as you have forgiven me. Amen.

Day 73

Mark 4:39; John 14:27; Romans 15:33; Ephesians 2:14; Philippians 4:7.

When there is a violent thunderstorm marching through the area, Daisy will be right at my feet! When the carpenters are pounding on the side of the house - as they are doing right now - adding on a sunporch, with brief interludes of racing to the window to bark, she returns to my side. She is right now asleep at my feet, though the pounding continues!

Where our Master is -- is Peace!

Years ago, a dog was shipped by sea to his master in New York City. The dog was restless on its journey! The crew took it from its crate, and allowed it to roam freely with them about the ship, but it found no peace. Only when it arrived in port, and was reunited with its owner did he find peace!

Where our Master is -- is Peace!

The disciples were caught in a violent storm on the Sea of Galilee. The winds blew, the waves billowed high, then crashed across the deck! They were terrified! Then they remembered Who was with them in their boat -- it was the Lord! He arose, and spoke peace not only to the sea, but to them as well!

We all have times when we are caught up in life's storms, and we are sure we are going to perish! Then the Master of the sea rises and speaks "Peace!" – and there is a great calm.

Daisy teaches me that where my Master is -- is Peace!

Prayer: Lord, I thank you for my Daisy that often teaches me lessons about her real Master and peace. Grant us peace amid the storms of life today. Amen.

Day 74

John 16: 25-33

It is difficult for me to even write about it, but Daisy came very close to losing her life at the hands of her first owner. She and her siblings were placed in a trash bag and left in front of a home. Fortunately the homeowner arrived home, saw the bag, and rescued Daisy and one other pup. You would never know today by looking at her of all she has been through! Daisy teaches me a lot about being a victor, not a victim!

But more, Daisy reminds me that our master in life determines the life we live.

- If our master is money – we will live anxious lives!

- If our master is sex – going from one partner to the next – we will live lonely lives!

- If we are our own master – we will live lives of fear!

- If our Master is the Lord of history, then we can live victorious life!

Thank God that the Master of the winds and waves is our Master – for because of that we know that all is well!

Prayer: Lord, thank you for being the God of Love who has reached down to us, and rescued us from sin and death! Thank you for being the Rock we can stand on! Amen.

Day 75

Mark 6:30-34

Sixty-five percent of my dog's waking hours – are spent -- asleep!

Daisy teaches me the importance of rest!

With the wonderful advances in technology, we are at the same time robbed of free time! We live such frantic lives! Always on the go! Calendars full! No time to hardly breathe.

Jesus said: "Come away to a lonely place, and rest awhile. For many were coming and going, and there was hardly time to eat!" (v.31) You know the feeling!

Someone has said: "You can accomplish more in eight hours than you can in twelve, more in six days, than you can in seven, more in eleven months, than you can in twelve."

Creativity, insights, clearer focus, avoiding burnout – all grow out of quiet times – a rested mind and body.

Henry Ford had an employee who always had his feet up on his desk. Another worker complained to Mr. Ford, but the famous car maker replied: "The last great idea this company had come from George – while his feet were on his desk!"

Prayer: Lord, help me to learn the lessons rest and relaxation – of lying back in your everlasting arms. Amen.

Day 76

Psalm 145:8-14

My beloved dog teaches me about faithfulness! Wherever I go – she wants to go. Wherever I am she wants to be! Her faithfulness knows no limits!

Our world desperately needs – not more "love," but more faithfulness. The problem with a live – in relationship is its lack of faithfulness.

We all desperately need someone to be there for us - when we lose our job - when we lose our health - when we succeed, and need someone to share the good news with. We are made for fellowship with others, and not on a superficial level, but on the deeper level of a committed relationship -- even as friend-to-friend.

We need to give the word "love" a rest. For it can mean everything from lust to liberty without responsibility. We need Love with a capital "L!" We need committed Love! Without such life is lonely, and incomplete! Daisy reminds me of this every day!

Prayer: Lord, help me to value the lessons of faithfulness – that I might know, and those around me might know, the beauty of real Love. Amen.

Day 77

Jeremiah 7:21-23

Daisy teaches me in a backward kind of way the importance of obedience! She is not always obedient mind you – but when she is not it reminds me of how important that is!

Once she bounded from the car at a filling station beside four lanes of heavy traffic. I was terrified! Fortunately she ran away from the traffic. I chased her - which was a mistake! After all she is a three year old pup, and I'm not! So, I had to resort to a trick to get her to come. I reached into the trash, and got a piece of paper, then called and waved the imaginary treat. Only then did she come.

The problem with disobedience is not that we break some law – but that we can be broken by our disobedience! Daisy reminds me of this truth ever so often.

Prayer: Lord, help me to obey, above all, your law of love, not because the Bible says for me to do so, but for my own sake and that of others. Amen.

Day 78

My three year old pup, Daisy, teaches me: It is OK to drool when you drink. (For a man getting on in years that is good news!) When Daisy drinks the water gushes from your jowls! She makes the experience look inviting - like the water is the best drink in the world! She enjoys the time she spends drinking! (I often have to mop up after her, but the point is made!)

She teaches me that life is lived much too neatly – too perfectly – too safely. We spend a way too much time worrying about what others will think, rather than being and doing what God has made us to be and do!

A woman once said: "If I had my life to live over again, I would take more chances, climb more mountains, cross more ravines – I would be freer to be myself!"

How would you live your life if you had only an audience of One watching? Daisy knows that lesson well!

Prayer: Lord, help me to remember that it is you alone that I shall seek to please today. Amen.

Day 79

Hebrews 12:1-3

My best friend teaches me that the Joy is in the chase. She once spied our neighbor's cat in our backyard. She exploded across the yard like a bullet! The cat, realizing it was caught, turned and hissed, hunkering down to do battle!

Daisy slid to a halt a foot short of her prey. At that point she realized: "Cats are to be chased – not caught!" She kept her distance, simply barking. I intervened to rescue not only the cat, but the naïve dog. Both were glad to be rescued!

Could we not say that the best part of Christmas is the anticipation of the day? The anticipation of a meal shared around a table with loved ones, may be more joy-filled than the actual meal together. The anticipation of seeing a loved one open a gift, may be the better part of the gift exchange itself.

It was said of our Lord: "Who for the joy that was set before Him – endured the cross ..." Looking ahead to the salvation He was bringing to the world brought the Christ great joy – while He was enduring great pain.

Daisy has taught me that the joy is in the chase.

Prayer: Lord, help me to remember that life is not all "cherry pie" – but difficulties too. Help me to discover today the joy of depending on you – part of the chase for Heaven's glory. Amen.

Day 80

Philippians 4:4-7

Daisy teaches me the importance of the simple pleasures of life. She loves to take a walk. When we first got her, we had developed a way with our other dog of getting him to go out and "tee-tee." First, when we said, "Tee-tee," to Daisy she looked blank, but soon caught on. Now at the signal, she jumps as high as my head! (I still don't know but what "tee-tee" means to "go out and play.")

She also enjoys quiet cuddling on the divan. Just being together without a lot going on – just being!

My most blessed times with God are when we go for a walk, sit quietly viewing a sunset – just be! With nothing really going on we do our best communing: spirit to Spirit!

Daisy has taught me the joy of the simple pleasures.

Prayer: Lord, teach me the value of the small things: silence … a quiet walk… just being with those I love. Amen.

Day 81

Matthew 11:28-30

If I'm having a bad time Daisy senses it. She climbs up in my chair beside me, nuzzles me gently with her nose, and all my problems begin to fall into perspective. She is my therapist, and connector to our Maker. She is a Godsend!

Sometimes I feel the nuzzling of the Holy Spirit – saying: "Come unto me all you who labor, and are heavy laden and I will give you rest." And – as I listen – an inexplicable peace comes over my being. Trials that at times are overwhelming, are cut down to size! "When God is for us who (what) can be against us?" (Romans 8:31) Yes, "the Lord is my Shepherd, I shall not want!" (Psalm 23)

Daisy senses the presence of a rough day, and gives me her upmost attention!

Prayer: Thank you, God, for the lessons you teach us through your creatures. Help me to sense the nuzzling of your Holy Spirit when life seems overwhelming. Amen.

Day 82

Genesis 31:11; Daniel 2:3

Over the years I have experienced several dreams that I came to realize were of God. Not all dreams are of God by any means, and I'm thankful that my nightmares - that come on rare occasions - are not of God! I have come to realize a dream is from God when it meets several criteria:

- It is a vivid dream that I recall the next morning.
- It is a dream that gives me a sense of the Divine.
- It is often a dream where I engage characters with dialogue.
- It is sometimes a dream where God gives us instructions of things to do.

Several years ago I had a dream. I dreamed that a man, I will call Bob, in the congregation had lost his job. In my dream he was in worship. I noticed he cried through the whole service! Then the thought came to me, "Bob has cried every Sunday for a long time!"

I awoke the next morning – remembering this vivid dream. I had the distinct impression: "I must call Bob!" I should see how he is doing after months of unemployment, and offer financial assistance from the church.

I called, and got Bob. I told him some of my dream, and I offered financial assistance from the church. "Maybe later. We're getting by right now," he said. I persisted: "Bob, don't let pride stand in your way of a gift God wants you to have. I feel the church should give you $1,000, since you all have been so generous with the church in the past!" "That would be awfully nice!"

I took the check by. He and his wife insisted I come in. She said, "Bill, I wanted you to come in because I heard a scripture quoted on TV shortly after you called. It was Psalm 20:1-2: "The Lord [will] answer you in the day of trouble. The name of the God of Jacob protect you! May he send you help from the sanctuary, and give you support from Zion. May he remember all your offerings, and regard with favor your burnt sacrifices!"

We wept with joy with all God had done that day to sustain and encourage his faithful servants!

Prayer: Lord, thank you for speaking to us today. Thank you for your provision when we are in need. May my heart sing your praises today for all your goodness! Amen

Day 83

Romans 8:15-16

Can I know I am saved? If you say, "Yes," some will say: "How self-assuming of you!"

But the affirmative answer is not based on one's goodness – or great faith – or anything else that you can boast of. It is based solely and completely upon God's goodness! It is like one beggar telling another: "I have received this bread from the woman who lives down on the corner." He has no boast, just a testimony of what was given him!

Methodism was born, we know, when in 1738 John Wesley had such an experience of God's grace! He went forth to tell all who would listen that God loves, forgives and saves us from death to life - and you can KNOW it!

What else would explain the first Christians hiding in fear in Jerusalem, then – after Pentecost – after receiving this assurance - going out to boldly proclaim the Good News of Jesus Christ?!

Am I lost if I don't have this assurance? Absolutely not! If you have faith in Christ you are saved! Whether you feel/know it or not! But this is the first step. Coming to know that you are saved is the second.

For some such assurance comes gradually over a long walk with the Lord of many years. For others it comes, as with the first Christians, (Acts1:1f) after a time of intense prayer. Prayer is key! But whichever way, the point is you can "know in whom you have believed!" (II Timothy 1:12)

Prayer: Lord, help me to bask in your Love daily, that I may come to know that you Love even me! Help me to have the assurance of my salvation, that I may know your peace. Amen.

Day 84

Philippians 4:4-7

We repeat a lesson of several days ago, that merits further mining for its nuggets.

What is this peace Paul speaks of which "passes all understanding?" (v.7a)

It is the peace that the disciples could have known while in the storm at sea, before the Lord spoke calm to the waves. It is a peace amid the storm. It does not make sense to the world, because it "passes all understanding."

It is the peace Paul writes about here from a prison cell – while facing the possibility of death.

It is the peace you may feel amid tears! It doesn't make sense! Again, it "passes all understanding."

It is a peace based in our God of grace and Love. It is a peace that was founded (paradoxically) at Calvary, and more clearly in the empty tomb! It is a peace that keeps you centered in Him who suffered, died, arose, and is present now with us in His Holy Spirit.

May the Peace of God – which is beyond all explanation – keep your heart and mind anchored in Christ Jesus!

Prayer: Lord, help me to know this peace, for the worries of the world are very near. Help me to take my eyes off of those things that cause me anxiety, that I may focus on you, the Source of all peace, and calm. Amen

Day 85

I Thessalonians 5:16-24

"Pray without ceasing," Paul writes. But we say, "How?! I have things to do and places to be! If I 'prayed without ceasing' I'd have a wreck – be a wreck – or worse!"

Praying without ceasing is not with head bowed and eyes closed, but being in an attitude of prayer while we are doing our daily chores. It is ultimately seeking God's will in all decisions. It is loving as He loved - doing as He does. It is being in communion with our Maker at all times.

Praying without ceasing is what Nicholas Herman, Brother Lawrence, meant when he spoke of: "Practicing the Presence." He became famous for this form of prayer, while he did the dishes in the monastery kitchen. As he did these menial tasks, he was aware that God is near. It had become second nature for him. He did not bow his head, or close his eyes, but, while working, he sensed God! It had taken him years to arrive at this habit.

Not all prayers are word prayers, but rather are being aware of God's Presence in ALL circumstances - at all times!

Praying without ceasing is reaching the point where you live in thanksgiving - continually. "Give thanks always!" Paul wrote. (II Thessalonians 2:13; Philippians 4:4; I Thessalonians 1:2)

It is prayer that comes as natural as the tasks that we are doing.

Prayer: Lord, help me to pray always: in words – in spirit – in deeds – that I may come to know you more fully and love you more deeply. Amen.

Day 86

Genesis 13:1-7, 14-18

Abraham and Sarah set out for an unknown destination. They did not know where they were going, nor what it would be like when they arrived! They lived in tents, so they could be on the move to where God would have them go.

We yearn for permanent dwellings with deep foundations – strong walls – solid water-tight roofs! But such does not exist!

We too live in tents! Temporary homes God has entrusted to us.

All this stuff is transient – entrusted to us for a brief while, while God calls us to: "Go!" to places we don't know where, to do tasks that are yet to be revealed. He bids us to be His People amid an alien world!

Someone has written:
>I do not know where God may lead
>But that His People may be freed
>From sin and death and doubt and fear
>That our hearts and others cheer.

Prayer: Lord, help me to realize I too live in a tent – that I may be free to do your bidding. Amen.

Day 87

Psalm 23

Mabel was celebrating her hundredth birthday. Gathered around her were her children, grandchildren, great grandchildren - even one great, great grandchild. There were also folks from her Sunday School Class at church. There was a lot of laughter and storytelling going on.

Mabel had sown joy along her path throughout her life, and now it was much in evidence!

The psalmist writes: "Surely goodness and mercy shall follow me all the days of my life"... (v.6a) What follows you in your journey? Goodness? Mercy? Love? Laughter? Joy?

For Mabel, love and laughter were the primary gifts she left in her wake. They followed her as she traveled the path of life. These things were much in evidence in her progeny at the birthday party that day!

What will I leave behind me today?

Prayer: Make me a contagious Christian, Lord. Fill me with your joy, that those who follow after me, may benefit from my witness. Make me an instrument of your hope and love, Lord, that others may see you in me. Amen

Day 88

II Chronicles 7:11-14; Philippians 2:1-11; Matthew 5:2, 3, 5 & 7

The least talked about aspect of the Christian walk is humility. Dare I say it is the least valued of all virtues! Yet, the more humble we are, the less worry, fear, and exhaustion will possesses our lives.

The beginning point of prayer is humility. For we are not ready to pray until we cease counting on our own resources, and discover what it is to truly rest in the Almighty. If you do not know what it is to be utterly and totally dependent on the Lord, then you do not know what real prayer can mean!

God says in II Chronicles 7:14: "If my people, who are called by my name, humble themselves, and pray ... then I will hear from heaven..." Our Lord says it again in Matthew 5:2: "Blessed are the poor in spirit ..." The Greek word translated "poor" is abject poverty, utter helplessness, or complete destitution. Such a person, Jesus says, is "blessed!"

How do we get humility? It is a by-product of suffering – suffering that leads us to lean wholly on God. It is the result of pondering the Cross, and sensing our own unworthiness. It is the result of prayerful realization of our limits.

Paradoxically, humility is not something you realize you have lest you be proud: "I'm humble and proud of it!"

Be careful about praying for humility. For often suffering follows. For God gets His greatest saints from the highlands of affliction!

Go with me to the nursing home to visit Aunt Minnie. She is bedfast now. Listen to this humble say, "God is so good!" and you will hear the angels sing!

Prayer: Lord, make me yearn for nothing more than a humble heart. Amen.

Day 89

Luke 23:42

Let me say more about the lost virtue: humility, that we dealt with in part yesterday.

Humility always precedes salvation. You cannot be saved if you feel you are self-sufficient. You must first cry: "Lord, remember me," as the thief on the cross did. (Matthew 9:20) You must sense your abject poverty before life and death, or you will not seek salvation to start with.

"Love" without humility is paternalistic, condescending. It places the recipient of our love beneath us. It states to some "poor soul:" "Let me fix this for you," rather than an attitude of one beggar telling another where he/she found bread. Thus, Jesus, who was and is humble love, washed the dirty feet of those who should have been washing His feet! (John 13:5) His was humble love!

Paul, who was the greatest missionary/evangelist of all time, was humbled by a "thorn" in the flesh, that caused him great anguish. Yet, it was a big reason for his effectiveness as a witness to the Gospel of Jesus Christ! (II Corinthians 12:7-9)

Humility is vital for salvation, love, and witness.

Prayer: Lord, you save us – you love us - you witness through us – through humility. Make us more humble that we may know that blessed life. Amen.

Day 90

Hebrews 11:8-12

"He looked forward to the city which has foundations, whose builder and maker is God."

Abraham looked forward to that city that John saw, as recorded in the book of Revelation 21:1-4: a city coming down out of heaven from God.

Soren Kierkegaard, the Danish philosopher, said: "Life can only be understood backwards, but must be lived forward." When we look forward, sometimes all we can see is gloom and doom – wars and rumors of war! Whereas in hindsight we see much more clearly the hand of God at work in our own lives and in history.

It is by hindsight that our faith is increased and confirmed! For we see now that God was in a time of trial that we went through. So that in practicing "rehearsal theology" – as it has been called - we confirm the activity of God in the past, and in the future.

Abraham could see all the way God had brought him, and thus could trust God for where He was leading him!

Prayer: Lord, I see your hand at work in my past – help me to trust _____ to your care now too! Amen.

Day 91

Psalm 139:1-12, 23-24

Mark Twain wrote that he spent $25 to have his family history researched, and then $50 to try to get it covered up again!

The Psalmist writes: "O Lord, you have searched me and known me …"

Yes, God knows us well! Yet, seeks us still!

"Where can I go from your Spirit, or flee from your Presence. If I ascend to Heaven, you are there; if I make my bed in Sheol – you are there. If I take the wings of the morning, and settle at the farthest limits of the sea, even there your hand shall lead me, and your right hand shall hold me …" (v.10) Face it, says the Psalmist, you can't get away from God no matter what!

God is in your past! He is in your present! And God will be in your future! He is going to keep you close!

Prayer: Lord, your grace is beyond all my imaginings! It is love "so amazing, so divine, [that it] demands my soul, my life, my all!" Amen.

Day 92

Matthew 7:21-27

"Not everyone who says to me, 'Lord, Lord' shall enter the kingdom of heaven, but he who does the will of my Father in heaven." (v.21) How do I know that I am on my way to Heaven? Jesus says, by the fact that I do the will of God.

The Protestant Reformation went too far! It taught that salvation is all about faith. Thus, it is commonly understood that all we have to do is "believe" - i.e. believe that Christ died for our sins, and arose to give us life eternal – then we are "in" -- Heaven is ours! But that is not what our Lord teaches!

Faith IS central to our salvation! But if our faith does not work – it is broken. Or as James put it: "Faith without works is dead!" (James 2:20) If your faith does not result in works of love, then it is of no account.

The Lord reaffirms this in Matthew 25:31ff, declaring that we will be judged by how we treat the "least of these [our sisters and our brothers]!"

Yes, all of us fall short! (Romans 3:23) Thus, we all must depend on the grace of God! But this must not lead us to complacency, but give us such gratitude that it makes us want to please our God of grace! It should lead us to works of love!

Prayer: Lord, help me this day to live out my faith through faithful obedience to your will. Forgive me of my sins, and give me an overflowing gratitude for your grace. Amen.

Day 93

Jeremiah 32:1-3a & 6-15

"And I bought the field at Anathoth". (v.9)

Back in 588 B.C. Jeremiah was imprisoned in Jerusalem for preaching – charged with treason! The Babylonians had the city surrounded – and were closing in!

One afternoon Jeremiah's cousin came to the prison with a strange offer: He wanted to sell to Jeremiah the family farm up at Anathoth.
Now let's go over this:

- Jeremiah is in prison facing the real possibility of death.
- Anathoth has already fallen to the enemy!
- The family farm is no longer in possession of the cousin.
- The cousin comes and offers a "real bargain" to Jeremiah.
- Jeremiah takes it!

Jeremiah is either a fool, OR a person of great faith who believed in God's ability to reverse what appears to be certain doom!

I believe it was Judy Collins who sang: "Where are the clowns?" We think of clowns doing such ridiculous things as to make us laugh. Jeremiah was a Godly clown, for he did something so laughable – yet daring, and faith-filled! For he believed in a God of possibilities who acts in the face of impossibilities!

Prayer: Lord, help me to lean on you as I look at the earthly possibilities before me. Amen.

Day 94

Psalm 137

Between yesterday's lesson and today's, Jerusalem has in fact fallen. The Hebrew people have been taken into exile in Babylon, and now on the occasion of Psalm 137, they are back! They are back lamenting their days of captivity and the destruction of their holy city! They are wishing vengeance on their enemies.

Self-pity is an attitude that is no stranger to us! It is a great enemy, one of the greatest we face in the Christian life!

- Before we fall to temptation usually it is preceded by numerous statements of "poor me!"

- Pity is the opposite of gratitude – thus it turns us inward rather than Godward.

- Pity saps the joy out of life!

Think of the past week: have there been times when you felt sorry for yourself? Then imagine the good things ahead – beyond your sight – that God has in store – just as he returned the Hebrew people to their homeland, and in time rebuilt the temple.

Prayer: Lord, help me to see the grave dangers of self-pity. Help me to avoid it "like the plague!" Fill me with a grateful heart – that I may sing your praises in times of trial. Give me the eyes of faith to see the good things you have in store for me. Amen.

Day 95

Jeremiah 1:4-10

Jeremiah lay down under an almond tree. He had finished his chores, now he could retreat to his favorite place. (Do you have a favorite place of retreat?)

He lay down under the tree, and looked up into its pink and white blossoms. The sun made it glow with a brilliant incandescence. For a few moments, time stood still!

"Jeremiah!" – He thought it was his mother calling. (How often we understand too soon!) He thought he heard someone in the tree – but saw no one!

"Jeremiah!" It sounded like his mother's voice and yet it didn't.

"Before I formed you in the womb, I knew you, and before you were born, I consecrated you; I appointed you a prophet to the nations."

You have heard this voice! Calling you in unexpected moments – in unexpected ways – in unexpected places. Calling you to be ... to do ... The Voice often comes when we are quiet enough to listen – still enough to hear!

"Lord! ... I don't know how to speak, for I am only a youth!" We often make excuses – for good reason – it usually doesn't make sense to us, and to many near us. "Calling YOU ... to do WHAT?!"

But God promises to be with us, and that alone makes it doable – makes it somewhat sensible!

We may all be tongue-tied prophets, but we serve an eloquent God!

The phone has rung. The Voice is God's! And it is for you!

Prayer: Lord, help me to hear, help me to do the tasks you have for me today. Help me to see where You are at work – and join in. Amen.

Day 96

Matthew 2:1-12

A puzzling group of men – these wise men from the East!

- They were not Jewish.
- They were not "church" people.
- They were astrologers of the occult!
- They were outsiders!

Yet, they were led by God! AND God used them to tell those "in the know" where He – who was to be worshipped – was to be found.

It is amazing how the Christ of Eternity is able to speak to those of differing faiths, or no faith.

Our job is not to take Him to them, but to simply name Him who is already there!

Prayer: Lord, humble me that I might realize that I am, as a Christian, not the only one with a "hot line to Heaven," but YOU have a way of coming/speaking to all peoples. Help me this day to name Him to another. Amen.

Day 97

Jeremiah 31:31-34

Michael Williams tells how in his first church, in Tennessee, as part of the "Mule Day Festivities," he entered the "liars contest." Now it is all right for a pastor to enter such a contest, but to WIN it could prove embarrassing! Win it he did!

Thus, the following week the town newspaper headlined: "Local United Methodist Minister Wins Liars Contest". AND, if that wasn't enough, they pictured him in the paper – so all would recognize the lying preacher, AND one of his Sunday School teachers who came in second! (You know the Baptists had a big laugh over that!)

Seriously, we prefer to talk about others' sins, but each of us has "sinned and [fallen] short of the glory of God".

Some of the best of the Good News comes from over in the Old Testament in Jeremiah 31:34b: "[Where God says] "I will forgive their iniquity, and I will remember their sin no more"

We preachers have been known to like a three-part message, and here we have it:

- God forgives.
- God forgets it!
- God forgives and forgets – forever!

Where in the Bible does it say that God can forget? Jeremiah 31:34b.

How often do we pray again – and – again: "Lord forgive me of that." And the Lord says: "Of what, Bill." For when God forgives he forgets it – forever!

Prayer: Lord, I thank you for your forgiving grace! Help me to forgive myself. Amen.

Day 98

Luke 10:25-37 (v.27)

"Love the Lord, your God with all your heart, all your soul, with all your strength, and with all your mind and your neighbor as yourself." (REB)

Jesus gives us three persons to love here: God, neighbor, and self. My guess is that of the three, the most difficult to love is yourself.

Sigmund Freud once wrote: "It is a good thing that we don't love our neighbors as we love ourselves, because if we did, we'd have a lot of dead neighbors!"

The antidote for this is to pause often before the Cross and repeat this truth: "God loves me THAT much! I am a child of the King! I am somebody very special!"

What can you do to make God love you more? Absolutely nothing! He already loves you with a love that is cruciform!

Prayer: Lord, thank you for loving me so. Thank you for coming in the flesh – for dying on the Cross – and for rising from the dead – for ME! Amen.

Day 99

Psalm 139:1-12, 23-24

We all carry baggage with us in life: good and bad. God is aware of it all, for He knows us well! (vs.1-3)

Yet, God seeks us still. (vs. 7, 9 & 10)

Francis Thompson, who died in 1907, was addicted to opium much of his life. In 1893 he wrote the poem, "The Hound of Heaven." That poem was his testimony of how he had tried to run from God, and yet how God remained in hot pursuit!

Each of us can look back, and see God's hand in our lives. In time of danger we see Him protecting us - in time of trial – seeing us through. He seeks us still!

Finally, this Psalm is telling us that God will not let us go! (v.8) You may let God go for awhile, but wonder of wonders, God will never let you go!

Prayer: Thank you Lord for your never-ending pursuit of me. Thank you for not being willing to let me go. Help me to live today as one who has been caught by your Holy Spirit. Amen.

Day 100

Matthew 5:38-48, especially verse 48

Does the Lord really expect perfection from us? He says here: "Be perfect as your heavenly Father is perfect!" Wow!

John Wesley, founder of Methodism, rightly interpreted verse 48, I believe, when he saw in it a reference to perfection in love, for immediately preceding this verse, is the Lord's discourse on love, climaxing in this command. Thus, the Lord is saying: "Be perfect - in Love - as your heavenly Father is perfect in Love."

But how can we attain perfection in love? Not by our own resources! For it is impossible for us to love persons who have caused us great harm! We cannot attain to this Love apart from the Love we encounter in the Cross of Christ.

That is why we have the Cross at the center of our worship each Sunday. That is why I have a crucifix on my Study wall - for I need a regular reminder of a Love like that, come from the God of creation! Only when we meditate upon that Love, do we come to more-and-more Love as He has loved. I have a long way to go, but hopefully I am on my way.

John Wesley never claimed perfection in love, but felt if that is not our goal, then what is it? We must aim high!

Prayer: Lord, help me to know the Love that enabled you to pray form the Cross: "Father, forgive them ..." Amen.

Day 101

Matthew 17:1-9

Strange things happen in this text! Two dead men, Moses and Elijah, appear to Peter, James, John, and the Lord – all on the Mt. of Transfiguration.

Though we do not see the dead in Christ, we do believe in what the Church has called the "Communion of the Saints" – i.e. those who die in the Lord surround us in a great cloud, and especially when we/they gather in worship. (See Hebrews 12:1a) Sometimes their presence is so real to me that tears come to my eyes!

Those who die in the Lord are not off in some distant heaven – they are here – all around us – cheering us on in the "race that is set before us" (Hebrews 12:1b). Wow! What a glorious reality that is!

We sing: "Praise God from whom all blessings flow; praise Him all creatures here below; praise Him ABOVE YE HEAVENLY HOST…"

Thus we can say: "There were TENS of thousands present for Holy Communion today!" Though the preacher can't count them as part of his/her congregation that Sunday – nevertheless they are present – they are HERE! – Praise God!

Prayer: Lord, thank you that we can pray: "Therefore with angels, and archangels, and all the company of heaven we laud and magnify your Holy Name.." Thank you that we too can commune with the saints as Peter, James, and John did of old. Amen.

Day 102

Romans 9:1-5

In September of 1992 we were having special services at St. Luke's United Methodist Church in Raytown, Missouri. The Reverend Gene Atkins was preaching and leading a Bible Study.

To prepare for these days, we had a 12 hour Prayer Vigil. I took a thirty minute block of time along with twenty-four others. It was, as it always is, a blessed time! Toward the end of my allotted time, I "saw" the sanctuary without pews, and the congregation face down on the floor. They were in earnest prayer to God. Anguished praying - as we see the Apostle Paul doing in the Lesson for today - that all might come to know Christ!

My spirit was deeply moved! I had been in the Presence of the Mighty One, and He had spoken!

The sense was: God was saying, "Such prayer is going to be the future of my Church. It will be known as a praying Church!"

Since, I have witnessed a growing movement in prayer, and a deep hungering for the same across the Church, and beyond.

Prayer: (Spend some time in prayer. Allow God to direct you in how long this should be.)

Day 103

John 20:19-31

All of life is lived by faith! We eat our cereal – by faith – that the manufacturer didn't allow something bad into the mix. We crossed a bridge this week – by faith – that it wouldn't collapse.

We trust our government officials – most of the time – and it is such faith that keeps our democracy intact – saving us from anarchy!

Thomas has gotten the title of "doubting Thomas" – because he doubted that the Lord had risen.

He was not going to take someone else's word for it, he was going to have to see the risen Christ with his own eyes! Thank God for Thomas, because he has helped to confirm our faith in the risen Christ!

Thomas did not conform to a cheap faith of "I believe - I believe!" I am glad the Biblical record includes him in the story.

Thomas is an important part of the saints of glory!

Prayer: Lord, I thank you that you make room in your kingdom for doubters. Help me to move, like Thomas, from doubter to one who is willing to give his/her life for the faith. Amen.
(See: II Timothy 1:12b)

Day 104

I Peter 1:3-9

What is Christian joy? Is it freedom from sadness? No. We will all have sadnesses in our lives, yet paradoxically we can rejoice. Is it being in a state of continual happiness – i.e. "happy all the time?" No! Happiness is dependent on outward circumstances. It comes and goes. Joy is constant.
(See Philippians 4:4)

The Greek word, here in verse 6, that is translated "rejoice" is "khar-ali." It means "calm" or "serene." Thus, I can be grieving, yet have a serene confidence that all is well – that God is still in control through Christ. Christian joy is founded in an inner relationship with the Lord!

In the early days of our nation, a pioneer was making his way westward in the dead of winter, when he came to the Mississippi River at evening time. The sun was setting in the west. Across the river was a log cabin with a light in the window. The river appeared to be frozen, so, with no place to stay, he decided to crawl across the ice – to spread his weight out - lest he break through. Half-way across he was frozen in his tracks by a loud noise! Then realizing it was behind him, he looked back. Coming out across the ice was a coal wagon piled high with coal, and a black man high atop the load – driving six horses, and he was singing as he made his way toward the other side!

Some persons crawl through life locked in fear of what the future holds. Others, with heavy loads, go toward the other side singing, for they know the Joy which comes from a sure foundation! (I Corinthians 3:11; II Timothy 2:19a)

Prayer: Thank you Lord for being a sure foundation. Thank you that in prayer I can be reassured of that fact, and grow confident of your faithfulness. (Spend 5 minutes thanking the Lord for specific blessings He has sent your way.) Amen.

Day 105

Psalm 23; John 10:11

My father was a sheep herder in eastern Wyoming back in the 1920s. He used to tell me stories of the month he spent "40 miles from nowhere" caring for the sheep. He often drew parallels with shepherding and Psalm 23.

Dad taught me these things about sheep, in light of the portions of the 23rd Psalm.

- The Lord guides to greener pastures. (The shepherd must continually move the flock to where the forage is.)

- He leads beside the still waters – because sheep are afraid of running water.

- He prepares a table before them in the presence of their enemies. (A "table" is a flat area, important so the Shepherd can watch over his flock. Further, he prepares the table by chopping out – noxious weeds, killing any rattlesnakes present, and he does all this in the presence of enemies: coyotes and wolves that can prey upon the flock.)

- He anoints the sheep's head and around the eyes with oil when they are irritated.

Therefore, the sheep "shall not want." (The shepherd provides all their needs.)

Through it all we can take heart, for "we shall fear no evil..." For we have a wondrous, and capable Shepherd and His name is Jesus!

Prayer: Lord Jesus, thank you for being my shepherd. Leading, guiding, providing, and protecting me insures I shall not want! Help me to sing your praises this day. Amen.

Day 106

II Timothy 4:6-8

Paul was in Rome in prison on death row. He knew that the time for his execution was near. So, unlike the rest of us, he could say when he would die. He expressed it by saying: "The time for my departure has come." The Greek word here translated "departure" was used by a captain of a ship when he gave the order to loose the mooring-ropes, so that the ship could sail toward its destination. Paul knew where he was going!

He writes to Timothy, his beloved son in the faith, "I have fought a good fight." Here we have the imagery of an athlete who has finished a race, and looking back, can say: "I have done my best." Paul knew he fell short of perfection (I Timothy 1:15), but he could say, "I have given it my best shot!"

He goes on to declare: "I have finished the race. I have kept the faith." He hadn't "kept" it to himself, but had shared the faith, while remaining faithful to it.

"Henceforth, there is laid up for me a crown..." In Greece the laurel wreath was placed upon the head of the victor - he was "crowned" with it. Though that wreath would wither, Paul knew that the crown he was about to receive from Christ would be eternal!

Paul says that this is not only true for him, but for all persons of faith who finish the race.

Prayer: Thank you Lord for the victory you give to us all who love you. Amen

Day 107

Romans 8:26-39, especially verse 26

"But we do not know how to pray as we ought" (v.26b). "We" here includes the apostle himself, and the Christians in Rome. "We do not know how to pray as we ought." "I thought I knew how to pray," we say. But, do we?

Too often our prayers – especially our public prayers – are focused on the wrong audience. Someone once described an elaborate prayer spoken in a prestigious Boston church as: "the most eloquent prayer ever offered a BOSTON audience." Who are we praying to?!

Further, our prayers too often are like Christmas lists sent to Santa Claus. But do we know him personally? Do we spend time listening, or repeating a mantra like: "Jesus, Jesus, Jesus," as we center on Him – draw close to Him – get to know Him?

Jesus says the heavenly Father is eager to give Himself, i.e. the Holy Spirit, to us who ask. (See Luke 11:13)

We do not need to voice our prayers at all, for the "the Spirit intercedes with sighs too deep for words." The Spirit forms the words to our wordless prayers.

Prayer: Lord Jesus – come. (Repeat this for the next two minutes as you center upon Him.)

(See also: Psalm 46:10)

Day 108

Genesis 1:20-31

The Irish teacher, John Scotus Eriugena, spoke often of God having two books: the Bible, and the universe. He believed that just as God speaks to us through the pages of scripture, so God speaks to us through His creation.

Have we not all experienced this? As a child I enjoyed lying on my back in the grass in the yard, and looking up at the great blue vault of the heavens with fluffy clouds floating by, and thinking how great is God's universe!

When I walked through the woods, and saw the squirrel scamper between the trees... the birds in their nests... and heard the cardinal singing nearby -- I sensed the Presence of God everywhere!

All this was not created out of nothing, but out of God! And God saw it, and pronounced it "very good." (v.31)

Spend some time today enjoying God's creation as you sit on your deck, walk in your yard, or drive in the countryside.

Prayer: O Lord, our Lord, how majestic is your name in all that you have made! In the wonders of your creation I sense your Presence. Thank you for creating me, and this vast glorious world! Amen.

Day 109

I Kings 19:9-18

Elijah had a price on his head! Jezebel, the Queen, was out to get him, so the prophet decided it was best to run for it! He fled south, over 250 miles, into the Sinai Peninsula to Mt. Horeb, climbed up the mountain, and went into a cave.

Elijah was disappointed with his plight as a faithful servant of the true God, Yahweh! He was tired of serving – burned out! He had been faithful, but what did it get him? A price on his head!

We like caves. They give us a place to hide out. We like them because they become so familiar. Illness is a cave for some people. Maybe it was the only time as a child she/he got attention. Thus, they enjoy poor health, for it still gets them needed attention. Others retreat into various addictions: drugs, sex, workaholism ... Several times I considered quitting the ministry – climbing Mt. Horeb – hiding!

But caves are poor places to live! So, God tries to blow Elijah out of his cave with a mighty wind! But the old wiry prophet hangs on. If he won't listen to the wind, how about an earthquake accompanied by fire and smoke?! Yet, Elijah remains in his hideout!

Then God does something interesting, He causes the place to fall silent. (See NRSV) Only then did the prophet crawl out of his hole to see what was going on. God then speaks to him, and he went forth with new resolve to serve his Maker.

Prayer: Lord, cause me to crawl out of my cave, and trust you wholly, as a Elijah of old, that I too may see your greatness in this time. Amen.

Day 110

Matthew 5:38-48, especially verses 44 & 45; Romans 12:14-21

Most of us have enemies. We did not choose it to be this way. Maybe it was for our stand in the Faith. Maybe it was because they offended us, or did some great harm to us. We do not live life very long without having some enemies.

The issue before us is how we are to deal with our enemies.

We can seek to ignore them. Sometimes this is an appropriate response for someone who simply seeks an eye-for-an-eye, or is seeking to get under our skin. Jesus says there is a time when it is appropriate to "shake the dust off of our feet," and leave! (Matthew 10:14)

We can seek revenge. Though tempting, this is inappropriate for us as followers of the Crucified One.

Finally, we should at least try to befriend them. "Love your enemies," Jesus says in our lesson for today. This may involve us saying, "Hello, Mary," when Mary does not return our greeting. (It also can "heap burning coals upon her head." Romans 12:20)

One of the greatest challenges of the Christian life is this: how am I to deal with my enemies?

Prayer: Lord, help me to know when to speak, and when to walk away. Above all help me to do the loving thing. In your name I pray. Amen.

Day 111

Deuteronomy 8:1-10 (Read this in Today's English Bible)

After the people of Israel crossed the Jordan into the Promised Land, they were told to gather twelve large stones and pile them up on the river bank as a reminder to generations to come of the blessed crossing of the river. The stones were called their "Ebenezer."

In the hymn, "Come Thou Fount of Every Blessing", we refer to this act by singing: "Here I raise my Ebenezer."

Where would you erect your Ebenezer?

- Maybe it would be at a church camp you attended.
- Possibly the church building of your youth.
- I would place one at Missouri State University where I met my wife.
- And one in St. Joseph, Missouri where our sons William and Wesley were born.

Prayer: Lord, if we started erecting Ebenezer's we would soon run out of rocks – even in these Ozark hills - for our blessings are as countless as the stars! May our lives sing your praises this day for all your mercies. Amen.

Day 112

Hebrews 12:1-2

Why was there "Joy" in the Lord's heart as He looked ahead to the Cross?! We could understand dread! Even fear. But Joy?! That is incomprehensible!

But the Lord realized that the Cross would bring salvation, hope, and peace to generations that followed.

The Crucifixion was the decisive: "Battle of the Bulge" – as was that battle in World War II. Now He was being called to participate in D-Day that would culminate in the Battle of the Bulge. He looked forward to it – as any team member who was getting to play the "super bowl" with Evil, for He was confident of victory!

Thus, He went to Golgotha's Hill and suffered the anguish of crucifixion. AND to all it appeared that Evil won!

But, there was an overtime battle being waged, and on Easter He came dancing and leaping – butting chests – if you will - with His followers!

There are other battles to be fought. The Battle of the Bulge in WWII did not end it all, but it was so decisive that the allies knew that victory was in their grasp! You and I will have to endure skirmishes with the Devil – if you will. He will cause us pain. He will even crush us down into a grave someday!

But we remain, with our Lord, joyfully confident! For we shall rise and go to be with the Lord – sharing His Victory!

Soldiers! "Put your armor on! Strong in the strength which God supplies through His eternal Son!" (From the hymn: "Soldiers of Christ Arise").

Yes, "In all these things we [too] are more than conquerors through Him who loved us. For I am sure that neither death, nor life, nor angels, nor principalities ... nor anything else in all creation, will be able to separate us from the love of God in Christ Jesus our Lord." (Romans 8:37-39)

Prayer: Lord, thank you for that truth! Help me in my trials to rejoice with You in the Victory that is mine! Amen.

Day 113

Romans 15:5-6; Hebrews 12:1

Carlyle Marney coined the phrase "balcony people." Balcony people are your cheering section. They are there for you through the valleys to be traversed, and the mountains to be climbed. They watch you run the race of life! They are persons here below, as well as the saints above who root for you! They surround you like a stadium filled with fans.

Life has an ample supply of critics, but far too few encouragers! It is great to know that regardless of the response of your earthly audience, you have one in Heaven that is cheering wildly for you every day!

Try to give honest encouragement to five persons today. It will bring joy to your soul, and to theirs as well!

Prayer: Lord, the Gospels are filled with instances where you encouraged others. Help me to profit by your example as I seek to be an encourager too! Amen.

Day 114

Hebrews 13:1-8

Being burdened down with things that in the end prove petty can consume a lot of our energy! Dr. Arnold Prater once shared in a sermon three things that can help us overcome our worries.

First, some things don't matter! Having a perfectly kept house – doesn't matter. Having perfect children – doesn't matter. Doing the perfect job (usually) doesn't matter. (Perfectionists need not apply.)

Second, some things don't happen! It would be revealing to keep a journal of our worries, and then see how most of them never happened!

An elderly gentleman said: "I know worry works, for over the years most of the things I worried about never happened!

Third, some things don't change! "Jesus Christ is the same yesterday and today and forever!" (v.8)

The earth may change; the oceans may change; but God's love, Presence, and Power – never change!

Prayer: Lord, Help me to remember that you are the same yesterday, today and forever! Teach me to trust in your unchanging Presence and Love. In Jesus' name I pray. Amen.

Day 115

Colossians 2:6-15, especially verse 9

When we trace our roots in the faith it leads us to Jesus, which, in turn, leads us to God, for you cannot, according to scripture, separate the two!

We acknowledge the human side of Jesus in the modern era. We readily think of Him as living among us - even being "Son of God." But today most Christians, I would dare say, fail to see Him as God Almighty! They, without realizing it, believe in two Gods: God Almighty, and His boy: Jesus Christ.

Yet, Colossians 2:9 tells us that: "... in Him [i.e. Jesus] the whole fullness of deity dwells." (See also: John 1:1; 20:28; Isaiah 9:6; Matthew 1:23; and Colossians 1:19)

Why is this important? If Jesus was not God, then God was not "in Christ" (II Corinthians 5:19), and if God was not in Christ, then we do not know if God loves us or not. Jesus loved us, but does God?

But because God was in Christ we have glorious Good News! We know we have a unique Savior, the Mighty God, who has come to us in flesh, and who loves us with a love that is cruciform!

Prayer: Thank you, O God, for caring enough to come yourself to save us, and even now to dwell with us as Risen Christ in your Holy Spirit! Amen.

Day 116

I Samuel 3:1-10

In Arthur Miller's "Death of a Salesman", Willie Loman's wife cannot figure out why he has committed suicide. She cries: "For the first time in our thirty-five years we were just about free –and–clear. He only needed a little salary! He was even finished with the dentist!" A friend replies: "No one needs: 'Only a little salary.'"

Too often we set our sights on trivial things, rather than the eternal ones. We want to sustain an existence, rather than the real life God intends for us!

Our lesson out of I Samuel is one where God is calling young Samuel to a life of meaning and purpose. As Samuel takes up the mantle of doing the Lord's bidding, his life will have great worth! He will be living for what his Creator made him for!

Thus, we too need to cry: "Speak, Lord, for your servant is listening."

Prayer: For your prayer time repeat: "Speak Lord, for you servant is listening" - followed by a minute of silence. Repeat this until you get a word – an inclination – a prodding concerning something you are supposed to do today.

Day 117

John 12: 20-33

A leading laywoman, we will call Mary, was experiencing burnout in her Christian walk. She had so many persons for whom she was concerned about their souls.

One night Mary had a dream. In her dream, the Lord came to her, and said: "Mary, I have been listening to you lately. You are sounding more like the public prosecutor, than the public defender." "But Lord!" Mary protested, "I want to reach others for you and your Kingdom!" In her dream God answered: "But, Mary, you must just love them and believe in them – I will take care of the rest."

When she woke, she determined to give up her Judge's Bench, and let the Lord love these folks through her into His Kingdom. In time, she was amazed at the results!

The world is crying: "Sir/Madame, we wish to see Jesus." (v.21)

Prayer: Lord, we are so quick to want to fix people, and forget your patient plodding on their trails. Help me to remember, and trust you more. Amen.

Day 118

Luke 24:13-35

Strange that He walked with them to Emmaus, and they – who had been so close to Him for all those years – did not recognize Him! Why?

But wait! He walked with you yesterday – but did you recognize Him? Did you recognize Him when he met you in "the least of these?" (Matthew 25:40) Did you realize He was there in the child's gaze? Did you recognize Him in that urging of you spirit to do a loving deed?

They DID recognize Him as they broke bread together! (v. 30-31 & 35)

Sometimes in the breaking of bread, we too sense His Presence so powerfully! Yes, we DO recognize Him at times!

Remember: He will walk with you again today also.

Prayer: Lord, keep me sensitized to your Presence – so that the trials and sorrows of life may be kept in perspective, so that I may hear you speaking, and so I will discover worries cure. Help me to tap your Resurrection Power, that I may live victoriously – and others will want some of what I have. Amen.

Day 119

I John 2:18-24, especially verses 18 & 19a

We are all guilty of idle talk – even hurtful gossip. It is one of the more common sins among Christians – and the pain it can cause is too underestimated.

Many years ago Alexander Whyte of Edinburgh, Scotland suggested we submit all conversations to three tests – to determine their appropriateness.

- Is it true?

    It is easy to repeat something without knowing its truthfulness. I once had an old saint in the church tell me right before worship one Sunday that a man – who rarely came to worship - had died. I announced it, only to find out he was very much alive. I made a beeline to his house to apologize! (After that I had to see the body!)

- Is it kind?

    This is an easier test to check. If it is not kind – it should be left unrepeated.

- Is it necessary?

    How much conversation about others – is not necessary? For example, Mabel is in the hospital. The Prayer Team does not need to know she had six inches of her colon removed. They should be able to pray for her anyway! And God is perfectly capable of locating the problem area without our detailed explanations. Most gossip resides in sharing the gory details of a person's malady.

Prayer: Lord, save me from idle chatter about others' maladies. Help me to first ask: Is it true? Is it kind? Is it necessary? Amen.

Day 120

Acts 1:12-14

Harry Denman, a great man of God, told of visiting a man in Meridian, Mississippi who was fondly called: "Praying Brother Brown."

Brother Brown was a widower, who had experienced many sorrows in his life. He was an humble man, who radiated joy in his life. Several miracles had happened in the lives of persons for whom he had prayed.

After dinner together, Brother Brown took Harry into his prayer room. He explained that he didn't let many persons into the room, but he sensed that Harry was a deeply spiritual man. It was a place where he went to be alone with God.

When was the last time you were truly alone with God?

One reason we do not know the Power that flows through prayer, is because we neglect being alone with God.

Prayer: Lord, in the stillness of this moment – I pause … to be alone – wholly alone – with you. Amen.

Day 121

Mark 4:35-41

All of us have been in "the boat!" God is there – for "storms" in our lives attract Him like a Mother is attracted to her baby's cry.

But note, in our Lesson for today, that the Lord is asleep! Have you ever – in the midst of a trial – felt God must be asleep? Many of us have.

Thus, it behooves us to "awaken" the Almighty – through earnest prayer. (v.38) Remember what Jesus teaches us about prayer? (See Matthew 7:7f) He teaches us to "ask" and keep on asking (for there is a continuum in the Greek that is translated simply as "ask"). "Seek" and keep on seeking. "Knock" – and keep on knocking.

Jesus is saying: "Keep on calling until the Master of the wind and waves awakens, and gives you what you need. (See Luke 11:9-13, especially v.13b)

What is it that we need? Healing? A job? Guidance? No–No, we need above all else the Holy Spirit – God with us! (Luke 11:13).

Prayer: Lord, teach me to look beyond all the things I could ask of you, and seek what I need most of all: your Presence! Amen

Day 122

I Samuel 17:32-49

David had his giant to face! I imagine that the boy, David, was possible 5'4" tall and weighed all of 100 lbs. The giant: 7' tall and weighing in at 325 lbs.! David had an impossible task!

From David we learn how to face those giants in our lives.

First, we have to face them - not denying their existence – nor pushing them down in our subconsciousness, but admit their existence and prepare to deal with them.

Second, David bows down to find five smooth stones – he bows before his Maker. I am sure he asked God's help, for we do not defeat life's "giants" without prayer!

Finally, he ran toward the giant with his sling whirring over his head – looking to the God of possibilities in spite of realities. Then releasing – trusting God for the results – and watching as the giant crumples to the ground!

Friends, ours is a God who is bigger than we often think – larger than life – greater than sickness – more powerful than even death!

Prayer: Lord, remind me of your greatness when I get focused on life's problems. Help me to trust you when the odds overwhelm me. Amen.

Day 123

I Corinthians 10:6-13 / Jude 24

Paul says here that temptation is common. If you are not aware of any "big" temptations – praise the Lord – but go easy. For are you tempted to gossip? Are you tempted to take the easy road – rather than going out of your way to care for another? Are you tempted to be critical of others – rather than offering encouragement/praise?

We are all tempted! Being tempted is not a sin – giving into it is where the sin lies!

Leo Tolstoy wrote of a man in a rowboat. Pushed off from an unknown shore, he rows out into the middle of the stream where lots of other boats are. Most of the oarsmen have thrown their oars away – just to "go-with-the-flow!" He too drifts along – until he is awakened from his day dreams by the sound of a waterfall! He leans against the oars, and manages to get his little craft ashore!

Paul is saying that our temptation is conditional, for God does provide a "way of escape" – if we are alert – and take the way out that He gives us!

Finally, Paul declares that temptation is conquerable! God will give you a "way of escape that you may be able to endure it."

What are some of the ways of escape? Prayer ... Christian fellowship – especially small group or one-on-one fellowship ... Worship ... Keeping my marriage healthy ... Staying close up to date in my relationship with God! Through these means of grace, God enables us to endure temptation.

Prayer: Lord, temptations bombard me hourly. Make me aware of them, and keep me mindful of the "oars" you have given me to row hard to safety. Keep me close, that I may be ready for the next onslaught, and forgive me when I fall short. Amen.

Day 124

II Samuel 7:1-11, 16-18

David, as newly anointed king, wants to build a temple in Jerusalem for God. He talks with his pastor, Nathan, and he of course, is elated!

But that night in a dream God tells Nathan to withdraw his building permit. So, what was the problem? The problem was David was getting too "big for his britches!" He was feeling he could take care of God! And that never works!

So, David had to learn to sit! (v.18) Is not that the most difficult thing we have to do? - i.e. Sit waiting on someone to return from surgery. Sit waiting on a doctor's appointment. Sit!

We feel so useless! We have to give up control! It reminds us who is God – when we just sit! So, "David went in and sat before the Lord."

That's a beautiful description of prayer: sitting – surrendered – silently – before the Lord! And it is there we – like David of old – get the bigger picture of what God has in store!

Prayer: Lord, help me to learn to sit and wait on you. Save me from running ahead. Teach me the lessons of patience. Amen.

Day 125

Mark 8:27-38

Jesus and His disciples were on their way to Caesarea Phillipi. As they walked and talked with each other, Jesus asks: "Who do persons say that I am?" They tell Him that the latest gossip being whispered, is that He is another John the Baptist, or some prophet. Then He turns it back on His disciples asking: "But, who do YOU say that I am?" Peter, speaking for the rest, answers: "You are the Messiah." (But their idea of Messiah was a political figure who was going to lead an uprising against the Roman occupiers, and throw them out – set up a kingdom – with Jesus as King!)

We do little better in our answers! We think of Him as One who will bring us great material blessings – even wealth. One who rubber stamps our political views. One who is there for us when we need Him, and stays out of our way the rest of the time.

But, is He our God and Savior? One who is known for His humble, sacrificial, service to others.

We declare each day who we think He is by the lives we live!

Prayer: Lord too often we try to make you into the god we want you to be. Forgive us! Help us to surrender again to the God and Savior you are. Make us into the servants you would have us to be. In Jesus name we pray. Amen.

Day 126

II Samuel 24:18-25, especially verse 24

Riverside Church in New York City has been for many decades one of the most prestigious churches in America! It has the largest carillon in the world, 14 kitchens, 8 chapels, a bowling alley, a theater, a radio station, and a gymnasium. In addition its décor includes fine sculptures and other works of art.

Riverside Church was built by the Rockefellers in the 1920s. When it opened the famous Baptist preacher, Harry Emerson Fosdick, was called to be the first pastor. On his first Sunday, Fosdick stood before a packed house; looked around at the multi-million dollar edifice, then announced: "It is strange to remember that all of this was built in honor of a Galilean carpenter who had no place to lay his head!"

Yes, we need places of worship – but not places TO worship! But more, we need places where we can worship God each day – as we find places to serve Him.

King David said, "I will not offer ... offerings to the Lord my God that cost me nothing!"

Prayer: O God, help me this day to seek out places where I can show my commitment to you by acts of sacrificial love. Amen.

Day 127

Philippians 4:4-7

It is A.D. 63, and the apostle Paul is in the Mamertine Prison in Rome. His cell is a hole in the ground into which he had been lowered on a rope. There were no windows – no ventilation – only a small hole in the center of the stone that now covered the pit. Through this aperture what food and drink he was given was lowered. If this were not bad enough, Paul was awaiting execution.

Yet! He writes to the Christians at Phillipi: "Rejoice in the Lord always, again I say rejoice... Do not worry about anything, but in everything by prayer and supplication, with thanksgiving, let your requests be made known to God. And the peace of God which passes all understanding will keep your hearts and minds in Christ Jesus."

Paul had learned – through many hardships – to lean on God, and to know that God never failed him! He had learned to keep his mind focused in Christ through much prayer, with the result being a peace that is beyond the understanding of the world, because it doesn't make sense in human terms!

What does this say to you about the trials, fears, worries, hardships that weigh you down today?

Prayer: Lord, help me to let go, and wholly lean on you. Give me that peace that is beyond the world's understanding, that I may experience the victorious life. Amen.

Day 128

I Corinthians 12:1-13 & 27

Paul writes: "You are the body of Christ!" (v.27) You are the only Christ the world will ever see! Through you, and only you, the world come to know the love of Christ. So suddenly, as far as we are concerned, the mission field has moved to our doorsteps!

This is all a compliment and a great challenge! For example we can see on television those who depict Jesus as the great Wall Street Broker, who can make you rich if you only send your "seed money" to them.

Eugene Peterson says: "We are living in golden calf country! It is both easy and attractive to become a successful pastor like Aaron."
(Read again Exodus 32)

The temptation is great for pastors, and individual Christians, to justify their riches as a gift to the neglect of the tithe, and the true following of the crucified One who had "no place to lay His head!" (Matthew 8:20) (See also: Matthew 16:24-26)

"YOU are the body of Christ!" We must never forget who we are, and whose we are!

Prayer: Lord, enter into my flesh, and help me to be the true reflection of yourself. Enter in, Lord, and help me bear the cross you have for me to bear. Enter into my flesh, that I may share the glory of your Presence to all I meet today. Amen.

Day 129

Acts 16:6-10

Paul was on his second missionary journey. He headed into present day Turkey when it says that he and his companions: "Were forbidden by the Holy Spirit to speak the word there." So, they go north into Bithynia. Again it says: "The Spirit of Jesus would not allow them (Note the interchange here: Holy Spirit equals Spirit of Jesus). Disappointed Paul, Silas, and Timothy go west to the coastal town of Troas. From there they would go across to Europe to start the spread of the Gospel there.

Paul was ill. (See Galatians 4:13-15) His antecedent ties with Luke, the physician, was probably designed to keep him going. What was his illness? It may well have been malarial fever. We do not know, but that would come with debilitating headaches, etc. that would be a trial for him and his hosts.

A roadblock! We all have faced them, and like Paul it was not because of any evil he had done, but for a greater good that is part of God's plan! As Julie Andrews sings in "The Sound of Music:" "When God closes a door – He opens a window!"

Yet, we are prone to understand life's roadblocks too soon as: "the end of the road" _ "an insurmountable tragedy" ... could it be that there is no loss or pain that is beyond God's redemptive power?! That is the story of the Bible. It is Paul's story here. It can be our story too.

Because of Paul's disappointments, the Gospel was proclaimed to modern day Europe!

Prayer: Lord, help me to see the barriers I confront as bridges to greater service. Help me to discern when it is time to change direction, and when it is time to keep-on-keeping-on in spite of the obstacles, that You may be glorified in all things. Amen.

Day 130

John 6:1-14

The feeding of the 5,000 is the only miracle in all the New Testament that is recorded in all four Gospels. John Maxwell, when he looked at this and other miracles of the Bible, concluded that miracles happen when:

- There is a need
- Sensed by a few
- And each understands his/her responsibility
- And gives his/her best regardless of the odds
- Then the Lord will work a miracle.

God does not always work a miracle under such circumstances, but when He does these are the ingredients. Thus, we must pray to discern God's will, for God does do mighty deeds through us – even in spite of us!

I thank God that the lad in John 6:1f was willing to give his lunch over to the Master, and thus to be a part of a miracle.

Prayer: Lord, help me to not put limits on what you are able to do. Guide me that I may be a willing participant in your miracle-working power. Amen.

Day 131

Mark 16: 1-8

"Go and tell His disciples – and Peter." You see Peter had backslidden – he was no longer a disciple! He had denied the Lord three times.

How often do we deny the Lord by what we say and do, OR – more often – by what we fail to say or do!

It is comforting to know that the Lord still loves us – forgives us – wants fellowship with us!

My professor of homiletics in seminary, Dr. John Brokhoff, was preaching in a small town in Florida. One evening, before the service was to begin, he was guest for supper in the home of one of the members. As he arrived, he noticed his hostess' license plate read: "Even Me." Around the table she told her story: one of unfaithfulness to her husband – a resultant break-up of marriage – of turning to drink to drown her guilt and pain. Then one Sunday her children talked her into going to church. The preacher spoke on this text emphasizing the verse: "Go tell His disciples AND Peter" – suddenly the message pierced her soul, and her life was transformed!

In honor of her newfound life, she had her license plate changed to read: "Even Me".

Prayer: Thanks be to God for His wondrous grace extended to each of us! Amen.

Day 132

Luke 19:28-41

Why is God so powerless on this day as He enters into Jerusalem? He weeps over the city! He rides in on a humble donkey!

Where is the victorious General of the Universe riding His snorting steed into victory?!

Some things cannot be forced – and love is certainly one of them!

On the 100th anniversary of the birth of Abraham Lincoln in 1909, H. T. Webster celebrated the occasion by imagining two Kentucky frontiersman meeting in the snow. The two paused to visit, as folks did in those days. "What's new?" one asked. The other replied, "Nuthin'… 'cept a new baby was born down at Tom Lincoln's cabin."

In the silence of eternity – God works! Through humble love He transforms lives! Through resurrection Power, the Mighty One shakes the very foundations of the world!

Prayer: Thank you, Lord, for the many times you show yourself to be in charge! Amen.

Day 133

I Kings 19:1-4; 8-15

Remember the dual Elijah had with the prophets of Baal (Elijah 18:20ff) where he called down fire from heaven? Well Jezebel, the Queen, was very unhappy with her spiritual advisors being shown up in such a public way! This puts Elijah's life in danger, so he becomes a man-on-the-run.

Here God has just performed a miracle and embarrassed the prophets of Baal, yet Elijah is not sure if God can do it again – and protect him. Why couldn't he believe now?

Elijah was burned out! He had faced a formidable enemy with an evil queen on their side – and won! He had cared so much for the people who were being led astray by the prophets of Baal – and what did he get for all his efforts: a price on his head!

Have you ever experienced compassion fatigue? Have you ever felt you were doing God's bidding – yet receiving little or no thanks?

Elijah is ready to quit! Feeling very sorry for himself, he decides to head south. He is sick and tired of fruitless preaching – tired of standing up for God's way – tired of caring! AND he is more than a little forgetful of God's past mercies!

He hides out in a cave. There God seeks him out through a mighty wind – to blow him out, through an earthquake to try - to shake him out, but then came the shear silence (v.12 NRSV), and Elijah comes out to see what's going on! There he hears the "still small voice" of God. There he leaves self-pity behind and goes to do God's bidding.

Prayer: Lord, it is easy to get burned out – to give up – to feel sorry for ourselves! Speak to me in the stillness of Eternity that I may find your way again. Amen.

Day 134

Acts 26:24-29, especially verse 28 KJV

We once lived across the street from a woman who told me one day: "I'm a Christian. I'm just not practicing it at present." Can you be an "almost Christian" – one who either almost believes - almost serves?

I think not! (Matthew 7:21) John Wesley, the founder of Methodism once said: "The revival out of which Methodism was born began when we resolved to be, not nominal, but real Christians!"

This is summarized by the late Dr. Marvin Piburn, who had served many years as a medical missionary to Africa. In his last assignment he served in a hospital in Nigeria in 120 degree heat seeing on average 110 patients a day. As he was sharing some of his experiences, he stopped, stared off into space, and added: "I wish I could have done more!"

We might say that he tried to do too much, but we cannot say that Dr. Piburn was an almost Christian – he was an all together one!

Prayer: Lord, make me an altogether Christian: in word and in deed. Amen.

Day 135

I Corinthians 9:19-23

"I have become all things to all persons, that I might by all means save some." (v.22)

Paul was a humble man. He didn't flaunt his intellect – though he was a very intelligent man!

To "become all things to all persons" does not mean that he became like all persons, but in humility entered into their sufferings and questions without condemnation or a holier-than-thou attitude. Paul suffered with the suffering, and affirmed the doubter – without himself becoming such.

I have shared with you before, but it illustrates the point: Early in my ministry I was given a suit of clothes by an anonymous parishioner. I went to get the gift. The clerk, knowing that the recipient was a pastor, said: "I don't believe in God!" I found myself replying: "That's all right, God believes in you!" It was the Spirit giving me the words to speak.

I became one with him by saying: "That's all right ...," while affirming God as well. The clerk became very quiet, and said no more.

Prayer: Lord, give me the words to speak that you might save some. Amen.

Day 136

Acts 9:1-20

Saul who became the Apostle Paul was struck blind on the road to Damascus. The Lord calls Ananias on a dangerous mission of mercy to find Saul, the killer of Christians, now converted. Ananias is to lay hands on Saul that he might receive his sight. (The task was like someone to go, and lay hands on a lion!)

Ananias finds Saul, and lays hands upon him, and Saul receives his sight. For the first time he looked out with eyes of compassion, joy and peace! He was a different man!

Sometimes God sends us on dangerous missions:

- To take a moral stand against the forces that use and abuse persons.
- To take a stand against injustice and oppression.
- To go to lost souls that have no grasp of the Love God!

When we look upon Jesus we see a different world. We experience new life!

Prayer: Lord, we praise your name for the vision of a better world. Help us to never give up on any lost souls in our circle of influence. Amen.

Day 137

Luke 14:25-33

"Which of you, intending to build a tower, does not sit down first and count the cost, whether he has enough to finish it." (v.28)

Charlie, we will call him, came forward one Sunday morning and announced he wanted to accept Christ, and begin a new life. He had been a part of the drug scene for years, but this was to be a new beginning. We welcomed him and his wife into the church. They attended every Sunday for about ten months.

One evening I was watching the news and they announced a bank robbery. They had caught the guilty party: "Paul Johnson." Then they showed his picture, and it was Charlie! I called to report that they had the wrong name, but, by the time I had called, they had already figured out the real identity of the person they had in custody.

It is one thing to begin a race, and another to finish it. Charlie could not finish! How sad!

Thus it is important for us to count the cost of becoming a Christian, and then practice the disciplines of prayer, study of God's Word, and Christian fellowship lest we fall away.

Prayer: Lord, keep me near. Give me strength to stand while others fall. Amen.

Day 138

John 1:29-42

"They said to Him, 'Rabbi…where are you staying?' He said to them, 'Come and see.'"
(vs. 38-39)

What a glorious thought to be able to stay where the Lord was residing! And yet, He lives today:

- In loving hearts – "Come and see!"
- Where you find joy amid pain – "Come and see!"
- Where persons speak against injustice – "Come and see!"

Martin Luther King, Jr. was a reluctant leader of the Civil Rights movement. Yet because of his charisma and speaking ability, those near him pressured him into that leadership role. He was one who went and saw where the Lord was living, and great things resulted!

An imperfect man was inhabited by the perfect Christ! "Come and see!"

Prayer: Open my heart and life, O Lord, to the indwelling of your risen Presence. May your Holy Spirit take up residence in me, so that the world may come and see what you are like. Amen.

Day 139

John 16:25-33, especially verse 33

It is politically correct to criticize the Christian Faith! Commentators, motion pictures, and television media consider Christianity as fair game!

It is not politically correct to criticize Islam, Buddhists, or even atheists in our society today. Not that we should be party to criticizing any of these. All need to hear the Good News of Jesus Christ - not to be torn down by an attacks on their beliefs. (Yes, atheists believe too! They believe in human resources to meet their basic needs!)

All this is nothing new! For after all we are followers of a Crucified Lord! That is why He declared: "In the world you will have tribulation; but be of good cheer, I have overcome the world!" (v.33)

This is to say that we must not become masochistic about our world situation, for persons of all faiths suffer somewhere in our world. We do not have to seek it, persecution will come!

Prayer: Lord, save me from self-pity. Help me to remember your Cross, and to not waiver from bearing my own. Give me love for all peoples - that I might win some for you. Amen

Day 140

I Corinthians 2:1-10

Paul was a great intellect of the first century. He had studied under Gamaliel. (Acts 22:3) Yet he says, in his first letter to the church at Corinth, that his preaching didn't come from human wisdom – but in "demonstration of the Spirit and of power!" (vs. 4-5)

He was an attorney – a student of the law – of the first degree. Yet he did not rely on his great intellect to convince his hearers – but on the wisdom of God and the working of the Holy Spirit.

Human knowledge and insight cannot save souls, nor change lives, it takes the Power of God to do that!

Thus when we have persons who want to argue with us about the Faith, it is best to back off and pray for them. If they are open at all to God – He will convince them of their need for Him! And lay it on our hearts when, and if, it is time to speak about our faith.

Prayer: Lord, make of me your witness – not with human knowledge – but with the Power of you Spirit! Amen.

Day 141

Mark 6:45-52

Here Jesus "MAKES the disciples get into the boat ..." (v.45)

That runs contrary to our modern way of thinking, for we think of God as having a laissez-faire attitude toward the world. That is, we tend to be agnostic in our view of God.

The agnostic is one who believes that God made the world, but then ran off and left it to run on its own. To think that God makes anything happen is quite foreign to us. Thus we sing, "Que sera, sera – whatever will be will be."

But that is not the God of the Bible! For He is the God who "disciplines [the one] He loves." (Hebrews 12:6)

If a father sees his four year old running toward a busy street, he will race to intercept her, and if necessary snatch her by the nap of the neck in a rough manner to stop her. So God has to sometimes jerk us back from the edge of disaster!

He sometimes MAKES us get into the boat!

Prayer: Lord, thank you for caring enough that you discipline us. For loving us enough that you sometimes get rough with us to get our attention. Help us to profit from those times. Amen.

Day 142

Matthew 5:21-26

"If you bring your gift to the altar, and ... remember your brother or sister has something against you ... First be reconciled with [that person], and then come and offer your gift." (v. 23-24)

Here the Lord is pointing out how dangerous grudges are!

Studies have shown how holding animosity against someone can take its toll on your health!

Here Jesus is lifting up the spiritual implications of such – not to mention the negative witness that results.

Now this does not mean if someone abuses us, we should pretend nothing happened and go get abused again! But it does mean that, for our sake, we forgive so we can move on with our lives.

How can we forgive? By praying for our enemies. (Matthew 5:44) First, it will be begrudgingly, but later more sincerely, and forgiveness will come in equal proportion.

Prayer: Lord, help me to forgive _____. May you, as the crucified Christ, be seen to dwell in me. Amen.

Day 143

Colossians 1:15-26

We have a mystery here! Paul says: "I now rejoice in my sufferings …, and complete in my flesh what is lacking in the afflictions of Christ …" (v.24)

What is lacking in Christ's sufferings? What could be lacking?!

In every age it is necessary for there to be "little Christs," as Martin Luther coined the term. Little Christs are persons who bear the cross for that age – innocent sufferers. Persons who due to illness, persecution, or the sins of others, suffer as a result. They complete what is lacking in the sufferings of Christ -- for THAT age.

Such persons would include: Abraham Lincoln, Mahatma Gandhi, Rosa Parks and Martin Luther King, Jr. to name a few.

Abraham Lincoln said in his second inaugural address, in essence: "Great sins require great suffering. Thus the centuries of slave trade required the sufferings of the Civil War." He was saying that in that horrific war, they were completing what was lacking in the sufferings of Christ.

Prayer: Lord, help me to bear the cross in my time – to complete what is lacking in your sufferings for our time. Amen.

Day 144

Genesis 5:21-24; Psalm 90:12

What a difference when we have walked with God on our journey through life as Enoch did! (Genesis 5:24)

Roy Angell once said: "The best sermon I ever heard Dr. George McDaniel preach was from the back of a horse!"

The two of them were out fox hunting. They turned the hounds lose and soon they were on the trail of a fox. So Roy and George rode their horses over to a cave where the fox often sought refuge.

Once in sight of the cave, they hid in some underbrush. Sure enough the fox came trotting up to the cave well ahead of the dogs. He licked himself off. Then, as the dogs drew near, he trotted on into the cave.

Dr. McDaniel leaned over, and grasped the pommel on Roy's saddle and said with deep emotion: "Roy! When you have a safe refuge, the hounds of life don't worry you that much!"

Enoch walked with God 365 years, then God said, "Enoch it is closer for you to go Home with me, and so he did.

Prayer: Lord, thank you for being our safe refuge from all that would destroy us. Amen.

Day 145

Mark 10:32-34

Jesus is going to Jerusalem to die. He is walking ahead of the disciples. He has set His face "like a flint" (Isaiah 50:7) – walking with great determination!

The disciples were afraid (v.32b) as they followed Him. He had talked about dying, but they could not comprehend something so heinous happening to so great a Man!

Following Him is not easy! It can be downright frightening!

I was about eight years old when I came upon a copperhead snake in our garden. Dad was nearby hoeing the corn, so I ran to get him. He immediately went with hoe in hand to find the poisonous snake. I followed at some distance terrified of what lay ahead. My father found the snake, killed it, and returned to his work.

"God is able!" (II Corinthians 9:8) He is able to destroy the Destroyer! He is able to hang on a Tree and transform it into an instrument of redemption. He is able to rise from the grave, and come in His Holy Spirit to walk ahead of us into life's uncertainties!

Prayer: Lord, we praise you for being our God! We thank you for leading the way into the tomorrows. We are blessed! Amen.

Day 146

Psalm 37:1-9

A pastor saw a young lad trying to sell a lawn mower. Since he needed one, he stopped to look it over. He told the boy he was interested, but first he wanted to see it run. He pulled and pulled the cord, but to no avail. Finally, the youngster said, "Sir, you usually have to curse it to get it going." "Well son, I am a pastor and cannot do that!" "Keep pulling, Mister," said the lad, "and the words will come!"

The Psalmist declares that we must "wait patiently for [the Lord]." (v.7) Yet, that can be one of the most difficult things we have to do when we are hurting.

But there is good news from the prophet Isaiah for those of us who find patience slipping away, he writes: "They who wait for the Lord shall renew their strength!" (Isaiah 40:31a)

It is like exercise, the more you do it the stronger you get, and the more you practice patience with the Lord the more patient you become, because you learn that it is worth the wait! In the end, He does give us blessings.

Prayer: Lord, give me patience and give it right now. No! Lord, help me to wait on you so that I may get better at it, and be more blessed. Amen.

Day 147

Acts 12:5-17

Everything was going against the fledgling church! Peter was in prison and the enemies of the Church seemed to have the upper hand. (Does that sound familiar for the Church in the Middle East today?!)

Peter was sleeping, chained between two soldiers, with guards at the prison door. An angel came and woke him and led him past the guards to freedom.

Wow! When God is on your side you have nothing to fear!

I love the part where he then goes to the house where the Christians were praying for him. He knocked. They don't believe it could possibly be him! (Isn't it amazing how we fail to believe that God is going to answer our prayer?) No, it wasn't "possibly" him, it was impossibly him! And there was much rejoicing!

Our God delights in impossibilities, and asks: "Is anything too hard for me?" (Jeremiah 32:27)

Prayer: Lord, we can expect the unexpected when you are involved. Give me faith in the divine possibilities today. Amen.

Day 148

Psalm 95:6-7; Luke 4:8

"O come, let us worship and bow down", wrote the Psalmist. Again, our Lord Himself declared: "You shall worship the Lord your God".

But, why?!

I remember going with my parents to worship when I was about four years old. It was a very formative experience in my spiritual walk. I studied the older folks seated around me, and realized there was something here very important – even vital! The way they sang – their attitude in prayer (Yes, I was peeking!) – the way they loved one another – all had a tremendous impact upon me!

We need to worship for the sake of our young. We need to worship for our own sake, otherwise we will worship things all week, and forget God!

More – worship is not something you get, but give. From Old Testament times worship was the offering of a lamb, or some other animal, up to God, and later the offering of our voices in praise to God!

The fact that He is our God demands that we make the sacrifice of worship!

Prayer: Lord, help me to always want to worship you in response to all you have done for me in Christ Jesus my Lord. Amen.

Day 149

Deuteronomy 32:1-12

When young eaglets are mature enough to fly the mother eagle will swoop down on the nest, high on the bluff, and force them over the precipice. Then, if they struggle and begin to plummet earthward, she will drop below them and catch them on her back, and carry them back to the nest to try again another day.

When God thinks we are mature enough to fly spiritually He gives us a big shove. We think the world is coming to an end – that we will not survive this one! But again when we begin losing it – he swoops down below us and catches us, and lifts us back to the ledge where it is safe – to try our wings again another day.

Yes, "underneath are the everlasting arms!" (Deuteronomy 33:27)

Prayer: Lord, flying can be frightening! But that is how I find out what you meant for my life, and that you are faithful when I fall. How wonderful is your name, O God! Amen.

Day 150

Luke 18:1-8a

"Jesus told his disciples a parable to show them that they should always pray and not give up." (v.1)

Prayer is the breath of the soul! Without it we die spiritually! Persistence in prayer is like persistence in breathing – again you cannot live very long on one breath – it takes keeping-on-keeping-on.

Jesus uses His story of the widow to get this point across, and more – to impress upon us how God answers persistent prayers.

Thus, the question: "Should I stop praying, and leave the matter in God's hands?" is answered here with a: "No!"

Why? Because the tenacious prayer keeps us centered on Who is the Source of all blessing. And as God blesses us – we don't forget to thank God for the gift.

Prayer: Lord, your saints have been unflagging in their prayers. Help me to learn from this lesson, and their example, that I may see the glorious blessings in store for me and others. Amen.

Day 151

Zechariah 4:1-7

"Not by might nor by power, but by my Spirit," says the Lord of hosts." (v.6)

I cannot live the Christ like life – my feeble attempts are only by the Spirit at work within me.

I cannot be strong – but by the Spirit being strong within me.

I cannot have an effective witness in the world – only the Spirit can through me.

It is not by our nation's military might that we are truly strong, but by the Spirit working in and through our country.

Imagine that we are preparing for take-off aboard a 747. Here we sit in this airliner that weighs tens of thousands of pounds! By itself it is bound to the earth by gravity. It cannot fly! Yet, because of the spirit of petroleum it is set free from the power of gravity!

So, the Spirit of God sets us free to live the victorious life in Christ Jesus!

Prayer: Lord, help me to never forget: It is not about me, but all about you at work within me. Amen.

Day 152

Luke 4:1-13

Someone has said, "Satan aims high." Here he takes after the Christ tempting Him in various ways. Later he will get the lead disciple to deny the Lord three times. He always goes after the Christian who has risen through the ranks of the Church to a place of leadership, and still has time to tempt all the rest of us as well!

It is not until we become a Christian that the Devil begins to work on us – tempting us with all manner of evil. Up until we are saved, Satan has us – so temptation is no issue.

Because we as Christians are all the subject of Satan's seduction, therefore, we must "watch and pray... [for] the spirit indeed is willing, but the flesh is weak". (Matthew 26:41)

When you reach the pinnacle – look out! Pray often lest you come crashing down!

Prayer: Lord, keep me near. Help me to be grounded in prayer, for temptations are ever around and within me. Amen.

Day 153

Isaiah 6:1-8

Back in the 1700's in the great Evangelical Revival that swept across England, John Wesley called for volunteers to go to the American colonies and take the Gospel to them. Francis Asbury stood up as one who was ready to go, and go he did, spreading the Gospel far and wide!

We are Christians today because of persons like him. All Christians are called to be witnesses for that same Gospel. Hopefully our response will be "Here am I, send me." (v.8b)

Not all hear the call, for there are so many voices vying for our attention. Some hear, but respond: "It is time for the younger people to do that – I've done my part!" But the only retirees in the Lord's Army are out in the cemetery! The rest of us – especially older persons with all their reservoir of experiences and insights – are called to: "Go!"

Prayer: Lord, the need is great, and willing witnesses few. Help me to hear your call and respond with my own: "Hear am I! Send me." Go before me to the persons you would have me to bring your message to. Prepare their hearts for your Good News. Go beside me to know the words to speak, the deeds to do. Then go behind me, to continue your work in the lives of those I meet. Amen.

Day 154

Matthew 6:24-34

We spend a lot of time and energy fretting about:

- Getting our fair share
- Our health
- The welfare of our children
- Having enough for retirement

These are all important concerns and should require our attention, but many of us are prone to allow our worry to go off the scale!

Jesus says to us: "If God ... clothes the grass of the field ... will He not much more clothe you, O [persons] of little faith?" (v.30) ... "But seek first His kingdom ... and all these things shall be yours as well." (v.33)

He closes by giving us a humorous thought when He says in essence: Be satisfied with the troubles you have today – they are enough without borrowing more from tomorrow!" (v.34)

Prayer: Lord, help me to trust more in you, and rely less in my own ability to answer all my needs. Help me to be satisfied to simply surrender to your will, knowing you will give me what is best. Amen.

Day 155

II Kings 6:8-23

Elisha's servant announces to his master that they were surrounded by the Syrian army! The servant was panic stricken! What were they going to do?! They were surely going to fall to the enemy!

But what does Elisha do? He prays: "Lord open his eyes that he may see." And the Lord opened the eyes of the young servant, and he saw the mountain was full of God's cavalry and chariots of fire -- they were everywhere!

We need to pray that prayer for ourselves that we may see that we are not alone against all that would do us harm! God does not leave His servants defenseless!

Yes, we face foes within and without – all around: i.e. doubts – fears – illnesses – terrorist threat! But our God is bigger, and will not to be defeated!

Prayer: Lord, open my eyes that I may see beyond the obvious to the unseen. Help me to realize your saving power. Amen.

Day 156

II Corinthians 6:1-13

Paul writes that he is "sorrowful, yet always rejoicing". (v.10) What a paradox!

Be patient with yourself and your friends when they experience a time of sorrow or depression, for such is not a stranger to the faithful of the Bible! Moses got so depressed that he cried out for the Lord to "kill me at once!" (Numbers 11:10-15; especially v.15) Elijah, considered the greatest prophet of the Old Testament, became depressed to the point of wanting to die! (I Kings 19:4) The Psalmist often showed signs of depression. In Psalm 42:3-11 he tries to talk himself out of it three times, but to no avail. Paul showed signs of both, and we all experience the former – if not both! Even Jesus wept! (John 11:35)

Nevertheless Christian joy supersedes all this. For you can be sorrowful – even depressed – and still know in your heart-of-hearts the joy of the Lord. For this joy is not cheaply bought! It is founded on a Rock like a massive lighthouse. Storms will come. Their impact will be felt – but our confidence is sure for we know Him who is our Rock!

Sorrow – yes! Yet, rejoicing!

Prayer: Lord, help me to be more patient with myself. When I am sorrowful help me to claim it – experience it – and regain my footing. For I have full confidence in You – my Rock and my Redeemer! Amen.

Day 157

Exodus 20:1-21

God is content to keep certain things from us. Oftentimes it is things related to suffering, but it can also be the heights of joy that come only after a long walk with the Almighty! Mysteries!

Moses has just received the Ten Commandments. Now Moses draws near to the "thick darkness where God was." (v.21)

When we went through the trials we had with our mentally challenged son: seizures ... frustrations with not being able to do things his twin brother was doing – it was amazing that amid the dark cloud – again-and-again – God revealed Himself to us! God's tears – His strength seemed very near!

Yes, there were many hours when all we could see was the black cloud, but dark clouds are where God is! Moses found this to be true, and many of us have also.

So, when you enter a period of darkness, get ready! God is coming - like a Mother running to her crying infant!

Read: I Peter 4:12-13; Philippians 3:8-11; & John 11:35

Prayer: Lord, I do not like dark clouds. But I love your Presence that comes amid those clouds. Thank you, Lord! Amen.

Day 158

Luke 5:1-11

Think of it: the itinerant preacher, Jesus of Nazareth, telling the real fishermen how to fish! (v.4) (There are lots of humorous occasions throughout Scripture, if we move away from thinking that the Bible has to be all seriousness, and see especially the humor of God!)

Peter protests: "Lord! We have fished all night and caught nothing" – we are tired – ready to call it a day!

Yet, Jesus has said: "Put out into the deep and let down your nets for a catch." So to humor Him they launch out.

It is in the deep water that the fish – in this instance – are to be found!

How many persons live their lives in the shallows! i.e. In the shallows of prayer – never probing its depths – content to rattle off a rote verse to the Almighty – while avoiding a real relationship - the real Power!

Out into the depths of silence is where we find God – where we – if you will – come back with the real Catch – as the Lord directed that we would.

Prayer: Spend five minutes in silence. If it is helpful to keep you centered repeat the name: Jesus, Jesus … Or: Come, Lord Jesus.

Day 159

Matthew 15:21-28

Jesus had withdrawn to the area of Tyre in Sidon when a woman approaches Him and asks for help with her daughter who was sick. But Jesus did not answer her.

Have you ever experienced the silence of God? You went to God with an urgent need – and there was silence!

This woman had great faith, because she did not give up! She didn't give up even when the Lord gave an abrupt: "No!"

She had great faith because she continued to believe in the Love of God! Jesus, noting her faith, announces that her daughter is healed – and she was!

We must persist when God seems silent – when God seems to say, "No!" And God will give us what we need -- not always what we want, but always what we need!

Prayer: Lord, give me patience when I'm met with silence. Persistence when the answer seems to be: "No!" that I may see your glory. Amen.

Day 160

Mark 1:35-39

Very early in the morning, before daybreak, Jesus went to a lonely place to pray. (v.35) He prayed often!

In Luke 6:12 we find Him going off to the mountain, and praying all night. Then, in the morning, He called His disciples together, and named out of them those who would be apostles.

He prayed before He raised Lazarus from the dead. (John 11:41-43)

On another occasion, in the company of Peter, James, and John, He was praying, and as He prayed there appeared to them Moses and Elijah. We call this the experience on the Mount of Transfiguration. (Luke 9:28ff) Through this encounter they were all encouraged, and went back down the mountain to heal others, and to announce His coming death.

There are other examples of prayer in the life of Jesus, but why did God in human flesh need to pray anyway?! Remember He was fully human, and fully God. At times we see the human side:

- When He prays to the Father
- When He is tired.
- When He is hungry...

For God never gets tired or hungry...

We see the Divine side when He raises Lazarus from the dead... Feeds the multitude... Cures many from their maladies... Foresees His death... Forgives sin... The list is long!

In our lesson for today we see the human side as He prays, and what a lesson it is for us, for if Jesus the Christ needed to pray, how much more do we need to pray!

Prayer: Lord, teach me to pray as you did your disciples of old. Help me to make a habit of it. Help me to learn to pray without ceasing. Amen

Day 161

Luke 18:1-8

Jesus told his disciples that "they should always pray and not give up." (v.1)

I more than once considered quitting the ministry. I was burned out and "weary in well doing." (II Thessalonians 3:13) I even went so far as to consider how I would earn a living. Sell cars? Work in a funeral home? They both sounded good at the time!

Then in seasons of prayer I would regain my footing. I experienced the truth of our text for today: "[I] should ... pray and not give up." I went back to preaching and caring for my congregation with renewed vigor! I am thankful I did.

Martin Luther had a period of depression when he considered giving up. Katie, his wife, dressed in black and met him as he came home with the question: "Martin, is God dead?!" He regained his footing and went on leading the Protestant Reformation!

Prayer: Lord, we get care-weary sometimes. Help us to retreat, and claim a season of prayer for ourselves, that we may find our way forward. Amen.

Day 162

Romans 8:18-24

"I consider that the sufferings of the present time are not worth comparing with the glory that is to be revealed to us".

Good things are on the way! Yet suffering in the present is part of the birthing process. Like a woman in labor suffering birth pangs so that a glorious baby can be born, so our spirits are in pain until we experience the glory God is about to reveal!

A man visited his friend, who had beehives. The friend asked him if he would like to go see his hives. When the man said that he did, they donned the bee keepers apparel, and went out to the hives. The friend lifted the top back, and then pulled out a frame covered in honeycomb. Seeing a bee struggling to be born from the comb, the man pulled out his pocket knife to help it along. "Oh no!" protested the beekeeper, "If it does not struggle it will not be able to fly".

The sufferings of the present are but a harbinger of good things that God has in store – in this life – AND in the next!

Prayer: Lord, I thank you for the good things you promise to us – things that often follow a period of suffering. Help me to see and believe and find encouragement. Amen.

Day 163

Psalm 23:1-6

Back during World War II my father, Lynn Riley Moore, was in the Home Guard. Since Dad was blind in one eye, he was not allowed to be in the regular military service. So he was allotted the duty of checking bridges around our home town for bombs, planted by spies, and having practice drills of "Lights Out" in case of an enemy air raid. Those were uncertain times!

It was during those war years that the 23rd Psalm took on new meaning for my parents and others. Especially: "Thou prepares a table before me in the presence of my enemies" and "thy rod and they staff, they comfort me".

The rod was used by shepherds to protect the sheep. And the staff, with its hook on the end, was for rescuing a lamb that had fallen down a ravine – lifting it up.

"Even tho I walk through the valley of the shadow of death I will fear no evil; for thou art with me." If God is for us, who or what can be against us?

Down through the ages many have found comfort in this Psalm!

Prayer: Lord, help me to see how I am a sheep and you are the Shepherd ... and be comforted. Amen. (Read slowly the Psalm again trying to visualize this truth.)

Day 164

Hosea 14:1-9

It is glorious to think that our God is a God of provision!

When the Hebrew people were wandering in the desert, God provided water from the rock, and daily manna. But he only gave them enough for a single day. Why? So they wouldn't stray away. So they would have to rely on Him! So they would know Who it was that was the Giver of "every good and perfect gift!" (James 1:17)

There are times I wish God would provide for all the uncertainties that lie ahead, so I wouldn't have to be concerned about the needs that lie in the distant future. Then again I remember why it is best just one day at a time!

God said to Hosea: "I will be like the dew to Israel." (v.5) That is, the morning dew that brought the daily "bread" in the form of manna that sprung up from the soil like mushrooms!

Quietness brings the spiritual manna of joy, and peace, and hope, and a sense of the Presence.

Prayer: Lord, drop your dew of blessing on me this day. Then help me to remember Who is the Source, that I may give thanks. Amen.

Day 165

Luke 11:1-13

Prayer is the sunshine for the soul! It lifts our heads toward the Almighty. It gives us Life!

The disciples had observed, over their years with the Lord, that the Master was a Person of prayer! Seeing all it meant to the Lord, the disciples asked: "Lord, teach us to pray!" (v.1)

The Lord taught them three things about prayer:

1. They needed a Place of prayer. Not just a certain place in a room or closet, though that can be helpful, but a place in their day. Life gets so crowded that it is difficult to find room for prayer! It helps to declare that upon rising, or before going to bed, I am going to spend some quality time in prayer.

2. We need Persistence in prayer. Remember the continuum that is present in the Greek words we translate: "ask" (and keep on asking), "seek" (and keep on seeking), "knock" (and keep on knocking). Yes, we need to persevere in prayer!

3. THEN we will see the Power of prayer. A power that, paradoxically, is not based in my prayers, but in the Lord - for He is the Power behind prayer! (v.13)

Prayer: Lord, teach us to pray! Help us to remember the need to have a place for prayer, a persistence in prayer, that we may come to see the Power of prayer in our lives. Amen

Day 166

Isaiah 55:6-11, especially verses 10 & 11

As the rain and snow come down and water the earth making it sprout forth... giving bread to the hungry, so shall God's Word go forth to accomplish its purpose... (Paraphrase of v.10 and 11) That is to say: When God speaks things happen!

God spoke and the heavens and the earth were created! (Genesis 1:3-4) God didn't give the Ten Suggestions -- but the Ten Commandments which He spoke to Moses on the mountain, and they have become the moral code for three world religions: Judaism, Christianity, and Islam.

When God in Christ spoke, the blind received their sight, the lame walked, multitudes were fed, sins were forgiven, and the dead rose! Always when Jesus spoke things happened!

God has given us His Holy Word in the Bible. When it is taught in the classroom, or proclaimed in the sanctuary -- things happen! Lives are changed!

This is why we study the scriptures, because they contain Power! High Voltage! For within those pages is the Power of God - unto salvation! (See Romans 1:16; Hebrews 4:12)

Prayer: Lord, speak a fresh word to me, that I may be empowered to do your bidding. Speak Lord through the teachers and preachers of your Gospel this Sunday, I pray. Amen

Day 167

John 1:35-42

Andrew had been a disciple of John the Baptist. He had heard John speak of the coming of the Messiah. Then, suddenly, the Messiah was standing before him, and he could not believe his eyes! Jesus walks on by. If Andrew was going to learn more about the Messiah, he was going to have to follow Him, and follow he does. Wanting to make small talk, Andrew asks Jesus where He was staying. Jesus replies, "Come and see." Again He was saying, "Follow me."

Our faith journey is not like sitting in a classroom, and hearing the professor speak. It is more than learning theology. It is following in the footsteps of the Master. Ours is a journey of faith that leads to an assurance, and confidence that Jesus is all He said He was, for we have been there with Him, and have seen all He does in our life, and the lives of persons around us.

Andrew turns and finds his brother, Peter, and the scripture, in one of it most poignant moments, declares: "And he brought him to Jesus."

When we have walked with the Lord it becomes second nature that we too bring others to Him.

Prayer: How glorious it is to walk the road with you, O Lord! We begin with many questions, but soon find answers coming from being there with you - like Andrew found of old. Lord, help me to walk the walk with you today. Amen

Day 168

James 1:2-8

One of the great preacher/evangelists of the 19th century, Dwight L. Moody, said there are three kinds of faith: struggling faith, clinging faith, and resting faith.

Struggling faith is a faith that is constantly bombarded with doubts. It believes, then gives way to doubt.

Clinging faith is a faith that is afraid of doubts. It is not secure in its state. It believes, but is like an insecure child that clings to its mother - afraid she will walk away.

Whereas resting faith is faith that has doubts at time, but is not unduly threatened by the thought, and works through them. It is a faith that has an assurance that the Lord will remain faithful - will not leave us alone!

The fact is most of us have to have struggling faith and clinging faith before we come to resting faith. And again, we all slip back at times into one of these before we regain our footing in prayer – and once again find the faith that flows into peace.

Prayer: Lord, sometimes I struggle! But that just calls me to rely not on my faith, but on You! Help me to do that right now. Hear my prayer, O Lord. Amen.

Day 169

Hebrews 4:12-16

This was the text my father, who was a lay preacher, was speaking on when I was called into the ministry.

I had asked for a sign: "Lord, if you want me in the ministry, have Dad ask for testimonies." He rarely asked for testimonies -- maybe at Thanksgiving time he would ask the congregation to share something they were thankful for, but not in August! However, midway through his sermon he began to stumble – then finally I heard him say: "We must walk boldly to the throne of grace," then: "Well, I guess I'm going to have to ask for testimonies".

As shy as I was, I rose and told the crowd: "The Lord just called me into the ministry." Pretty good for a little church named "Sleeper!"

We all can "walk boldly to the throne of grace" through prayer. As we do, we will see the glories of God's grace in our time!

Prayer: Lord, help me to walk boldly before to your throne of grace. Save me from hesitancy – that I may see your wonders. Amen.

Day 170

Deuteronomy 31:1-13, especially verse 8

Think about what you fear most ... a speech to deliver ... a job interview ... test results ... guilt and shame that lurks behind you... Death...

Once I was going through a tough time. I was battling asthma, and I was depressed. The thought came to me: "Is this the way I'm going to die - gasping for air?"

Woody Allen famously said, "I don't fear death, I just don't want to be there when it happens!"

The scripture says: "It is the Lord who goes before you. He will be with you; He will not leave you or forsake you. Do not fear or be dismayed!" (v.8) Wow! What comfort!

He goes before you – into that job interview – into the doctor's office – yes, even into death! He has blazed the trail! Now He comes to walk beside you. You are not alone! Then He follows up - protecting you from what would attack you from behind. Forgiving you of past sins.

Prayer: Lord, fears lurk about in the shadows like jackals stalking their prey. Help me to surrender all that is beyond my control into your care – that I may know your Peace. Amen.

Day 171

Colossians 2:6-15

On our land southwest of Marshfield, Missouri is a massive white oak tree. It is approximately fourteen feet around at the base. Its branches reach heights in excess of 50 feet. It is the old patriarch of the forest!

I had the local forester out to look at the trees on our place. He was impressed by the size and obvious age of that giant oak! He said it would likely date back to Civil War days, if not before.

He said its roots would extend well beyond the drip line of the tree, and deep down to the bedrock beneath. It had survived droughts and storms because of its massive root system.

Paul, writing to the church at Colossae, directs: "As you received Christ Jesus the Lord, so live in Him, rooted and built up in Him." (vs. 6b-7) Remember as a Christian the Rock on which you stand! Nurture your "roots" through prayer that they may extend deep unto those things that abide! Encourage your "branches" through lifting them up to the Son in praise and thanksgiving, that you may know strength for the storms.

Prayer: Lord, Help me to grow roots deep down into those things that endure – that I may be truly rooted in You. Amen.

Day 172

Ephesians 1:15-23

Paul is grateful for the unity of the Christians at Ephesus! Their faithfulness to the Gospel is such an inspiration to him. He reaches the summit of his thankfulness, when in verse 16 he writes: "I do not cease to give thanks for you..."

Have you considered the worthwhile effect of a life of thanksgiving? Especially the habit of giving thanks without ceasing. Wow!

I do not claim to have attained such, but the closer I get, the more I see the benefits to my Christian walk and witness!

"Rehearsal theology" is the act of going over in our minds the actions of God on our behalf in the past. Protecting us in danger... Blessing us in countless ways... Giving us guidance when we had lost our way...

As we so reflect, it strengthens our faith; it fills us with joy! It gives us peace!

Prayer: Help me Lord to develop the habit of thanksgiving for all your goodness to me!

(Take 5 minutes and write down the things you are thankful for, not in any order, but just as they come to mind.)

Day 173

Revelation 22:1-9

Years ago Billy Graham visited the United States Senate. At mealtime he went with one of senators to the Senate dining room.

His host asked: "Billy, are you an optimist or a pessimist?" "I'm an optimist," Dr. Graham replied, "Because I've read the last page of the Bible." They laughed, but the senator got the message!

The Bible declares that God's people "shall reign forever and ever!" (v.5) That countless times in the Biblical story, God comes out the Victor, and in the End will do so again!

We can read newspapers and magazines and get to feeling pretty pessimistic. But if we spend time in the Word of God, we discover that the risen Christ conquered more than death and the grave. He vanquished hopelessness, meaninglessness, and lovelessness. He transformed lives!

Ultimately, to know Him is to be an optimist!

Prayer: Lord, thank you for the promises you give us in your Holy Word. Promises that you back up with your risen Presence! Amen.

Day 174

Psalm 119:65-72, especially verse 71a

When English nobleman, Lord Roberts, was having his portrait painted, the artist suggested that he leave some of Roberts' wrinkles out. "No, no!" protested the nobleman, "Put every wrinkle in. I have earned every one of them!"

"It is good for me to have been in trouble," writes the Psalmist.

Troubles have a way of causing us to live life to its fullest. They keep us mindful of what is really important. They enable us to help others who walk the same valley. They push us close to God!

Louis Banks tells of two men who were assigned to stand watch on a ship at sea. During the night a storm struck, and washed one of them overboard.

An investigation followed, and it was discovered that the sailor who perished, had been in the most sheltered place on the deck, and the one who survived was exposed to the storm! So the question was asked: "What happened?" The captain answered: "The man who was lost had nothing to hang on to!"

It does make a difference if you have One to hang on to in the troubles that come your way!

Prayer: Lord, hold my hand - keep me close, for the storms are all around. Teach me the importance of communion with you! Amen

Day 175

I Corinthians 13:1-13, especially verse 12

The first time I flew in an airplane, I was amazed at how different everything on the ground looked from my heavenward perspective! Houses were little matchboxes, roads tiny ribbons, and cars little specks!

A tapestry from below makes no sense - with its threads producing a hodge-podge pattern. But from the topside it is a beautiful masterpiece!

What does not make sense now will, when we look back upon it from heaven's perspective. For there we shall see the Master Weaver's plan.

"Now we see in a mirror dimly, but then face to face. Now I know in part; then I shall understand fully, even as I have been fully known."

Prayer: Lord, grant me patience – give me trust – while I await the view from above. Amen.

Day 176

II Corinthians 12:2-10

Paul asked three times, in deep anguish of spirit, that the "thorn," he suffered from, might be taken away -- that he might be healed. Three times the Lord said, "No. My grace is sufficient for you, for my power is made perfect in weakness."

Is God's "grace" - Presence - love enough, when you are hurting, as Paul was? It can sometimes seem inadequate. Then, in prayerful reflection we begin to see a glimmer of the truth of our dilemma. We realize that His Presence is ALL we have when all is said and done! And in His Presence is disclosed the very Power -- to redeem lives!

Think of it, all of the todays trials that Satan hurls at us... all of tomorrows difficulties... are strained through the Master Strainer which is Christ Jesus. He will let nothing through that would destroy us! What a comfort!

God promised Moses that He would hide him in the cleft of the rock. (Exodus 33:22) And He did! Christ, who is our Rock, hides us in Himself. Outside the storms rage, but we are safe in Him.

Vance Havener once said that "worry is like rocking in a rocking chair. It will give you something to do, but it won't get you anywhere."

But oh the glory! when we realize, with Paul, that His grace IS sufficient, for it has been sufficient throughout Biblical history, and I would dare say it has been proven to be adequate in our own experiences! In that is our peace!

Prayer: Lord, help me to remember that all of my fears about tomorrow will be strained through the Master Strainer - which is your Grace. Give me peace in the realization of that truth. Amen.

Day 177

Galatians 5:16-25

"The fruit of the Spirit is ... joy!" Paul did not say, "The fruit of the Spirit is happiness. For happiness is based in happenings, whereas joy is founded in Him who conquered the grave!

Thus, with our world falling apart, we can rejoice, for our God remains intact, and He is an overcoming God!

George Matheson, the blind Scottish preacher, wrote in 1882:

> "O Love that will not let me go,
>
> > I rest my weary soul in Thee ..."
>
> "O Joy that seekest me through pain,
>
> > I cannot close my heart to Thee,
> >
> > I trace the rainbow through the rain ..."

Yes, this Joy comes to us as we live in a vital relationship with the Lord of love – the conquering King!

Prayer: Lord, draw me nearer, for the world is very near. Fill me with your Joy and Peace today and always. Amen.

Day 178

Philippians 3:12-14

Forgetting the past! Reaching forward to what is ahead. "I press on!" (v.14)

Paul is saying that living the victorious life involves three things:

First, we have to leave the past behind. That is sins committed yesterday must not be allowed to haunt us today. We must accept God's forgiving love. For God has already cancelled every record of the debt! (Colossians 2:14). -- Press on!

Second, persons do at times put us down. As a result we can get down on ourselves. But Christ lifts us up – viewing us as His child – one of unutterable worth! -- Press on!

Finally, we can look at tomorrow with confidence. For we have His promise: never to leave us – never to forsake us. Thus we need not fear! (Deuteronomy 31:6) -- Press on!

Prayer: Lord, help me to press on amid all that would hold me back, laying aside guilt and shame, remembering that I am a child of the King! Thank you for being faithful to me, even when I am not faithful to you! Amen.

Day 179

Philippians 4:10-20

In the Fall of 1966 we went to Atlanta, Georgia, so I could start seminary at Emory University. My wife, Ginya, got her Master's Degree that year, then she began looking for a job. The job market was tight! All summer she applied – but to no avail. In late August we began to think that God must not have intended for us to be there! Did we get the wrong message, when we felt led to go there in the first place? We were at the end of our rope, when suddenly one day a wonderful job offer came from the Merit System of Georgia state government. We were ecstatic! The job exceeded our expectations. Ginya was a perfect match!

Paul, no stranger to trials and tests, wrote: "And my God shall supply every need of yours according to His riches in glory in Christ Jesus." One need we had, without realizing it, was the need for greater patience! God even provided a lesson in that in the midst of our trial!

Isn't God wonderful! He knows our needs better than we know them, and seeks what is best for us. He supplies our every need!

Prayer: Lord, thank you that when we are about to give up you never give up! Help me to trust _____ into your hands right now. Amen.

Day 180

Exodus 33:12-23

Moses had, by God's grace, gotten the people set free from slavery in Egypt. They had seen God perform a wondrous miracle when they had come to the sea, and met their first roadblock. How were they going to get out of this? Then God parted the water, and they passed through on dry ground!

Now, in our Lesson for today, they are in the Sinai Peninsula, and Moses is being tried by the very people that he had seen out of slavery! While he was away, they built a golden calf, and begin to worship it! Poor Moses, he is bound to be extremely disappointed, and ready to give up! But God said to him: "There is a place by me where you can stand upon the rock."

The Lord said to Moses: "There is a place by me where you shall stand upon the rock." (v.21)

People can disappoint us, but God appoints a place by Him for us where we can stand upon the rock, and regroup, and regain our bearings! And the Rock is Jesus! (I Corinthians 10:4)

When all around my soul gives way, how blessed to know that I can stand upon the Rock!

Prayer: Lord, people disappoint us – circumstances can threaten to overwhelm us – but you, the living Lord, are our Rock – our stay. Help me to stand by you today. Amen.

Day 181

Hebrews 2:1-4; Job 23:10; Isaiah 28:28

None of us want to be tested. Yet scripture tells us that seed must be buried before it can spring forth, and produce its fruit. Grain must be ground before it can become bread. Bread must be ground, and digested, before it can give life and strength.

Job, the epitome of suffering, speaks of how testing brings forth gold from the ore we have within us. (v.10)

The strongest trees are not to be found in the middle of the forest, but along the edge where they are impacted by the storms. Thus, as someone has put it, "God gets his greatest saints from the highlands of affliction."

None of us want to be tested, but surely all of us want to be made strong in the Lord. Sufferings produce just that! Thus, we must give the Almighty digging rights, so that He may unearth the nuggets in our lives. Yet, His digging can be painful!

Prayer: Lord, "melt me, mold me, fill me, use me*" – according to your will. Amen.

*From the hymn: "Spirit of the Living God"

Day 182

Hebrews 12:1-3

When I was in High School I went out for track. In one track meet, I remember running the mile. I can even now feel the burning in my lungs - the pain in my legs - as I put heart and soul into the race! I didn't complete the race in four minutes, mind you, but I did come in fourth out of about twelve runners.

Why did I do as well as I did? I had trained for the race certainly, but there was something else. Up in the bleachers were my parents - cheering me on!

The author of Hebrews declares that since we are surrounded by so great a cloud of witnesses -- a cheering crowd -- let us lay aside all that would hinder us, and run with perseverance the race that is set before us!

In this case, the cheering section is made up of all who have died in the Lord, who watch from above -- like a great stadium filled with fans!

It is one thing to begin a race – it is another to finish it. It is one thing to begin living for the Lord, and another to keep-on-keeping-on!

Let's not disappoint our heavenly fans, nor the One who runs the race before us: Jesus Christ!

Prayer: Lord, grant me courage and persistence in the race you have put before me. Help me to lay aside all sins that would hinder me, and run - and keep on running to your glory! Amen.

Day 183

John 20:1-18

Mary Magdalene was from Magdala in Galilee. It was there that Jesus met her, and cast seven demons out of her. From that time on she became one of the disciples that followed the Lord wherever He went. (Luke 8:1-3) Life was good!

Then they went to Jerusalem on that fateful day. The crowds welcomed Him crying, "Hosanna, blessed is He who comes in the name of the Lord!" She was ecstatic!

Then everything turned ugly: He was betrayed by one of His own, arrested, tried, and crucified, and in those few short hours Mary's life fell apart! All of her hopes and dreams were dashed!

If that were not enough, on Sunday she went to the tomb to anoint His body, and it wasn't there! Someone had stolen the body! As she sobbed by the tomb angels appeared and asked: "Why are you weeping?" Then Jesus appears, and asks the same question. Finally, He calls her name: "Mary!" and she recognizes Him! She runs to tell the disciples! -- Mary is the first witness to the resurrection!

The empty tomb cries out that nothing including death can defeat the purposes of our Lord!

Are you crying beside an empty tomb?

Prayer: It is so easy, Lord, to be slow of heart to believe. Help thou my unbelief. Remain with me Lord, until I come to know you and the Power of your resurrection! Amen

Day 184

Psalm 118:1-6, 24

"THIS is the day the Lord has made!"

- Suspending the earth in space!
- It rotates on its axis at 1,037 m.p.h.
- Hurtling through the universe at 67,000 m.p.h.
- Daily the sun "rises" and "sets."

God made this day! Thus, "let us rejoice and be glad in it."

In about 1960, God made a day out of chaos in Seoul, South Korea. Dr. Paul Cho started a church there. It started meeting in his home. But with the rapid growth of the congregation, came overwhelming responsibilities - as Dr. Cho tried to minister to all the needs! He found he was burning out! He suffered a nervous breakdown!

During the weeks their pastor was in the hospital, the laity began to take over the ministry. This strengthened the church, so that, after their pastor got out of the hospital, the church was stronger than it was before he went in, and was ready to grow! And grow it did to over 800,000 members today, and counting! It is the largest Christian church in the world!

Prayer: Lord, on this day that you have made, help me to find the ministry you have for me. Amen.

Day 185

Ecclesiastes 3:1

The seasons of the year provide opportunity for everything. They are a microcosm of life on earth.

Spring realizes the birth of new life. The flowers bloom. The trees regain their leaves. All of nature arises! Summer is a time for growth and productivity. Gardens flourish. Fruit forms on the trees. Fall is the time of harvest. And the beauty of autumn is unmatched! Winter is the time when all of nature lies down to rest. Trees drop their leaves. Bears go into hibernation. Oh the beauty of winter!

Our lives have seasons. We think that Spring is the time of youth... But each age has its own times of new birth, and creativity. Not necessarily when we are young. For Abraham was 74 when God called him to leave Haran and go to a land -- he didn't know where. A new venture in what we would call the Autumn of life?! Many Biblical characters would have similar stories.

"For everything there is a season..." Don't limit God by how young or how old you are! But stay attuned to the Spirit at all ages. For God has special purposes for your life today!

Prayer: Lord, help me not to limit you by my age, or what I perceive to be my abilities. Rather, guide me to dream your dreams, and share in your creative powers today, and in the days to come. Amen

Day 186

Daniel 3:19-28

Shadrach, Meshach, and Abednego are the Babylonian names of three young Hebrew men, Hananiah, Mishael, and Azariah. These three, along with Daniel were taken as hostages by King Nebuchadnezzar in 605 B.C. (II Kings 24:1; Daniel 1:1-4) They may have been of royal descent, and therefore their presence in Babylon was possibly to guarantee the good behavior of King Jehoiakim, back in Judea.

The names of the three were an affront to their Babylonian captors, because each of the names honored Yahweh. Daniel's name was changed, for the same reason to Belteshazzar.

Shadrach, Meshach, and Abednego, refused to bow before the golden image that King Nebuchadnezzar had erected. Threatened by the king with death, the three said they would rather trust in the Lord. So, Nebuchadnezzar had them thrown into the fiery furnace!

Sometimes faithfulness gets us into trouble! We can be good Christian persons, and still suffer.

But our troubles attract the mighty God!

Though they were thrown into the fiery furnace, this trio didn't have a hair singed on their heads.

Again, God does not promise a pain-free ride, but He does promise to be with us.

When the furnace-stokers looked in, they saw not three men, but four walking around in the flames, and the fourth looked like a Son of God! (Literally: "son of the gods.") (v.25) What a God!!

Prayer: Lord, the way can look bleak! The forces of evil seem to hold the upper hand. Yet, you come to us, and the unbelievable happens! Thank you, God. Amen.

Day 187

I Corinthians 15: 1-11

Paul declares: "By the grace of God I am what I am, and His grace toward me was not in vain." (v.10) That is a powerful statement by the Apostle Paul.

It is by God's grace that we were made - creatures of unutterable worth - with the finger prints of the Almighty all over us! Through grace we have been gifted, to do the tasks that God had in mind for us to do when He made us. By grace God has provided for our physical needs of food, drink, shelter... And it is God's grace that has protected us innumerable times over the years!

Paul could say that all this "was not in vain," for he had come to see the light (literally!), and give his life in service of his Lord!

Can you say that God's efforts on your behalf are not in vain?

We are not all called to be missionary/evangelists like Paul! We are not all called to be clergy - a few of those is enough! But we are all called to be ministers of Love -- called to see where God is at work, and join in!

None of us does our calling perfectly! We all fall short! But if we are seeking to live by His Love daily, then His grace toward us is not in vain!

Prayer: Lord, make me disciplined in my prayer life, so that I may remain in tune with your will. Keep me connected to your Power and Love that the world may see you in me. Amen.

Day 188

Acts 9:36-41

Dorcas was from Joppa of Judea, and noted for her acts of kindness, and self-giving. In verse 36 she is called a disciple of the Lord - the only time in the New Testament that the Greek for disciple is given in the feminine case. The Aramaic equivalent of her name would be Tabitha - the name that Jesus would have used for her as he spoke Aramaic.

When Dorcas died, Peter was nearby at Lydda. He was notified, and came immediately to the home where her body had been prepared for burial. He recalled a similar situation where Jairus's young daughter died. Jesus came, mourners were everywhere! He scolded them, saying she is not dead but sleeping. (Matthew 9:24) Nevertheless, the Lord went in, and called her back to life. Now Peter comes, prays in the name of the Lord, and calls Dorcas, or Tabitha back to life!

Do we have to have miracles to believe? Or can we like the disciple Dorcas believe because we have walked with Him, and gotten to know Him!

Prayer: Lord it is enough to know that you walk with me, and talk to me, and tell me that I am yours, and you are mine. How glorious is the thought! Amen

Day 189

I Samuel 3:1-10

Young Samuel was serving under the tutorage of Eli, the priest. One night God called, but he thought it was Eli. Twice this happened, then Eli said: "If you hear the voice again say, 'Speak, Lord, for your servant hears.'" (v.9) This time Samuel got the message that God was in fact calling him.

"As Samuel grew up, the Lord was with him, and everything that Samuel said was proved to be reliable. And all Israel... knew that was confirmed as a prophet of the Lord." (I Samuel 3:19-20)

This story has a many-faceted message:

1. We prefer to choose what we listen to.

2. We don't really expect God to speak here and now.

3. We often understand too soon.

4. It is those who are willing to obey who hear!

Do we have a hearing problem? Young Samuel didn't, he just couldn't believe it was God!

Do we believe that God can call us at any age? Do you realize that God has a special purpose for your life?

Prayer: Lord, give me ears to hear your voice, and a heart that is willing to obey. Amen.

Day 190

Acts 18:1-5

Priscilla and Aquila were a Christian couple that were likely converted under the ministry of Paul when he went to Corinth. They were tentmakers by trade, as was Paul. So, he probably used this as an entree to witness to them. Priscilla and Aquila are always mentioned together in the New Testament, with her name usually given first. (See: Acts 18:18, 26; Romans 16:3; & II Timothy 4:19) Priscilla was likely a leader in the church in Corinth, which may account for her name being listed first.

Both of these stalwart Christians were Paul's trusted coworkers and friends (Romans 16:3-4). When Paul left Corinth, they went with him to Ephesus where they likely remained to provide leadership for the church there.

Every pastor needs a few Priscillas and Aquilas! Most every church has folks like that, and they are the life blood of the congregation!

What role are you playing in the congregation where you worship?

Prayer: Lord, thank you for your faithful servants who brought the faith to me. Help me to profit from their example, that I may be a faithful witness to others in my circle of influence. I pray in Jesus' name. Amen

Day 191

Luke 10: 25-37

A lawyer put Jesus to the test. He asked: "What must I do to inherit eternal life?" Jesus points him to the love that is found in the parable of the Good Samaritan.

The feeling of the Jews at this time toward the half-breed Samaritans was like our view of a terrorist. Jesus was touching a raw nerve by using a Samaritan as an example of one who is to be emulated.

The excuses for not helping the man, beaten and robbed and left beside the road, would parallel our excuses: i.e. "I'm too busy" – "He doesn't deserve help" – "It is too dangerous to stop."

Yet, Jesus is paralleling the Samaritan's love with that of God! He is saying that to be in a state of salvation means that you care for the "least of these" (Matthew 25:40).

Who is it by your path today?

Prayer: Lord, give me the compassion of this Samaritan. Come Holy Spirit and love your world through me. Amen.

Day 192

Luke 14:15-24

Jesus is speaking of the great banquet in the Kingdom of God - a banquet that represents the rule of God here on earth in persons lives - and heaven's feast at the table prepared by God. He tells this parable to get across His point.

A man once prepared a great banquet. He invited many guests (in fact the whole world)! But the guests began to make excuses for not coming. Then the host got angry, and directed his servant to go invite the societal rejects. He did, but still there was room. So, the host ordered: "Go out to the highways and hedges, and compel people to come in!"

Compel?! Sounds a little foreign to our nonchalant approach to witnessing! But, yes, the Lord is directing that we should go out with such urgency that our love – our words – our deeds would make persons feel compelled to come in to the Heavenly Kingdom's Banquet!

Prayer: Lord, give me a sense of urgency for bringing in those outside your Kingdom. I pray this day for _____, _____, and _____ who do not know you as Savior. Help me to know the words to speak, and when to say them. Grant me humble love that woos these to you and your Kingdom. Amen.

Day 193

Luke 14:7-14

Here again Jesus lifts up the importance of humility. (See also Mark 9:33-37; Luke 18:9-14; Matthew 5:5) "Whoever exalts himself/herself will be humbled, while the one who is humble will be exalted."

Brother Lawrence was very disappointed when he was assigned to work K.P. duty in the monastery! But after a time of self-pity, he began doing the menial tasks as an offering to God. He would prepare meals – for God. Wash the dishes – for God. Through it all he "practiced the Presence" of God, as he referred to it, and made it all his offering of humble love.

For the last fifty years we have focused on developing our self-esteem. We have worried about our children's self-esteem. There is a place for developing a good feeling about ourselves, but Jesus was more concerned with servant-esteem. That is, self-forgetfulness while glorifying God in all things. That is humble love – Christ-like Love!

Prayer: Lord, help me to learn that it is the most humble tasks that help me to best identify with you. Help me to seek glory – not for myself – but for your name. Amen.

Day 194

Exodus 20:1-17

EVERYONE has a G(g)od! Atheists have gods: materialism, humanism ... from which they draw their security. Others are just good old fashioned idolaters – worshipping money, things, even children and family.

Why is it important to concern ourselves with this issue? Your G(g)od determines your destiny, and more: how you live life on the way toward your destiny.

The late Reverend Jay Purviance served alongside his wife, Ruth, as missionaries to Brazil. Once he told me of an elderly woman, Senora Valentino, who was in his congregation. Though extremely poor, she had saved up so she could have the Purviances for lunch one Sunday after worship. She had killed one of her valued chickens and fixed rice with it.

With the missionaries feeling so bad to be eating her precious foot – she broke the silence by saying: "Oh pastor, God has been SO GOOD to me!" Jay said he heard the angels sing!

Her God was the Lord Jesus Christ, who had come again–and–again to her on the edge of existence, to show her what was of utmost importance: i.e. our relationship with Him.

Prayer: Lord, too often we settle for trinkets and overlook what lasts. Forgive us, Lord! Help us to so center on you today that we may realize how good you have been to us! Amen.

Day 195

Genesis 32:22-30

Jacob is in trouble again! He got in trouble with his brother Esau, and then he gets in trouble with his father-in-law, Laban – in the land he went to, to escape Esau's wrath.

Jacob decides to go home and face his brother. So, he takes his family and herds, and heads out. Then word comes that Esau is headed toward him with 400 men!

Jacob comes to the Jabbok River, sends his wives, children, and flocks on across, and he beds down on the river bank worried about what tomorrow held for him! There he wrestles all night with a "man" who proves in the morning to be GOD! He tells this "man" (God) he will not let Him go until He blesses him, and bless him He does – with a tearful reunion with his brother Esau the next morning! (33:4)

Often we face the unknown with great anxiety! It seems we must wrestle a blessing from God – who is all too willing to bless us in the first place. Sometimes God's blessing comes with a "limp" (v.31) – a continuing reminder – a means through which God keeps us leaning on Himself.

Prayer: Lord, I am worried about _____. Help me to trust you more with this situation, knowing that you will bless me in the morning light. Amen.

Day 196

Ephesians 1:11-23

Many of us played "Ring Around the Rosie" as a child. Did you realize that for over 600 years children have played this game? Its beginnings date back to the great Bubonic Plague that swept across Europe – killing half of the population!

The telltale sign of having caught this Black Death was rings of inflammation around spots on your skin. (i.e. "Ring around a rosie...")

The whole little song, and accompanying game, was a coping mechanism – enabling children to make light of something very frightening!

Paul writes to the church at Ephesus: "I pray that your inward eyes may be opened, so that you may know what is the hope to which he calls you". (v.18a)

The New Testament is NOT the biography of Jesus who once lived and died. He is ALIVE!

Because he lives, we don't have to play games to distract us from the inevitable – death. We can sing songs of JOY of his Victory over death and the grave – and our Victory too through Him!

Prayer: Lord, how can we thank you for the hope you have brought us?! Help us to thank you with our lives! Amen.

Day 197

Luke 18:9-14

Jesus tells a parable about persons who trusted in their own goodness, and treated others with contempt.

"Two men went up to the Temple..." One was a very righteous man – a Pharisee – a keeper of the letter of the Law! The other was a tax collector. Tax collectors were known for cheating the people by charging extra on their taxes, then pocketing the amount. The tax collector was hated by the common people because of this.

The latter cries out: "God be merciful to me a sinner!" Jesus said that he – not the religious Pharisee – went home justified. (The hearers of this parable were shocked by this!)

Someone has said that "justified" means: "just-if-I'd" never sinned. I like that! That is glorious news! When in sorrow we repent of our sins, God views us as though we had never sinned in the beginning!

Prayer: Lord, your love is beyond all that we can fathom! It blots out our sin, and wipes the slate clean! How wonderful you are, O God! Thank you! Amen.

Day 198

Matthew 5:1-12

Our heroes are the great athletes, beauty queens, movie stars, those who have died in battle, the great intellects of the day ... But in this passage Jesus is declaring that God's heroes are the poor, the meek, the mourners, the persecuted!

A man found a turtle on top of a fence post. He pondered it briefly, and before helping it down, declared: "This turtle didn't get there by itself!"

Jesus is saying here that what really counts in life is not our ability – either physical or intellectual – nor our great acts – what counts is that we realize how utterly and totally dependent we are upon God!

Turtle on a fencepost - didn't get there by itself, and we didn't get where we are, but for the grace of God!

Prayer: O God, help me to remember that I am not God, and you are! Help me today to surrender up the throne of my life to you alone. Help me to be your hero by the life I live for you. Amen.

Day 199

Matthew 6:24-34

Life is filled with fears! We get rid of one, and along comes another! In the past were fears of: nuclear holocaust, aids, Y2K ... Now there is talk of catastrophic earthquakes, infections that do not respond to drugs, worldwide economic collapse, terrorist attack...

To us, Jesus says: "Do not be anxious about tomorrow." (v.34a). The Lord is not talking about positive thinking or transcendental meditation as solutions! For when you are up to your neck in a swamp filled with alligators, no amount of these will help!

His solution is having the right master! (v.24) Most of our worries center around the false gods we worship, be it money, things, health, etc. In fact the Lord's answer is seen in the "bookends" of this passage: verses 24 and 33. Or put simply: seeking to wholly trust in God and His will for our lives.

Prayer: Lord, help me to let go, and wholly trust all things to your care and keeping this day. Enable me to see beyond my resources to the Divine supply, that I may know your peace. Amen

Day 200

Exodus 14:10-15; 21-22

The Hebrew people have had a miraculous escape from slavery! On their way to the Sinai peninsula, they arrive at the sea. They can't go forward – or so it seems! There's an ocean out there!

But God says to Moses, in verse 15, "Why do you cry to me? Tell the people to go forward!" Moses had been apparently offering prayers that were little more than whining! Whining about how impossible their situation was.

Moses had seen the miracles God had performed! But, with no assurance of what is going to happen next, God simply is saying: "trust me! - Tell the people to go forward!"

It is easier to live in the past! Easier to turn away from the challenges God places before us in the present! Easier to say: "I don't have the ability" or "Call someone more capable!" But God says: "[You] ...go forward!"

They did, and God parted the water!

Prayer: Lord, give me the courage to step forward where you lead. Help me to be brave enough to get my feet wet in the sea before you part it! Remind me of miracles in my past, so I can step forward in faith into your future! Amen

Day 201

John 4:5-26, 39-42

The Samaritan woman came to Jacob's well with her empty jar.

Have you ever felt you were running on empty? Burned out – not even feeling like praying. God understands, and comes to us – just as Jesus met the woman at the well.

She came expecting to just get her jar filled with water, but got her soul filled up too! She came with a jar, and went home with a well!

One of my childhood memories is following my Grandfather Holman, who was blind, down into the barn lot to get water for the cows. I remember wondering, how he would know when the stock tank was full. He turned the water on, then placed his thumb inside the top of the tank. Soon his thumb felt the cool water, and he turned off the spigot.

The Samaritan woman's "jar" was overflowing after she met Jesus at the well!

Prayer: "Fill my cup, Lord, I lift it up, Lord come and quench this thirsting of my soul…"* Amen.

*From the chorus: "Fill My Cup, Lord"

Day 202

Ezekiel 37:1-14

Ezekiel's vision is a powerful one! The Spirit transported him into a valley – a valley filled with human bones. God then asks: "Can these bones live?" (v.3)

We have all stood by an open grave, and asked the same question. God answers His own question by asking Ezekiel to preach to the bones – that they might live!

Over the years I have preached to a few – fortunately only a few – congregations that were as dead as a sanctuary filled with bones! It makes preaching very difficult when the people have not prepared through prayer, and are not expectant of the Spirit to move/speak.

But like a valley of bones – if we maintain our expectancy God can move mightily and raise the "dead!"

Through the Word become flesh (John 1:14), Jesus Christ, God does in fact raise our loved ones up into Heaven's glory!

Prayer: Lord, we praise your name for that glorious Good News that you can still stir through our valleys, and bring hope and life out of death and despair. Grant us faith – grant us assurance – for the living of these days. Amen.

Day 203

John 1:29-42

Back around the turn of the last century, two missionaries, a husband and wife team, sought to bring the Gospel to South Africa. They arrived in Cape Town, purchased an ox and a cart, and headed for the interior. For days they traveled the pathless plain, not knowing where they were going.

One day they came across a group of Hottentots headed for Cape Town to find a missionary! They had heard of this one called Jesus, and wanted to learn more. That day God began a mighty work among those people!

I cannot tell you where God is leading you, but I do know it is to reach another for Christ and His Church!

Verse 42 of our lesson for today, tells how Andrew – who had just met the Lord – immediately went, and found his brother, Peter, "and he brought him to Jesus." Wow! What a passage - what a powerful text!

Think what a difference just one convert, Peter, made to the Faith! We never know what the one person God has put in our path will do for the Kingdom!

Prayer: Lord, enable me to see those you have put along my way. Help me to tell them of your love, and that you have conquered death and the grave! Amen.

Day 204

Ephesians 4:11-16

You may have known someone who believed that accepting Christ as Savior was the end of the journey. They felt that they had nothing else to do! "I'm in!" they would say.

Actually it is just the beginning! It is like being born (i.e. "being born again"). What a tragedy if a baby remained a baby, and never grew or developed. We expect that child to eat, exercise, and grow into adulthood!

In I Corinthians 1:18 Paul writes how the Word of the Cross "is folly to those who are perishing, but to us who are BEING saved it is the power of God!" There is a continuum here. Salvation is a process of growing toward maturity in Christ. Thus, we are saved by faith in Christ, but then must "grow up in every way ... into Christ." (Ephesians 4:15b) (See also: Colossians 1:28-29) In this way we have faith, but it is growing into assurance. We have peace, but it is becoming more genuine. We have love, but we are growing toward Christ-like love.

We, who accept Christ as Savior, must nurture our spirits through prayer, worship, study, and service. So that we may grow up into Christ in every way, so that we can become little Christs ourselves!

Prayer: Lord, it is difficult to practice the spiritual disciplines that enable me to grow and be spiritually mature! Motivate me Lord, that I may become like you in every way. Amen.

Day 205

Isaiah 40:21-31

This passage lifts up the power of the patient!

Why does the Lord require me "to wait?" I prefer instant results - in life, and in my prayer life too! I want a God who, I put a quarter's worth of prayer into, and bingo out pops the answer I seek. But God does not function in that way, and for good reason. Soon I would take Him for granted, fail to be thankful for my blessings!

"They who WAIT upon the Lord, shall renew their strength..." (v.31), our scripture for today says.

Notice the Patience that is called for here! "They who wait..."

See the Providence involved here: "They who wait upon the Lord!"

Acknowledge with me the Power that is present here: "... shall renew their strength!"

He had an amazing amount of patience throughout his illness! Come uncertainty... long waits on test results... he was content. I thought: I could never be that persevering! But George was! He had had a life of many maladies. I often thought he was a living example of this verse.

Prayer: Lord, give me more patience. Make me stronger in my faith, and in you. When the way seems uncertain, let me rely on what is certain -- your Presence. Amen

Day 206

Matthew 6:24-34

Life has more than an adequate supply of fears! Yet, Jesus says some six times: "Don't be anxious!" (v.25) How can this be?!

Worry is a reflection of our gods. What do your worries tell you in regard to a god vying for your love and loyalty? If it is money, then you will have an exorbitant amount of fears concerning the same. Whatever the false god, fears come accordingly.

When I was 12 years old my folks went to a Board meeting at church. After dark my dog started barking like something was about to get him! I went to the back door, and now I could hear the rhythmic jangle of chains! It sounded like a large man in shackles shuffling toward the house! I was petrified!

About an hour later Dad came home. I told him what was going on. He got a flashlight, and started out the back door. I took his hand, and went with him. Sure enough the darkness revealed the same clang, clang, clang! We walked toward the barn in the direction of the sound, there in the shed on the side of the barn we saw it! A cow rubbing its head against some tire chains hanging on a nail on the wall. My "giant" was revealed for what it was!

When we realize that God is bigger than all our foes, then we walk with confidence into tomorrow.

Prayer: Lord, help me to take your hand, and know the peace of surrender. Guard my mind from borrowing troubles that often don't materialize. Grant me courage – for today. Amen.

Day 207

Romans 5:12-19

In Charles Dickens' "A Tale of Two Cities", a young Englishman, was caught trying to flee from France during the French Revolution with his wife and child. Because of the French hatred for the British, the young husband and father had been sentenced to death.

A few hours before his execution, a French friend of his, who had no family, visited him in his prison cell. There he insisted on trading places with the British man. Finally, reluctantly, the prisoner agreed. They exchanged clothes, and the waited.

Minutes later the guard came and unknowing escorted the Englishman to safety and a reunion with his family.

In the television version, a young seamstress, who was in love with the doomed man, rides with him through the streets of Paris to the guillotine. As they ride along she whispers: "Are you dying for him?!" "Yes, and for his wife and child".

God, the Mighty Maker, has visited our Prison Cell, and died in our place!

Prayer: Lord, we praise your name for your great Act of Sacrifice, that we might go free – forgiven – given Life forevermore. Amen.

Day 208

Jeremiah 15:15-21

Jeremiah was born in the village of Anathoth, about three miles northeast of Jerusalem. It was there that his cousin sold him the family farm. The problem was, that Jeremiah was in prison, and the area was surrounded by the Babylonians!

Jeremiah was a man of unbelievable faith, but, as a prophet, he was a denouncer of all the evils of his day too. There was nothing in need of denunciation that didn't get denounced by him!

Jeremiah battled depression. At a low point, he cursed the day he was born (Jeremiah 20:14)!

In today's lesson, he declares: "Your words [O God] were found, and I ate them. You words became a delight to me, and the joy of my heart (v.16)."

Sometimes God calls us to stand against the evils of our day. Other times, when we are feeling low, we find comfort in realizing the saints of old were at times depressed too! As we feed upon the Word, digesting it, it becomes a part of our very being - our very lives! Its strength becomes our strength...

Prayer: Lord, we often see ourselves when we feed on your Word. Help us to digest it, and make it our own, that we may be truly your own. Amen

Day 209

I Corinthians 1:10-17

Our Boxer / Australian Shepherd, Daisy Duke, is true to her instincts. She loves to go out into the backyard, and try to roundup the birds there. When I appear to be headed that way, she will guide me with bumps to my legs - even nips to my arm - to keep me going in the right direction. I have never had her around a flock of sheep, but I am sure she would catch on real quickly to the task of herding them. Daisy's deep instinct is to bring into unity what is scattered.

In 1994, when we visited Bethlehem on our tour of the Holy Land, I arose one morning, right after sunup, and went up to the roof of the dormitory that was part of the Bethlehem Bible College -- a Christian school. The flat roof with its walls around the sides, made a wonderful observation deck from which I could observe the ancient city as it came alive for the new day. In the street below, was a shepherd herding his flock of sheep down the street - with his faithful dog helping to guide the sheep. I felt I had gone back in time to Bible times!

In our Lesson for today, Paul is calling upon the church at Corinth to be united as once flock. Nothing is more important within a congregation than a unity of spirit! (See I Corinthians 13)

Prayer: Shepherd us, O God, that we may be united with other Christians in the faith and mission of your Church. Help me to be a reconciler, and force for unity. I pray in Jesus' Name. Amen

Day 210

Matthew 25:31-46

In over 1950 years since these words were written, how many deeds of love have been done because of this admonition? "Truly I say to you, as you did it to one of the least of these my brethren, you did it to me." (v.40)

It is said that Oberlin was making his way across the Alps when he got caught in a terrible blizzard! He would have perished had it not been for another traveller; who knew where shelter could be found. Once inside out of the storm, Oberlin asked his newfound friend, "What is your name?" His rescuer would not tell him. Oberlin kept insisting to know. But the stranger finally answered: "Do you know the name of the Good Samaritan?" "No, I don't." "Well, then, there is no need to know my name either."

Deeds of real love do not want to be commended. It is reward enough to see another rescued from grave danger!

We meet the Christ in all those in need, and as we do for them we are actually doing for our Master, who comes to us in the guise of the poor!

What will you do for the Lord today?

Prayer: Lord, it is good to know it is YOU who meets me in those in need. Help me to be more attentive to the needs of my sisters and brothers whom I will meet today. Amen

Day 211

Mark 14:66-72; 16:7

Peter had fallen away! He denied knowing his Lord not just once or twice, but three times! Isaiah declares: "All we like sheep have gone astray (53:6a)." Sheep do not stray because of evil intent. They just do what comes naturally: they simply feed away from the shepherd. In the vast majority of cases, we do not have evil intent when we stray from the Lord. We just get too busy doing important tasks to focus on Him, and gradually walk away.

One of the most common ways we stray is what I call cross-free religion, or faith without a price. Jesus declares that to be a contradiction in terms in Matthew 16:24, for we cannot be a follower of the Crucified One, and not make sacrifices ourselves.

Yet, there is good news in our lesson for today! For the angel at the empty tomb, tells the women: "Go tell the disciples AND Peter He is going before you into Galilee. There you will see Him." Our Lord wanted to forgive and have fellowship once again with Peter – who was no longer a disciple! That is Good News for all of us who have let Him down!

Prayer: Lord, how can we thank you for your grace shown to us? Help us to do so by the sacrifices of our time – talents – and money to your glory. Amen.

Day 212

Luke 12:13-21

"Fool! This night your soul is required of you; and the things you have prepared, whose will they be?"

In Egypt, in ancient times, the Desert Fathers had a very lovely custom. It was laid down that no monk might ever speak of "my" room, "my" book, "my" clothes... To do so would mean that the errant one would receive the sternest rebuke and discipline!

What is mine? Nothing, really. For all that I have is on loan from God - to be used while life lasts. To forget this is to receive the sternest of rebukes from the Lord, as is noted above: "Fool! This night your soul is required of you..."

Life is always shorter than we think. Remembering this, and who owns it all, will make us wise! The Psalmist expresses it: "Teach us to number our days that we may get a heart of wisdom." (90:12)

Is this not the opposite of the "Fool!" statement we began with? Wisdom lies in realizing Whose we are!

Prayer: Lord, help me to realize that this life is not unending -- whereas the Life you have for me is! Make me a good steward of the possessions you have entrusted to me. Amen

Day 213

Exodus 14:10-31, especially verse 15

We have looked at this passage before, but there are more nuggets to mine from its verses.

Have you ever felt trapped? Maybe your sense of entrapment came as the result of a job, an illness, or other circumstances that left you feeling that life was out-of-control. Then God's word to Israel is a word for you. "Why do you cry to me? Tell the people to go forward".

There is a time for prayer! But there is also a time to cease praying, and ACT!

From about eight years of age until I was eighteen I prayed on numerous occasions for God's guidance on what I was to do with my life. I can recall about a dozen times God telling me – through others, or through the "still small voice" – that He wanted me to be a preacher. There came a time in August of 1962 when I had to quit "crying to the Lord," and act! I have never been sorry!

Seek God's guidance through prayer, then act on what you discern His will to be, and you will no longer feel trapped, but set free!

Prayer: Lord, thank you for your freeing will revealed in your Holy Spirit. Give me the courage today to act upon what I know I should do in your Name. Amen.

Day 214

Romans 8:31-39, especially verse 28

Paul makes a most daring claim: "We know that in everything God works for good with those who love Him, who are called according to His purpose."

We would all agree that "some" things work for good – but "everything?!" Yet, Paul, who was no stranger to great sufferings, could write "in everything God works for good."

Note the apostle places two conditions on this working out: first this happens only when we love God, and second when we realize we are being called according to His purpose. Implied herein, is the assumption that we are willing to obey God's guidance.

God does not CAUSE all things, but He is able to USE all things for His purposes.

Joseph, who was sold into slavery by his own brothers, ended up – because of this – in a position to save his family from famine. Salvation always has a cross in it somewhere! Joseph, who was willing to bear the cross of forgiveness, saw: "You (i.e. his brothers) meant it for evil, but God meant it for good!" (Genesis 50:20).

The Lord enables us to bear our cross victoriously because He is working with us in this project! (Romans 8:28)

Prayer: Lord, help me to not give in to self-pity in the face of suffering, but to bear it for the good you can bring out of it! Amen.

Day 215

Matthew 14:22-33

Worry! We are all good at it! Some of us are better at it than others. A man once declared: "Worry works! For of all the things I worried about this past year, only a few came to fruition!"

Some things are within the vale of our ability to take care of, and we should do so, but other things are beyond our control so we should trust them to God – and leave it there!

In our lesson for today, Peter walks on water – for a while! Then, when he takes his eyes off the Lord, and begins to consider the waves, he begins to sink! Jesus had to rescue him!

There are some lessons here:

      1. If we prayed more, we'd worry less!

      2. When faced with a test, we must focus even more upon the Lord!

      3. We must do our best, and trust God for the rest.

Prayer Time: Pray the Lord's prayer, repeating it slowly. Bask in the light of each word.

Day 216

Romans 12:1-2

God has given each of us a bank account. In it is an unknown amount of time. What are we spending it on? That is the biggest question of our lives, for it strikes at the very core of meaning to life!

I have referred to it before, but it is so appropriate for this scripture! In Arthur Miller's "Death of a Salesman", Willie Loman's wife cannot understand why he has committed suicide. With friends gathered round trying to console her, she cries: "For the first time in 35 years we were just about free-and-clear! He only needed a little salary! – He was even finished with the dentist." A friend responds: "No one needs 'only a little salary!'"

We need more! So much more!! We need to lose ourselves in being "a living sacrifice" – to God - that alone counts/lasts/has meaning! That is life that is worthwhile - that has eternal significance!

Prayer: Thank you, Lord, for the opportunity to give ourselves sacrificially in your service. Help me this day to see those opportunities and act. Amen.

Day 217

Jeremiah 18:1-11

It is amazing how often God speaks to us in everyday situations of life! Think of what God has said to you today through nature ... another person ... some life situation.

In this lesson for today, God communicates with Jeremiah as he was visiting the local potter's shop. The potter throws the clay onto the wheel, and begins to shape it into the vessel he sees in it to be. Possibly Jeremiah's arrival distracts the potter. The clay slips off center, and the pot that was about to be created is spoiled, so he stops the wheel, and starts all over again.

My preacher mind reads this story and surmises: Made – marred – re-made!

God created Israel (us). They (we) slipped off center from His will, so, by God's grace in Christ, He has started the process all over again in making them (us) into the people He would have them to be. Consider the patience, and grace of God!

Prayer: Lord, forgive me for falling away from your will. Take me. Mold me into the person you would have me to be. Amen.

Day 218

Philippians 2:5-11; Hebrews 12:26

Joy is different from happiness. Happiness is based in outward circumstances. Joy is founded on an inward relationship with Christ. Happiness is more "happy-go-lucky" – a feeling bordering on laughing all the time. Joy can run on the edge of sorrow – even despair, yet stands on the Rock which is Christ Jesus. (I Corinthians 10:4)

Joy comes like a butterfly lighting upon my shoulder while weeding my flower bed. I didn't seek it, but it came while I was lost in meaningful activity.

Joy comes in five ways:

- It comes as we are counting our blessings versus pitying our plight in life.

- It comes through service. One cold, snowy, day in 1960, Mother said: "William, do you want to do something that you will enjoy remembering the rest of your life?" I said, "I guess so ..." "Go over to Mrs. Hough's and shovel out her driveway." I went. It only took 30 minutes, but it felt so good while I was doing it, and brings me joy every time I reflect back on it!

- Joy is found in being part of God's Eternal Purpose of self-giving, sacrificial love. It is often difficult – even frustrating – but O the Joy of knowing you are a part of an Everlasting Work!

- Joy comes while loving and being loved. This too has its frustrations, even sorrows, for loved ones die! And: O the Joy of loving and experiencing love from others!

- Finally, Joy comes from leaning on the Lord, and as you do, coming to know He can be counted upon!

Prayer: Lord, I thank you that you CAN be counted upon! I thank you for including me in your Eternal Purposes! I thank you for placing thanksgiving in my heart, and accompanying Joy! Amen.

Day 219

John 15:1-8, especially verse 7

Did you know that "Louie, Louie" is forbidden to be sung at Clemson football games?

Several years ago the stadium began to crumble, and after considerable research, it was discovered that the song sung by a stadium full of fans, gave off the same frequency present in the concrete, causing reverberations that had caused the concrete to crack. Thus, officials asked that it not be sung anymore.

Think of the Power generated when Christians join together in prayer! When, with one voice, we pray, great things happen! When the frequency of our spirits gets in tune with the frequency of the Holy Spirit, it causes reverberations that can be felt throughout the world!

Prayer: Lord, teach me to get my spirit in tune with your Spirit, that I may witness your Power in this time. Amen.

Day 220

Luke 13:6-9

The fig tree was a most valuable tree! It bore fruit throughout the year except for April and May. So, when Jesus tells this parable of the unfruitful tree, the hearers could identify with the story. For them Jesus was saying that the final opportunity had come. It was time for them to "bear fruit!" (See Luke 3:9)

Alexander Whyte told of a man by the name of Rigby. Rigby found it hard to talk about his faith, but he would invite persons to come hear Dr. Whyte. Several came to Christ as a result.

He didn't know all the fruits of his labors, but once he introduced himself to Whyte. The pastor invited him to his study. There he showed him a stack of letters from persons who had visited, and found the Lord, all because a man by the name of Rigby had invited them!

Rigby's witness had borne much fruit!

Prayer: Help me, Lord, to never underestimate what you are able to do with a simple invitation to come to worship. Grant me courage to step out of my comfort zone, and invite someone this week. Amen

Day 221

Psalms 90:12; Isaiah 26:1-4, 19a

When we were young we assumed we were invincible! O, yes, rationally, we knew we were going to die, but that was way off in the future! Then we could take foolish risks, and live as though there was no tomorrow.

The Psalmist realized the importance of knowing that we are mortals, when he declared: "So teach us to number our days that we may get a heart of wisdom." (v.12) Or, the Bill Moore translation would read, "Lord, make us aware that we are mere mortals that we may be wise in our living."

We live on Death Row! We do not know when our "sentence" will be carried out, but we know it will! Therefore we must live our lives as one who feels the need to make each day count!

What tremendously Good News it is to be able to rejoice with Isaiah: "O dwellers in dust! Sing for Joy!! For in the Lord your God, you have an everlasting Rock!" A savior who is Christ the Lord!

Prayer: Lord, how good it is to stand near our mortality, and yet do so with joy and confidence. For we have one who has conquered death and the grave! Thank you, Lord! Amen

Day 222

Matthew 11:2-11

John asks the Christ: "Are you He who is to come, or shall we look for another? (v.3) Everyone needs a savior! And if we do not discover the real thing, we will try all sorts of substitutes: drugs, illicit sex, numerous relationships, materialism ...

Jesus did not ask John to believe His words, He said, "...Tell John what you hear and see ..." (vs. 4-5a) In other words the Lord was saying: Note the radically changed lives, and the miracles, not just my words.

We aren't asked to believe someone's word, but to see for ourselves the difference Christ can make in a life! Then, experience that for ourselves!

Being lost is a terrible, frightening thing! Being found is glorious!

Prayer: Lord, thank you for coming to earth to find us. Thank you for showing the Way. Thank you for giving us life, and that eternal. Amen.

Day 223

I Samuel 3:1-10

Have you ever experienced the silence of God? You want to know God's will on a particular issue, yet the word of the Lord is rare (vs.1b). Most of us have experienced this!

From time-to-time God retreats into silence to remind us who is God!

God is not our vending machine in the sky where we put in a quarter's worth of prayers, and out pops our answer. No, God has to remind us at times who is God! Also His silence keeps us close – keeps us wrestling – to keep us engaged (Genesis 32:24).

So what is involved in our hearing the Lord?

- To be listening. Two persons seated on the same pew, one leaves saying: "I heard the Lord!" The other complains that the organist hit a wrong note.

    Eli, the priest, heard nothing! (v.10)

- To be surrendered to God's will no matter what that may be! In August 1771, at a Conference of Methodist preachers – Bristol, England, John Wesley stood before the gathering and declared: "Our brethren in America call aloud for help! Who will go?" Francis Asbury, age 26, felt God calling him. He went and Methodism spread in the colonies.

God does not call us all to be preachers, but does call all of us who listen, and are willing, to act!

Prayer: Lord, help me to hear and to see the opportunities you put before me this day. Amen.

Day 224

I Corinthians 1:18-31

The cultured Greeks and pious Jews of the first century considered the message early Christians had to tell as the sheerest of folly! Even the early followers of Jesus considered the idea of a crucified Savior a scandal! The Greek word translated in our scripture for today is "skandalon," meaning stumbling block, or an absurdity. How could the chosen One, the Savior go to the Cross and die?

In our day, some churches have taken the cross out of the sanctuary for this very reason! They do not want to offend the sensibilities of the worshippers! They prefer positive messages – a Jacuzzi Jesus – that soothes us, and expects little in return.

But it is only a Crucified Lord that understands our pain – atones for our guilt and shame – knows our death – gives us hope over the grave! Sadly, He is an embarrassment to many, but "to us who are being saved, [He is] the Power of God!" (v.18)

Prayer: Help me, Lord, never to be ashamed of you, or your Cross! Forgive me for wanting an easy way out when you chose the road to Calvary. Amen.

Day 225

II Corinthians 1:18-22

Frequently life tells us, "No!" Sometimes it is in school that a grade says, "No." Other times as we are considering a vocation, either "voices" within, or from persons without, say: "No, you can't do that!" We may be being led by God to tackle a task that we feel is too big for us, and the word is: "No, don't try it!" Finally, age and/or health situations shout at us: "It is all over, admit it! Quit!" Life has an overabundance of negatives, and far too few positives!

Paul writing to the church in Corinth says: "All the promises of God find their Yes in Him [Christ] (v.20)." For when life says, "No!" God says, "Yes!!" Or when life closes a door, God opens a window! Look for it! The answer will be what you need, or what someone else needs – desperately! God never meant for me to be a track star! But he did mean for me to preach and share His Gospel – His "Yes!" for me, and for others.

Dr. E. Stanley Jones while well into his eighties, and suffering from a stroke, dictated his book: "The Divine 'Yes!'" It was based in this passage for today, and is a glorious affirmation of the truth behind it.

Don't give up! God has a special purpose for your life today!

Prayer: Lord, I feel defeated when life says, "No!" Help me to see the Divine Yes in and beyond it all. Amen

Day 226

Acts 8:4-40

Philip was preaching in the region of Samaria (Acts 8:5). In one of the cities there, the Spirit was moving with such power that many miracles were taking place (Acts 8:6-8). Yet, Philip was not so taken by his glorious successes - or better God's successes - that he had to remain, and keep his glory days on a roll. For the Spirit had other plans - other tasks for him to do.

The Lord called to Philip to go to the south to the road that runs through Jerusalem toward Egypt. There he found a single figure, a eunuch in his chariot, the treasurer of the queen of Ethiopia. The Spirit called him to go over and join the eunuch. As he approached, he heard him reading from the prophet Isaiah. The eunuch was puzzled by what he was reading, so Philip explains it to him. In the process Philip leads him to Christ, and baptizes him.

Philip was always ready to proclaim the name of Jesus. He was even willing to leave a fruitful ministry to others, so he could go to the individual that the Lord wanted him to reach out to. That person would take the Word to another land, and proclaim it there.

Who is God calling you to go out of your way to witness to today?

Prayer: (Relax your body... Now spend some time centering yourself in the Lord.... Repeat His name over-and-over until your focus is upon Him... Spend some time thanking the Lord for specific blessings... Lift up certain concerns... Now seek His guidance for today...)

Day 227

Mark 14:3-9

We have a mystery in our Lesson for today. A woman, whose name is not known, comes into the room where Jesus is reclined at the table. She has a flask of good smelling ointment, breaks it open, and pours it on the Lord's head. The disciples protest the waste of the costly ointment, but Jesus quiets them telling them that she has done a beautiful thing. She has prepared His body for burial. Then He adds that what she has done is to be told throughout the world, so she will be remembered by generations that follow.

Who was this woman? We do not know her name. She remains anonymous. She did nothing spectacular, she preached no sermons, witnessed to no one, performed no miracles. Yet, this nameless person was to be remembered, not by name, but for her selfless action!

How often do we do service for the Lord, and want our name told, so that we can get proper credit - proper thanks?! Not her! What an example for all of us!

Prayer: I like to get credit for the things I do for others, Lord. Help me to be content simply to glorify your name. Humble me, Lord, that I may be satisfied to minister to you and your children selflessly. Amen

Day 228

Deuteronomy 26:1-11

We are most blessed! Yes there are times when finances are not what we wish, but compared to the Third World, we all have a lot to be thankful for!

When I have taken Mission Trips to Honduras and Nicaragua, I have never ceased to be amazed at how little those people have to live on, and how grateful they are for their little! They are the spiritual giants of our time!

Are we better off spiritually for our abundance? No, for the Church is strongest where the people are neediest. One African pastor said, "You Americans have blessed insurance, we have blessed assurance!"

In our Lesson for today, the Lord is reminding the Hebrew People that when they come into the Promised Land, they must remember to give thanks! The Lord was sounding a warning here, saying that there are dangers in a land "flowing with milk and honey." For it is easier to forget the Lord when you have all your physical needs met. Who needs God? many ask. Yet, how temporary is all we have, and how empty to think it is enough!

Prayer: Lord, make me truly grateful! Help me to remember that I have nothing, but what your strength and the mental abilities you have given me, have made possible. Amen

Day 229

Ephesians 3:14-21

We all hunger for protection from accident, disease, and violent acts of others.

A very religious woman awoke one night to a noise coming from her living room. She crept in, and saw a burglar unplugging her television. She cried: "Acts 2:38!" (Which reads: "Repent ... in the name of Jesus Christ... for the forgiveness of sins") Amazingly the burglar froze, and raised his hands. She then called the police, who came and arrested him.

"Why didn't you run away from this little old lady?" they asked. The burglar replied: "Well, she said she had an axe and two 38s."

We all have experienced the protection of God! He has been there for us in sickness, in danger, and threats to our well being in innumerable ways! When we rehearse those experiences over in our minds, it gives us renewed courage/faith in the protection of God. Ours is a God who can be counted upon!

Prayer: Lord, you have proven your faithfulness over-and-over! Help me to recount those blessings, that I may realize your care and keeping, and be renewed in faith. Help me to do that right now.... Amen.

Day 230

Matthew 13:47-48

This parable speaks of the Kingdom, and therefore of the Church, for the Church is the embodiment of the Kingdom on earth.

I shared earlier that denominations are dying. I believe this is a good thing, for it leaves the Church united as one. Further, the Church is not dying, for the "gates of Hell shall not prevail against it!" (Matthew 16:18) The Church is going through another massive Reformation -- a reformation of worship... of the centrality of prayer to our lives... and a distinct call to be a servant Church!

This parable lifts up how the Kingdom/Church gathers persons of all kinds: all races, economic standing, and creeds. Then enfolds them into one Body - one Faith.

During the Middle Ages there was a scholar by the name of Muretus. He was very poor. He became seriously ill. No one knew who he was, so they could not contact any family.

The doctors were discussing his case in Latin, the scholar's language. One said to the others, "It doesn't matter what happens to the poor wretch, since no one will care." To which Muretus rallied: "Call no one worthless for whom Christ died!"

And the net gathered fish from every kind -- so must the Church continue to do!

Prayer: O God, help me to seek persons of all kinds for your Church. That all may come to know the Good News which is Jesus! Amen

Day 231

Mark 4:30-32

Again Jesus speaks on a favorite theme of His: the Kingdom. He does so using another parable. He says that the Kingdom is like a mustard seed - the tiniest of all seeds.

In 1620 when The Mayflower sailed from England to America. It had only 101 passengers on board. Compared to ships of today with their thousands of passengers, she was a miniature vessel! Yet, that voyage had a greater impact upon history, than all the great ocean liners that traverse the seas in our time.

Out of little - much!

That is the story of the Church! Whether we speak of the twelve apostles, one Saul becoming the Paul, or Rosa Parks as a forerunner to the great Civil Rights Movement of the 1960s.

Out of little - much!

It can be the story of our lives as well! Not that we will be nationally known for our works for the Kingdom, but we can sow a seed that will multiply and produce changed lives, and who knows where that will lead!

Prayer: Help me Lord, to not underestimate what you are able to do through me when I give my little to your Kingdom. Help me to hear your voice, and do your bidding with faith. Amen

Day 232

Matthew 13:44

Palestine has been a place for wars for aeons! Thus, it became commonplace in Biblical times for persons to hide their valuables in the ground - in the backyard we would say. Therefore, Jesus is using an analogy that his hearers would be familiar with: the treasure hidden in a field.

Charles Spurgeon was a famous preacher of the 19th century. His story goes back to when he was fifteen. He was headed for church when he was caught in a blizzard. Unable to reach his Baptist Church, he came upon a Primitive Methodist Chapel. Once inside he learned that the preacher couldn't make it because of the storm, so a layman was filling in.

Spurgeon caught the preacher's eye, and he called out to him: "Young man, look to Jesus!" Though the layman had said little else, Spurgeon said he did, and suddenly the darkness in his soul was gone! "I saw the sun!" It was a life-changing experience!

Hidden in a "field" was a treasure within young Spurgeon! It was the grace of God at work! His life would never be the same, and the lives of hundreds of others would be changed as a result too!

Prayer: Help me, Lord, to never underestimate the Power of your Grace exposed by the humblest of vessels! Enable me to sell all to purchase that "field." Amen

Day 233

John 14:1-7

Heaven! How do we get there? When do we go? What will it be like? The scripture is not a book of systematic theology. In other words, it's pages do not answer such questions in a systematic way. Instead, we get bits and pieces. In relation to the questions before us, we find answers primarily in the New Testament. For the afterlife in the Old Testament was viewed as a shadowy place... possibly existence.

In our Lesson for today, Jesus is dealing most fully with the issue. He says: "I am the way." He, who alone conquered death and the grave, is the only One qualified to save us from the same! No one enters but by that "door" (John 10:7).

When do we go to Heaven? Is it at a Judgment Day, or at death? Jesus told the thief on the cross: "Today you will be with me in Paradise." (Luke 23:43) I don't think that the One who made us for fellowship would leave us in a grave for several hundred years or more. In fact Moses and Elijah, long since dead, appeared with Him on the mountain! (Mark 9:4) They were very much raised from the dead!

Finally, what will Heaven be like? Jesus tells us in the simplest, and yet most profound way, that Heaven is like a loving father's house. "In my Father's House are many rooms." (v.2) Fellowship! Joy! Love! A glad reunion day! All shared around a big banquet table (this part is my idea)!

Prayer: Lord, it is difficult to give up those who die. But it is glorious to think of all they will enjoy in their Father's House! Amen.

Day 234

Mark 12:28-34

Just as its human nature to long for happiness, so it is also human nature to long for peace. But how do we come to a state of peace?

Peace comes first of all from being forgiven. Jeremiah 31:34 records what God said on the subject: "I will forgive their iniquity, and remember their sin no more." God is saying that He not only forgives your sin, but He also forgets it! And if that is not enough He forgives it, and forgets it - until Judgement Day? No, No! He forgets it forever! So, that if you are still feeling guilty it is because you have not forgiven yourself!

Second, peace comes from forgiving others. Forgiving others is as difficult as forgiving ourselves. Yet, bitterness is the poison we drink in order to destroy our enemies. In the cross we find grace to forgive – and thus find peace.

Third, peace comes from being for giving. I like it, now that I'm no longer on the payroll, to be able to lift up the importance of giving without having my motives questioned. For there is a glorious peace and joy in giving for the sake of others – for the sake of the Kingdom of God!

Prayer: Lord, help me to know the peace of being forgiven – of being a forgiving person – and being for giving for Christ's sake. Amen.

Day 235

Ephesians 4:11-16

What are you going to be when you grow up? Ask a child that question, and you will get a multitude of answers! All are dependent upon that child having a family to raise it to adulthood. Without a family, the infant will perish!

Paul calls us, who are children of God, to mature to the full stature of Christ (v.13). Yet, to reach such maturity requires a Family also - the Family of God - the Church! For the Church alone nurtures in the Faith that it has passed down through the centuries. It has parented us! Thus, without it, we perish!

It happened at a Special Olympics track meet several years ago. The contestants lined up. The starting gun was fired, and Timmy was suddenly out in front of the rest! Then he fell hard! The rest of the pack passed him by, when, as if with one mind, they stopped, turned, came back, and helped Timmy to his feet, and then walked across the finish line arm-in-arm together.

That's what it means to be a part of the Family of God! Lesson learned!

Prayer: Lord, how often it is the humble that teach us the most about what it means to be Christ-like. Humble me that I too may grow to be Christ-like. Amen.

Day 236

Mark 2:1-12

What a beautiful story! Four friends heard Jesus was in town. Immediately they thought of their friend who was paralyzed. Could it be that Jesus could cure him of his paralysis?

They went and got their friend, and carried him in the direction of the commotion down the block. When they found Jesus, the crowd was spilling out of the house where he was speaking. So, they did something creative - or destructive - depending on your perspective. They cut a hole in the roof, and lowered their friend down on his pallet at Jesus' feet. Jesus then healed the man. There was much rejoicing!

Learn from this what is involved in a miracle: The friends saw a need. They faced the obstacles that were standing in their way -- doing all they could. They turned to the Lord in their need, and He performed a miracle!

God doesn't always perform miracles. Sometimes we are left with the Lord and mysteries. Yet, when miracles happen -- and they DO - these are the ingredients.

Prayer: Lord, help me to be able to see the possibilities beyond the obstacles I face today. Amen.

Day 237

Ezekiel 47:1-6, 12

In about 580 B.C. Ezekiel had a vision. In it he saw a river running out of the temple – out from under the door. He followed the stream – wading as he went. After about a third of a mile, the water was ankle deep. He went another third of a mile, and it was up to his knees. At one mile it was waist deep. Another third of a mile and it was deep enough to swim in.

Note that the further Ezekiel went the deeper he got!

We cannot go further in our faith walk, until we are prepared to go deeper! That is deeper in prayer. Prayer that probes the depths of listening to God... Prayer that communes: His Spirit with our spirit... Prayer that seeks His guidance... Prayer that enables us to know the Lord personally!

"There is a river whose streams make glad the city of God, ... God is in the midst of her..." (Psalm 46:4a & 5a).

Yes, there is a River – that IS God!

Prayer: Lord, help me to not be content to just wade in your Presence, but to plunge in whole heartedly – soaking – knowing as I am known. Amen.

Day 238

Romans 12:1-8

Nothing is more important than knowing God's will! If we really want to know God's will, then there are seven helps that will guide us.

First, we must be willing to DO God's will. God is not into magic tricks to impress us, but He is desirous to reveal His will to the one is ready to act!

Second, God's Word is an important help. If something is not in keeping with the repeating themes of Scripture, then it is not God's will!

Third, ask yourself, "What would Jesus do?" There is no better guide, than seeking to do what the Lord would do.

Fourth, is prayer. Can He who made mouths not speak? Of course God can! We must listen for that "still, small voice" within.

Fifth: watch for open doors. Often guidance comes from an open door. Then when we look back – we see Christ behind the door!

Sixth: Gideon put down a fleece, and got the sign he needed from God. When God lays a sign on your heart to ask for, then He is ready to reveal His will to you by giving you the sign. (See Judges 6:36-40)

Seventh: Seek out other Christians' wisdom and insight on the issue at hand.

Prayer: Lord, give me the patience and persistence to glean your will for my life. Then help me to know the joy of being in your will. Amen.

Day 239

James 1:17-27

General George McClellan was an impressive sight to behold, galloping about on his magnificent horse! He was just thirty-four years old when he was appointed by President Lincoln to be supreme commander of the Union Army. Yet, for all of his charisma and abilities, he did little for the cause! He hesitated to engage the army in battle!

Lincoln was exasperated! "If General McClellan doesn't want to use the army, I would like to borrow it for a while," the president said.

There are many persons in the pews of a Sunday morning who are very capable. They are financially able to do wondrous things for the Kingdom. They are led by some of the most gifted clergy in the history of the Church. But are we really engaging the enemy? Are we taking on the forces of lovelessness, poverty, and meaningless living? Or are we simply maintaining the "form of religion while denying its power (II Timothy 3:5)."

James warns: "Be doers of the Word, and not hearers only, deceiving yourselves (James 1:22)."

Prayer: Lord, it is easy to put my spiritual life on cruise control, and just let things slide by. Help me to be more than one who wears the badge that says, "Christian," but who does little to show I am a person who believes in you. Motivate me to be a doer of your Word, Lord -- witnessing and serving each day. Amen

Day 240

Matthew 25:14-30

Back in the 1700s Susannah and Samuel Wesley had nineteen children. Two of them died in infancy, but the rest lived to adulthood. Can you imagine trying to raise seventeen children today - even with all the modern conveniences?! Yet, Susannah would spend time with each of the children, one-on-one, each day. In that time she taught them to read the Bible, and what it meant to be a Christian. She did all of this while the others played quietly nearby!

Two of these children were John and Charles – who grew to be the instruments of the great evangelical revival out of which Methodism was born.

It is difficult to discipline ourselves as adults, not to mention the same in our children. Yet, Susannah serves as an inspiration for us all! She took what the Lord had entrusted to her, and invested it in her children. It took countless hours on her part. It took tremendous discipline! But she persisted, and her life proved to be fruitful. When her life was over, the Lord is bound to have said, "Well done my good and faithful servant (v.21)!"

It is easier to live life in the shallows of come-what-may. Susannah did not settle for life lived so cheaply, and she was greatly rewarded for her efforts!

Prayer: Lord, help me to serve you with discipline, that I may know your sufficiency in all of life. Amen.

Day 241

Hosea 3:1-5

History is filled with famous couples who served the Lord together: Samuel and Susannah Wesley, Martin and Katharine Luther, and the list goes on. But few can match the story of Hosea and his bride, Gomer. In fact their saga is unique in the Biblical record! It is an unbelievable story of love, crushing separation, and steadfastness!

Hosea marries Gomer. They have children together - giving them each a name that signifies a divine message. Then Gomer leaves Hosea, and pursues her lusts - living as a prostitute. Hosea is devastated! But then God calls to Hosea, and tells him to take Gomer back as his wife!

"Why!" we ask! God wants to present to Israel a living parable of their unfaithfulness to Him, and how that He is willing to take them back. Here we see the "hesed" of God, i.e. the everlasting love!

C.T. Studd, preacher and pastor of the nineteenth century, once said: "No sacrifice is too great for me to make for Him who gave His life for me."

Hosea paid a great price in his obedience to God!

Prayer: Lord, help me to learn from the faithfulness of Hosea! Enable me to be willing to make the sacrifices that such steadfastness to you requires. Keep ever before me your Cross as an inspiration - especially in these times when faithfulness to you is lacking. Amen

Day 242

I Corinthians 15:12-19

I have a friend who is – if not an atheist, then an agnostic. I enjoy talking with him about the God he doesn't believe in. The other day he declared: "I believe when I die I will just become worm food." I smiled and asked: "What's the meaning of life then? What gives life value now – other than the figment of our imagination?" He grew very quiet. Never answered. So, I left him to ponder his thoughts as he changed the subject.

Paul, writing to the church in Corinth says: "If for this life only we have hoped in Christ, we are of all men most to be pitied." (v.19)

Pray for all those wonderful people who struggle with faith issues. We all know of names that come to mind. They are searching, and we may speak a word that will enable them to find the Way. Pray for them, for prayer taps into the very power of God, which can change lives. Let the Spirit lead you as to when to speak, and when to simply listen.

Prayer: Lord, grant me wisdom and courage to engage the world today in humble love, for many are lost and struggling. Amen.

Day 243

Luke 15:1-7

The shepherd was a most lowly occupation in Bible times. It is interesting, therefore, that Jesus lifts up the shepherd for a lead role in his parable, and even declares: "I am the good Shepherd (John 10:11."

Sheep on the other hand were rarely kept for their meat, but for their wool. Thus, the relationship between shepherd and his flock was a very special one. Sheep could recognize their shepherd's call, and would respond. H.V. Morton, on visiting Palestine, tells how he saw sheep being put into a communal pen. He wondered how they would ever get sorted out, but in time a shepherd would call, and his sheep would come, then another... (See John 10:1-3)

In Jesus' parable, one of the sheep strays. The shepherd leaves the ninety-nine sheep, and goes in search of the one. (It is a wonder that the rest didn't go astray!) But the point is: the love the shepherd has for each one of his sheep.

Jesus is saying you are important to God! Further, we should be concerned about the one person that goes astray, and seek to win him/her back to the fold.

Prayer: Thank you Lord God for your great love for me! Help me to value the lost ones of our time who go astray, and in prayer and witness seek to woo them back to yourself. In Jesus' Name I pray. Amen

Day 244

Matthew 21:28-32

Which of the two sons in Jesus' parable did the father's will?

The meaning is clear, the first son represents the tax collectors and sinners who were not doing God's bidding when Jesus came, but who then responded positively to the Lord's invitation. The second son stands for the scribes and Pharisees, who declared their willingness to serve God, but when the Son of God came, they refused to follow Him.

Which child are we?

Henry Drummond spoke on a street corner in London. His hearers were young men who had no use for the Church. A man passed by, and one of the youngsters said: "That man is the founder of the Atheist's Club." "How can that be?" asked Drummond, "He is a leader in the Church." "Yes," said the youth, "And that is why we have nothing to do with the Church."

Our negative witness can have a big impact on impressionable minds!

Prayer: Lord, grant me a pure heart, that none can say, "He/she is why I have nothing to do with the Church!" Amen

Day 245

Luke 9:23-27

William Booth, the founder of the Salvation Army, was once asked the secret of his success. "I will tell you ... There were persons with greater intellect than I; persons even with better opportunities. Yet, from the day I got the poor of London on my heart, and a vision for what Jesus Christ could do there; I made up my mind that God would have all of William Booth that there was!"

Before Christ turned the water into wine, someone had to first fill the jugs with water. Before He fed the multitude, a little boy had to give up his lunch. Before Christ raised Lazarus from the dead someone had to roll the stone away from his grave, and then "loose him and let him go!" (John 11:39, & 44b) We can have a role in miracle making!

Does the Lord have all there is of you? What is He calling you to do today, that He might perform some wondrous work?

Prayer: Lord, help me to give all there is of myself to you. Enable me to believe in your Power to do great things in our time. Amen.

Day 246

Isaiah 58:1-12

The Bible teaches us the importance of fasting. Jesus assumed His followers would practice it. (Matthew 6:17)

When we fast we usually will do without food for a meal, or a day - as health permits. The purpose of which is, not to lose weight, but to be able to discipline ourselves in regard to a basic appetite. Therefore, we are then better able to discipline ourselves in regard to temptations that would destroy us, or our relationships with God or others.

But in our lesson for today, God is saying there is a different kind of fast. It involves, not doing without, but DOING. That is: sharing your bread with the hungry -- your home with the homeless -- your clothes with those without...

Herein is a fast of a different sort, but a very Christ-like one! How are we doing with such fasting?

Prayer: Lord, help me to look beyond myself -- not to give up food necessarily, but to give something to those less fortunate than myself. Amen

Day 247

Malachi 3:1-4, especially verse 2b

How often the Lord moves upon us like a great blast furnace to burn away the impurities in our lives, and in our relationship with Him.

As I mentioned on Day 54, my wife, Ginny, was diagnosed with an aggressive form of uterine cancer back in October of 2009. The news sent me reeling! I began to run ahead to what may come next. It was terrifying! It caused me to stop and take a spiritual inventory, to see where I was in regard to the Lord. That inventory showed me that yes I loved the Lord and was walking with Him, but not as closely as I could be! I began to take steps to correct my path, so that I didn't walk so much parallel to the Lord, but flung myself into His arms!

Though I do not believe God gave Ginny cancer, I do believe He was using that experience to burn away the ore of my soul, and call me to a closer walk with Him. It worked!

Ginny's cancer was caught early, and after five years she has had no recurrences. We are grateful! At the same time I am walking closer to God, and am even grateful that He has used this evil thing for His purposes.

Prayer: Lord, thank you for the refiner's fire. Thank you for making me purer in my relationship with you. Thank you for being my God amid the storms! Amen.

Day 248

Psalm 63

John Wesley, the founder of Methodism, came to the American Colonies in 1736. His desire was to proclaim the Gospel to the Native Americans in Georgia. His efforts were a miserable failure! He returned to England a broken man!

In London in 1738, he went, rather reluctantly, to a Prayer Meeting on Aldersgate Street. As the leader of that meeting stood, he began to read Martin Luther's Preface to the Book of Romans. (A rather boring reading!) Wesley described how suddenly he felt his "heart was strangely warmed..." (It is amazing what God can use in His purposes!) He received assurance of his salvation, and a new lease on his ministry! It was the birth of the great evangelical revival out of which Methodism was born!

Discouragements come to all our lives. In fact, the more you seek to do for the Lord - the greater the number of setbacks! But such discouragements are calls to prayer! For in prayer we regain our footing, and see where the Lord is leading.

Prayer: Life's setbacks are painful, Lord! They make us ask, "What's the use?!" But you meet us there in the dark night for our souls, and lead us to the sunrise. Keep me mindful of that, Lord, when we face such in my life. Amen

Day 249

Nehemiah: 6: 1-9, & 15

Sometimes God asks us to do something foolish (See I Corinthians 4;10; II Corinthians 12:11). Nehemiah was called to do something many would say was foolish even impossible if you have ever seen the massive stones that were part of the Temple in Jerusalem - stones as big a boxcars!

But there is more to the story!

The people of Israel had been driven from their homeland by the Babylonians. The years passed, and Nehemiah got concerned because he had heard that the walls of Jerusalem were still in ruin. So, he asked the King of Persia for permission to return, and rebuild the walls. The king gave his permission. So Nehemiah journeyed back to Jerusalem. There he began his work, though many opposed him – even threatened his life! Still Nehemiah persisted!

From atop the wall he supervised the work, as the wall, with its massive stones, rose out of the ruins. His detractors kept up their assault, trying to get him to come off the wall, but he declared: "I'm doing a great work, and I cannot come down (v.3)."

How often do we engage in the Lord's work, and there are those who want to meet with us in the plain of "Ono" (see v.2), to say, "Oh no, that can't be done!"

Thanks be to God for all the faithful folks who over the years refused to give up, against all odds, so that we might know the Good News of Jesus Christ, and be a part of His Kingdom in our time!

Prayer: Lord, count me in! Help me to see where you are leading, and then do your bidding regardless of the odds. Amen.

Day 250

Isaiah 43:18-25

Thus says the Lord, "Do not remember the former things, or consider the things of old. I am about to do a new thing..." (vs. 18-19a)

Do you remember drinking water out of a plastic bottle that had grown stale -- old water?

Our life with God can sometimes become stale. When we think of thanksgivings - it is mostly something out of the distant past. When we think of our work for the Lord - we think of things we have done yesterday. Our joy in the Lord is a thing of yesteryears - when we first gave our life to the Lord.

God is saying, "I am about to do a new thing!" He is saying I'm about to use you in new ventures -- new work -- that will produce new joy! For the Israelites of old he made a new path through the sea, so they could escape the Egyptians. He did a new thing in Jesus Christ - upsetting a cemetery by conquering death and the grave. He did a new thing when he radically changed the life of Saul into Paul the Apostle. He did a new thing when he poured out His Spirit upon all flesh at Pentecost - so all would have the privilege of knowing Him and the power of His resurrection! Ours is a God of new things!

How up to date are you in your relationship with the Lord?

Prayer: Lord, use me in new ventures. Give me ever new thanksgivings to praise your name with. Show me how to keep my love for you fresh as the morning dew. Amen

Day 251

Matthew 14:22-33

Two farmers, Bob and Jim, were out duck hunting. Bob had an amazing dog! He could hardly wait to show him off to Jim. They went to the duck blind, and settled in for the hunt. Finally, they called in some ducks. They both stood and shot, and each got a duck. Jim's dog jumped into the water and began swimming for a duck. Bob's dog simply walked on the water – beat Jim's dog to the ducks. Picked one up, and walked back. Bob couldn't contain his pride: "Did you see that, Jim?!" "Yes I did," said Jim, "Your dog can't swim!"

Sink or swim? It is the question Peter faced, and the one we face repeatedly in life.

We land our first job, and life cries: "Sink or swim?" We marry and have children: "Sink or swim?" We come midlife, and the proverbial crises raises its ugly head: "Sink or swim?" We reach the autumn of life - "Sink or swim?"

Why did Peter sink? After all he was simply obeying the Lord's command: "Come!"

Sometimes we sink because of lack of courage to try new things. Other times it is because of self-doubt or fear of what others will think. Sometimes it is due to lack of discipline and hard work.

But Peter sank because he took his eyes off of Jesus!

It is difficult to maintain focus on the Lord with so many things vying for our attention! But, oh so important!

Prayer: Lord, help me to center on you today. Help me to remember the possibilities you bring to life, and keep me focused on that. Amen.

Day 252

Philippians 4:4-7

"Laughter is the Best Medicine" – so the saying goes. Laughter releases natural painkillers into our system which boosts our defenses against disease and stress. It gives our spirits a lift, and provides us with a mini-workout of a good belly laugh!

A favorite picture of mine, that hangs in my study, shows Jesus laughing!

1. In my book, "Holy Hilarity: Joy for the Soul" I have a collection of humorous stories. Here is a a couple of them:
   - A grandmother asked her grandson how he liked the Thanksgiving turkey? He said, "The turkey was all right, but the bread the turkey ate was the best!"

2. The Reverend Dennis Bowling showed us at staff a meeting one Tuesday a picture of Da Vinci's "Last Supper." Then he asked: "Do you know what the Lord said to the disciples right before this picture was taken? He said, 'O.K. boys, everyone on this side of the table for a picture!'"

Pierre Teilhard De Chardin said, "The surest sign of the Presence of God is JOY!"

Paul believed that, when he wrote, while in prison, "Rejoice in the Lord always. Again I will say it, rejoice!"

Prayer: Lord, focus my attention on your Presence this day that I may rejoice with you, O God, my Strength and my Redeemer. Amen.

Day 253

Luke 24:13-32

Cleopas was one of the two men who was going back to Emmaus on the Sunday that Jesus arose from the grave. Though the other man is not identified, some have speculated that it was Simon Peter. Their hearts were heavy as the trudged toward their destination! For their dear friend, Jesus, had been brutally crucified on Friday, and though there were rumors that He was alive, they knew he was dead!

As they walked, a stranger caught up with them. Suddenly He was pointing out the various references in the Old Testament concerning the Messiah. When they arrived at Cleopas's home, it was late, so he invited the stranger to spend the night with them. At supper this Stranger took bread and broke it, and suddenly they realized who He was, and He vanished from their sight!

How often has He walked with you on the road, and you didn't recognize that it was the Lord! Watch for Him today as He will come alongside you again. Sense His Presence, and know in your heart of hearts that He is risen - He is risen indeed!

Prayer: Open my eyes that I may see, and know You, Lord God! Amen

Day 254

Luke 6:46-49

Jesus is saying that building your life upon His teachings is the only sure foundation! To build upon anything else, is to face certain ruin! There is no half-way about it. It is Christ, or destruction!

The story is told that Lord Nelson captured a captain, that had heard of his magnanimous ways. So when Nelson happened in among the captured, the captain extended his hand to shake hands. Nelson responded: "Your sword, and then your hand!" In other words he was expecting total submission from the captive. This is a parable from history that speaks of how the Lord expects total submission from us! Your gods, and then your hand!

Jesus is declaring that we are not just to be hearers of the Word, but doers. For in so doing, we are building our "house" upon the Rock - which is the Lord! (See I Corinthians 10:4)

On what is your life being built?

Prayer: Lord, you are my Rock -- my Life -- my all! I dedicate myself anew to you. As long as life lasts, I want to continually build my life on you. Help me to stay focused on that project. Amen

Day 255

Acts 4:36

Barnabus was originally named by his parents Joseph. He was later in his adult life given the name Barnabus by the Apostles. Why? Because Barnabus, ... means son of encouragement (v.36b), and Barnabus was an encourager! What greater compliment could be given a person than that?!

Barnabus was the one who took Saul by the hand, when everyone else was afraid of him, for Saul had been in on killing Christians! Barnabus believed in him, and introduced him to the rest of the Apostles (Acts 9:27). He spoke in his defense. He was a vital part of seeing Saul become the Apostle Paul!

I have been blessed with a half dozen or so Barnabuses in my life! One of those was the late Reverend Bill O'Quinn. Bill was twelve years my senior. We grew up in the same town, and in the same church. Because of our age difference we hardly knew each other until later in life.

When I began my ministry Bill became my mentor. He was one of those persons around which you felt good about yourself. He made you believe in yourself. He saw in you great potential. He was a true friend!

How beautiful along life's path are the footsteps of a son or daughter of encouragement!

Prayer: Lord, thank you for the encouragers I have known! Help me to be an encourager to someone else today. Amen.

Day 256

Genesis 32:22-30

We dealt with this passage on Day 195, but there are more nuggets to be mined here. So let us begin.

Scripture tells us that Jacob wrestled God to a draw! What is going on here?!

To wrestle with someone you have to be in close proximity with them. Jacob, it can be said, was very close to God!

After Jacob had wronged his family, and thought his brother might come in the morning light and kill him, he turns to God, and "wrestles" with Him all night long.

Have you ever had a restless night? Jacob sure did! It was God who came to him. Like a Mother running to her crying infant, so God came. He wanted to give his child what he needed so badly – God's Presence, assurance, and blessing. But first God had to strive with Jacob to get him ready to receive what God had for him.

"I will not let you go until you bless me," Jacob cries with such boldness as to be funny! Who can wrench from the Almighty a blessing?! But God is the Patient One – who lets Jacob even believe that he was in charge. Then blesses him with good news in the encounter with his brother in the morning's light. What a God!

Prayer: Lord, often we think we are in charge, and need simply to give you your marching orders through our prayers. Forgive us, Lord! Help us to receive your approach to us as we surrender to you. Amen.

Day 257

James 1:2-8

James, the brother of our Lord, states here not "if" you face trials, but "when." Trials, as we have seen in other lessons we have looked at, are a part of life - and no less so for the Christian.

James sees such testings as opportunities to see - whether we are made of Christly steel or not!

There will be tests of sorrows... of illness... of uncertainty... of persecution... of seductions... of disappointments... of dangers... of unpopularity... of weariness... These all come our way that we may defeat them -- not let them have the last word! They are not to weaken us, but to make us stronger. They are the blast furnace through which our iron ore becomes steel!

Yes, we can expect such trials (See also: John 16:33b), and though we do not realize it immediately, in hindsight we will see that the Christ has come to us in such times - never to leave us nor forsake us. (Matthew 28:20b)

Prayer: Lord, the scene you have painted for me, is one of victory! Help me to not falter, but to rise above the storm. Amen

Day 258

Luke 19:11-26

This parable seems to parallel the parable of the Ten Talents. Perhaps Jesus was repeating the parable in slightly different form. Nevertheless, the story offers us opportunity to discover more truths that our Lord holds for us.

Note that the nobleman does not require the same result from the three servants. The first two did what they could with what they were given, and were commended. The third one alone is condemned, because he did nothing with what he was given!

Jesus is saying, God does not demand the same from all His followers. He knows that we come with different abilities and opportunities. Thus, He was asking of them that they do the best they could. The first two were considered faithful in this regard.

A further point of the parable is: If we are faithful with what we are given, we will be given more -- a bigger job. Booker T. Washington is a case in point. He was not allowed into the university he wanted to attend, because of the color of his skin, but was offered a job of sweeping the floors and making beds in the dormitory. He did it so well, that he was offered an opportunity to become a student. With the added opportunity, he was able to prove himself as a great intellect, and would later become President of Tuskegee University.

Prayer: Help me to be faithful with what you have given me, O Lord, that I may be given greater opportunities to serve you. Amen

Day 259

James 3:1-12

James is saying that out of small things come great feats! A small blaze can make a great forest fire! A small horse's bit can guide/control a mighty steed! A ship's rudder, though small in proportion to the size of a great ship, is able to guide it through storms!

The tongue is another thing. It is like a small fire, that is able to do great harm! Think of the hurt caused by gossip, and negative attacks on others. Think of the careers that have been ended by someone's tongue. Consider the children's lives that have been warped by a parent's tongue. Consider the harm done by the negative political ads - as they stretch the truth, or leave it behind all together. The tongue doesn't even have to be present to do its harm! It can be miles away.

Of all the body parts, could it be that the tongue is the most difficult to control? Out of control it enjoys tearing other persons down - looking for the negative in them, and sharing with another a little juicy tidbit of gossip.

The tongue can do great good, and it can do great harm. Which is the case with your tongue?

Prayer: Lord, help me control this runaway steed - my tongue! Help me to see the harm that it can do, and help me to see the wonderful good it can do. I dedicate it to you this day, O Lord. Use it to build others up, and thus to better my world. Amen

Day 260

I Peter 1:3-9

What does the future hold? Does it not depend upon Who holds the future?! And we know Who holds the future our Risen Savior, Jesus Christ! We rejoice that His resurrection Power guards us -- looks over us! (v.5)

Christians in Peter's day were facing persecution. Yet, he reminds them of the hope and confidence they have.

When the worst comes to the worst, and endurance is holding on by a thread, then Christ will come to us, and His power will be displayed! As long as we cling to this hope, we can endure anything!

Peter reminds us that every trial is a test. When the athlete is tried to the limit, he/she becomes stronger. So, we become stronger when we are tested to the limit - for at our limit stands the Limitless Power of God!

Finally, we can stand the test, because we know that in the end the Lord will come to us in the winner's circle, and say, "Well done my good and faithful servant (v.7)!"

Prayer: Lord, test me, try me, empower me, use me to be your faithful servant. Amen

Day 261

I Peter 2:18-25

Peter writes that God is the Shepherd and Bishop of our souls (v.25). Interesting! Describing God as Shepherd is one the oldest characterizations of God. "The Lord is my Shepherd...," the Psalmist wrote (Psalm 23:1). Isaiah wrote: "He shall feed His flock like a Shepherd..." (Isaiah 40:11a) Jesus took this title upon Himself, when he said: "I am the good Shepherd." (John 10:11)

On the other hand, the Greek word here translated by some as "Bishop" is episkopos. It has various meanings, one of which is protector of the public safety. That is, according to William Barclay, the word means: Guardian, Protector, Guide, and our Director. Barclay adds: "God is the Shepherd and Guardian of our souls. In His love He cares for us; in His power He protects us; and in His wisdom He guides and directs us in the right way (The Daily Study Bible: The Letters of James and Peter p. 258)."

How comforting to know God on this level as Shepherd and Bishop.

Prayer: Lord, I submit to you as my Shepherd, my Bishop, and God. Make me worthy to claim you as my own Savior. Help me to turn all my cares over to you right now. Amen

Day 262

John 1:1-5

John starts off as Genesis does: "In the beginning God created..." and "In the beginning was the Word... all things were made through Him." Here John is lifting up the all important idea that the Christ was the God of creation (v.1b)! The focus continues on Jesus as the Word/God.

At the time of the writing of these words, the ancient world was believed to have a hundred thousand Greeks in the Church for every Jew. Christianity, by this time, had spread all the way to Rome. At Ephesus, John was thinking how he could communicate this Gospel to the Greeks. God gave him the idea of "the Word," or Logos, Greek for Word, for the idea was both Jewish and Greek. So John ran with it in this first chapter.

Thus, John is saying: "If you wish to see the Word in flesh, if you wish to see God, then look at Jesus Christ!

It is a glorious thought! God had prepared both Greek and Jew to hear and understand this way of grasping the truth about the Man/God of Galilee, and John was putting it to print!

Prayer: How glorious, O God, it is to realize how you prepare the hearts of women and men to receive the Gospel. Through one word so much was communicated, and you were, and are, glorified! I praise your Name, O Great God of creation and salvation. Amen

Day 263

Malachi 3:8-10

"Will a person rob God (v.8a)?" How can we rob God? God answers: By failing to bring the full tithe, or tenth, into the Temple, for the tithe is mine (v.8b). Then God adds: "[Try me and see] if I will not open the windows of heaven for you and pour down for you an overflowing blessing (v.10b)." The message: You cannot out give God!

A missionary once told of a native who brought a fish to his home. When the missionary looked a little puzzled, the young man explained that that was the tithe that he was sharing with his pastor. "Well, how many fish did you catch?" "Only one, I'm going to catch the others now."

The native was living on the divine possibilities. God promised that he would pour down blessings from heaven in response, and the young man was living expectantly!

I'm not sure about his theology, for God is not a vending machine that we put in a dollar, and get back ten! But I do believe, and have experienced how God takes care of those who put their trust in Him.

Persons of faith are persons who have repeatedly trusted God's Word, and found it and the Lord trustworthy. You can count on God!

Prayer: Lord, help me to do my best, and then trust you for the rest. Help me to be faithful with what I am and have, and then watch as you open the windows of heaven with untold blessings! Amen.

Day 264

Mark 10:17-31

Jesus was on His way to Jerusalem to die, when a faithful Jew came running up and asked: "Good Teacher, what must I do to inherit eternal life?" The Lord saw through his attempts at self-salvation, and pierced to the very heart of the man's need: "Go, sell all you have ... then come follow me." That is, he was going to have to surrender his all to the Lord!

If we don't make sacrificial gifts of our material wealth how can we claim to be followers of the crucified One? Thus, the Lord was saying, Go... sell... give... follow."

Someone suggested that instead of personal letters thanking persons for their pledges of XX dollars to the Church, that the pledges be posted in the narthex beside everyone's names, with a big "Thank You" across the top! THEN the truth of our sincerity will be known! This is shared in jest, but the idea of laying it on the line before the Lord is not.

Prayer: Lord, I don't like to think of sacrificing my money - for there is not enough to go around as it is. Yet, you sacrificed your very life for me! What does it mean to be a follower of a Crucified Jesus? Help me to reflect, and act on that. Amen

Day 265

Psalm 1

The Psalm speaks of two paths in life: the one road leads to blessing, the other to destruction.

And why not?! For if we choose to be our own god, then there is no future, but a grave in the local cemetery! But, if we choose the path that has the Lord's footprints on it, our way will be blessed, and ultimately will lead to Life eternal!

Martyn Lloyd-Jones told of a tourist to Ireland who stopped and asked a road worker directions to Dublin. The worker replied: "I wouldn't go there from here." The truth is we must always start from where we are right now. But many want to start the godly route from a different starting point. They want to wait until they get their life straightened out. But that is the business that the Lord is in: giving us a new beginning - a new life! Therefore, we must start the good life from where we are right now.

He/she is like a tree transplanted to the stream of living water! It will bear fruit there, and will not wither.

Prayer: Plant me, O Lord, by your river of living water! Cause me to bear fruit that will woo others to your stream - to your Life. Amen

Day 266

John 15:1-11

Lindsay Clegg owned a warehouse that he was selling. The building was in need of repair, it had broken windows, debris strewn floors, bricks that needed tuck-pointing – it was a real mess! Clegg admitted it would take a lot to bring the building back to what it once was.

A gentleman came along, and expressed interest in the place. So, Clegg gave him a tour, apologizing as they went for the conditions the place was in. The buyer smiled and said: "I don't want the building. I want the site."

In similar fashion, God doesn't want a broken down structure to repair – but a site to build on, and build He will! He makes our broken souls into loving, caring, hope-filled persons that are a beauty for all to see. He will make of us an inspiration for all who knew what was there before.

May we allow Him to build on our "soil," and on our soul.

Prayer: Lord, I give you the site. Build as you see fit. Help me to grow in love, faith, hope, and joy, that others will see what You are able to do, and want to be like me. Amen.

Day 267

I Peter 3:18-22, & 4:6

Here is where the Apostle's Creed gets the words: "He (Christ) descended into Hell." For "the spirits in prison" is understood to be the dead - i.e. those who died without the Lord - who are now given a chance to turn and accept Him. (See 4:6) So the days the Lord was in the grave were spent preaching to the dead.

Here we find hope for those who die without the Lord - that they may be given a second chance. Further, God's Word affirms that there will in fact be a time when "EVERY knee shall bow, and EVERY tongue confess that Jesus Christ is Lord." (Philippians 2:10) To say otherwise, is to believe that God is limited in love or power or both.

Yes, there is "no other Name by which we must be saved (Acts 4:12)." But the Savior is now, according to the Word, not limited to this world, for He is risen. He is in His spiritual body - omnipresent. Thus, there is not a corner of the universe where He is not, and where He is not at work!

Prayer: Lord your love is beyond my fathoming! It is fresh every day. It is greater than the universe, and yet more personal than a mother's tender touch. Fill my heart with gratitude throughout the day, and always. Amen

Day 268

John 15:1-11

Peter Gomes, while chaplain at Harvard, was host for Mother Teresa. She had come to Harvard to speak, and to receive an honorary doctor's degree. Before she spoke to the graduating seniors, she rested in Dr. Gomes' office. Trying to make small talk with this humble woman, he commented on the great work she was doing in Calcutta. But she seemed ill at ease with the compliment. She ducked her head and while fiddling with her beads, she said simply: "It is Jesus".

A branch cannot bear fruit apart from the vine (v.4)." Thus, in her humble way, she felt it was not her, but God! Yes, it IS all about Jesus!

Mother Teresa always felt that as she ministered to the poor, she was ministering to the Lord. (Matthew 25:40) Therefore, she was doing nothing, but offering back a drop of love to the Lord of Love who had poured forth a river of love upon her.

So it is with us too!

Prayer: Lord, help me to so connect with you, that you may live your life through me. Grant me the privilege of doing for one of the least of these today, that I too may do for you. Amen.

Day 269

II Corinthians 4:5-11 Jerusalem Bible

In 1925 the "New York World" celebrated the birthday of Abraham Lincoln with a cartoon. It depicted two Kentucky farmers talking. One asks: "Anything new?" "Nothing much. Oh I guess there is a new baby over at Tom Lincoln's place." Then adds: "But not much ever happens around here."

How often do we fail to see the great works God is doing in His own humble way! Oftentimes when he needs some wondrous deeds done, He has a baby born. Then He sits back and waits!

Wow! What a God!!

"We are only the earthenware jars that hold this treasure. To make it clear that such an overwhelming power comes from God, and not from us." "Nothing much!" I am sure that even Tom Lincoln had no idea of what was about to come to fruition through that baby! Yet, in that earthenware jar was a Treasure, and His name is Jesus!

Prayer: Lord, help us to never underestimate the potential that you place in each child in our lives. Help us to encourage that potential to come to the surface. Then help us to step back, wait, and see your greatness in our time! Amen.

Day 270

Psalm 46

You need to know the rest of the story, as Paul Harvey would say. In 1527 Martin Luther was facing the most difficult year of his life. He was having serious health issues - on one occasion he had to stop preaching in the middle of a sermon, because of dizziness. With physical weakness, heart problems, and depression, he began to think the end of his life was near.

On top of all this there were the constant threats to his life. If that were not enough, Duke Frederick, his protector, began wavering. Someone asked Luther: "If you lose the Duke's support, where will you be?" Luther replied: "I will be right where I have always been, in the arms of God!"

During all of this, Luther was inspired by Psalm 46 to write: "A Mighty Fortress Is Our God." "A mighty fortress is our God, a bulwark never failing... And though this world, with devils filled, should threaten to undo us, we will not fear, for God has willed His truth to triumph through us... " WOW! What a man, no, WHAT a GOD!

Prayer: When all around my soul gives way, Lord, help me to remember that you are a bulwark never failing! Help me to surrender up to you my fears right now. Amen.

Day 271

John 21:5-6

Bob Buford, in his book, "Half-Time," points out that in the game of football half-time is the point where the team takes a break, and the coach analyzes how the first half has gone. Then they make changes, so the second half may be more successful.

Mid-life is a time to pause and consider, in light of our Heavenly Coach's input, how the first forty or so years have gone. Then make changes so the second half may be lived more fully.

The risen Lord asks: "Have you caught any fish?" If not it is time to change your strategy, and make a different approach. Has life been meaningful? Or have you simply been chasing it, but never quite gotten there. "Have you caught any fish?" Are your closest relationships fulfilling, or have you bogged down into routines without satisfaction? "Have you caught any fish?" No one lives life "happy-all-the-time" - but do you have a sense of peace and joy about life and living? "Have you caught any fish?"

If not, then it is time to "cast your net on the other side." Learn the meaningfulness of service to others. Determine to give more attention to your closest relationships - talk things out - praise each other more - express your love often. Then give the Lord your yesterdays with their failings, and determine to spend more time in prayer... more time in counting your blessings. -- Cast your net on the other side -- determine to make the changes.

The second half of life can be a winning half!

Prayer: Lord, help me to reflect on my life thus far, then to make changes – with your help – to live life more fully and completely to your glory. Amen.

Day 272

Acts 4:36-37; 9:26-27; 11:22-24

The late Dr. Fred Craddock said, "If my children remember something I've said, I would want it to be: "I'm sorry!" We all have an abundance of things we are sorry for! None of us live perfect lives. All of us fail, especially those we love the most. But we don't have to live in the past. We can ask forgiveness, and then forgive ourselves.

Barnabas, "Son of Encouragement", had lots to be proud of – not the least of which was how he befriended Paul and encouraged him! He could be proud of the fact that the apostles gave him the name: "Son of Encouragement!"

We may not be a daughter or son of encouragement - YET - but we can be! If we but let today be the first day of the rest of our lives, then starting today we can become an encourager! All those in close relationship with us will appreciate it, and we will feel good for having done so.

Even Barnabas – being human – had regrets! Yet, it is us for which grace is intended. (See I John 1:9; Romans 5:8) Accept it, and begin again!

Prayer: Lord thank you for your grace for me a sinner. Help me to accept the same, and begin anew today. Amen.

Day 273

I Peter 3:13-22

"Be ready to make a defense to anyone for the hope that is within you." (v.15b)

How do we go about this?

First, use reason. Ours is a reasonable faith! But it is not reasonable if we have not come to know the Christ who meets us in prayer. To be a good salesperson, we need to know our Product! Without such we are speaking in speculation, but not out of experience. Sharing what is secondhand is of little value. Our faith can only be reasonable when we have come to know the Lord!

Second, Peter says our defense should be done with gentleness. Many state their faith with an arrogant belligerence. Anyone that does not agree with them is a fool. They seek to ram their beliefs down others throats, but to little effect. Our faith must be shared in gentle, humble love. We must give others space to think, and let the Spirit act. It is not up to us to change them, but to simply share our experience, and let it be.

Third, this leads us to respect. We must be respectful of the other person - even of their negative thoughts/beliefs. Such negative beliefs should not make us defensive. Ours is a God who can take care of Himself! We should part as friends.

Prayer: Lord, help me know when to make a defense for the hope I have, and when to be quiet and listen. I prayer for _____ . Show me the way to help them be open to your Spirit. Amen

Day 274

Psalm 3

Here David has fled from a coup pulled off by his own son, Absalom. Feeling betrayed, and like the whole world was against him, David writes this Psalm.

Realizing that his foes are many! He repeats "many" three times in two verses (v. 1-2). Revealing how distraught and vulnerable he is feeling!

His enemies' taunting claims cry out: "There is no salvation for him (v.2b)!" This is followed by "Selah" which is probably a musical pause to give the people chanting this Psalm time to pause and reflect on the seriousness of what has been stated.

Still God brings David back with an affirmation: "You, O Lord, are a shield about me!... I cried aloud to the Lord, and he answered me from His holy hill. Selah"

When we feel overwhelmed, we, like David, feel despair. Yet, as we have time to reflect we get centered once again in the Almighty, and cry: "Salvation belongs to the Lord!... Selah"

Prayer: Sometimes I feel like I am being crushed, O God. It seems like my foes are so many! But then I come back to my moorings in you, and realize that I am not alone. Thank you, Lord! Amen

Day 275

John 13:33-35

Our son, William, who is a doctor, and myself were part of a medical mission team to Honduras, after hurricane Mitch had struck. My role was that of finding some over-the-counter drugs in our medicine trunk, or helping to organize the patients in order of arrival, etc.

One day a woman came to the makeshift clinic in the heat of the day. She was carrying her three month old baby – which she had carried for three miles to see the doctor. I offered her a bottle of water. She took the bottle, said, "Gracias," and first gave her baby a drink, then she drank. I was deeply moved by the love of that mother for her baby - something we might take for granted - yet in her I saw the face of Christ!

Often He shows His face in the love of humble souls, and why not, for He washed the disciples feet. Jesus said, "A new commandment I give to you, that you love one another ... by this all will know that you are my disciples ..." (John 13:34-35)

Prayer: O God, help me to love as the humble Honduran mother loved. So that all will know that I am a disciple of the Lord of Love, Jesus Christ. Amen.

Day 276

James 2:14-26

Are we followers of Jesus or Paul? Some scholars believe that Christianity has been taken over by followers of Paul. I would have to agree.

Jesus says that at the Final Judgment those who will go away to eternal life will be those who "did for the least of these (Matthew 25:31-46)." That is: persons who are known for their works.

James, who was the brother of our Lord and a key leader in the New Testament Church, writes: "Faith without works is dead." (James 2:17)

Whereas Paul often lifts up the role of faith alone as key to salvation. (Ephesians 2:8)

Is it faith, or works? As I have said earlier in these pages, I believe that the key is a faith that works. If your faith does not result in works of love, then it is broken! Dead!

Thus it is important to help others in the Church see that salvation involves more than faith, it requires works of love too.

Prayer: Lord, help me to move away from a cheap faith that says, "I believe, I believe!" to a faith that is known for its works of love. Amen

Day 277

Acts 26:6-10

It was little Jimmy's first time at scout camp. Having grown up in a big city, all the sights and sounds of the rural setting were new to him. By the second day he was covered in chigger and mosquito bites. That night he saw his first fireflies. He was heard to say: "Now they're coming after me with flashlights!"

On Thursday the scoutmaster decided he better call Jimmy's mother. He told her about the insect bites, and added: "He is homesick and has been befriended by a stray dog, which sleeps in his tent." "What about the smell?" "Oh don't worry" said the scoutmaster, "the dog seems to be getting used to it."

Trials! Paul was facing a great trial. He had wanted to take the Gospel into Asia, modern day Turkey, but was "prevented." It could have been poor health. We don't know. But he ends up down at Troas, where Luke, the physician lived. (Probably Paul went there to see his doctor!) There he would hear a call to go over to Macedonia, modern day Europe, and proclaim the Gospel.

Sometimes barriers become bridges to greater things!

Prayer: Lord, help me to keep on believing when the way is blocked, and the path is steep. Enable me to keep my ear tuned to your Spirit, that I may see the new way forward. Amen

Day 278

Philippians 4:4-8

This lesson ends with: "think on these things". We tend to become what we think, so it is vital that we think on things that are positive - things that center on the Lord.

Think of it:

- God made you – you are special!
- God made you – so you are beautiful!
- God made you – so your life has an eternal purpose!
- Christ died for you – so you can be forgiven!
- Christ died for you – so you are of unutterable worth!
- Christ died for you – so even though you die – you will live forever!

Think on these things and LIVE!

Prayer: Lord, save me from negative thoughts. Help me to see all you bring to life for me. Amen.

Day 279

Amos 7:7-10; 14-16a

"We dare not strut through the cosmos... as if we owned the place," was a warning given by the International Conference of Scientific Planners back in October 8, 1967. Their admonition parallels that of Amos in about 760 B.C.

Amos was a layman, we would say, when he received his prophetic vision of a plumb line against the wall, which was Israel. The plumb line showed that the wall (i.e. Israel) was in danger of falling. In a time of prosperity, Israel had declined morally and spiritually. Because of this God's patience was running thin!

Are there not parallels with our society? We strut our stuff among the nations of the earth, while we crumble morally and spiritually.

What can we do? II Chronicles 7:14 tells us: "If my people who are called by my name will humble themselves, and pray and seek my face and turn from their wicked ways, then I will hear from heaven and will forgive their sin and heal their land."

Prayer: Lord, help me to do my part - which seems small, but is large with you! Help me humble myself, and pray. Amen

Day 280

Ezekiel 37:1-14

After my granddad, Luke Holman Sr., lost his eyesight, his old car was parked in the barn behind his house. We grandkids loved to play hide-and-go-seek in that barn. One day when I was eight years old a cousin and I decided to hide in the trunk of the car. We got in and closed the lid. When we heard the click it dawned on us that we were trapped! We began to yell, and beat on the lid! Finally our other cousin heard us and came and turned the latch freeing us from our tomb! Were we ever glad!

"Can these bones live?" God asks Ezekiel in his vision. The answer would have to be: "No, it is impossible!" - if we consider human resources. But seeing the divine possibilities, Ezekiel answers, in essence, only if help comes from the outside – from Heaven's gate!

Prayer: Lord, we are trapped in these mortal bodies! The limits of our ability to solve our problems is troubling. It is only from you that our hope and help can come. We are grateful you have come in Jesus to do just that for us! Amen.

Day 281

Matthew 5:13-16; John 8:12-19

When I was a boy, we were listening to the local radio station one night, when a special announcement was made. The announcer said that a small plane was over our town, and was low on fuel. The problem was that our small airport had no landing lights! So, the request went out for all who could get to the airport in the next fifteen minutes, were to do so. The cars that gathered were asked to shine their headlights across the runway, so the pilot could see where he was landing.

I went with my father as we raced to the airport. There a policeman had positioned his patrol car at the beginning of the landing strip, and was directing the rest of us to line up about 30 feet apart to illumine the rest of the runway. Within a few minutes about 40 cars arrived, and the pilot was able to come on in for a safe landing.

Jesus said, "I am the light of the world." (John 8:12) Again He said, "You are the light of the world." (Matthew 5:14) We are to let our light so shine that others may find their way Home!

Prayer: Lord help me to be your light that others, who are lost in the darkness, may find their way Home. Fill me with your love and zeal to be faithful. Amen

Day 282

Deuteronomy 6:10-13

We have all drunk from wells we did not dig! We have all eaten the fruit from trees we did not plant. This is the message of our lesson for today.

Think of it: our lives, our land with its vast natural resources, our personal resources both mental and physical along with our capacity to work and earn a living – are all gifts from God. In fact, if time permitted, we could fill a book with the blessings that we receive as a handout from Heaven on a daily basis!

Thus, we are called by God to be well diggers for generations to come. We are called to plant trees, the fruit of which we will never eat. How do we do this? It is through the gifts we give - the faith we share - the service we perform today and in the future.

Prayer: Lord, give us grateful hearts for all the blessings we have received. Help us to be good stewards of these for the present day, and generations to come. Enable me, Lord, to show my gratitude through the wells I shall dig today. Amen

(Spend five minutes writing down the things you are thankful for.)

Day 283

Matthew 5:13-20

"You are the salt of the earth, but if salt has lost its flavor, how shall its saltiness be restored?"

Jesus was paying a high compliment to His hearers in these words. If we want to praise someone we say: "People like that are the salt of the earth."

In the ancient world salt was highly valued. Sometimes it was even used as currency. It was always treasured for its ability preserve foods, and flavor the same.

If Christians are to be the salt of the earth, then they are to preserve what is good in our culture - what is Christly. They are to make life more palatable for suffering folks.

But sadly not all Christians do these things. Oliver Wendell Holmes once said, "I might have entered the ministry if certain clergy I knew didn't act and look like undertakers."

Our faith by its very nature should be joy-full! It should radiate love into a world of hate. It must lift up hope amid despair. It should "flavor" the world with all this and more. Yet, as Vance Havner said, "We are the salt of the earth, not the sugar." Our witness must change the status quo, not just make lovelessness more palatable.

Prayer: Lord, help me to be the salt of the earth through my loving ways and witnessing. Help me to make the Faith flavorful, so that others will be drawn to you. Help me to be a part of preserving what is good and beautiful in the world. In your name I pray. Amen

Day 284

Isaiah 43:1-3a

The t-shirt reads: "No fear!" but you wonder. For there is so much to cause anxiety within us!

The late Harriet Hutchins, a former member of Wesley United Methodist Church in Springfield, Missouri, told me one Sunday morning of an experience she had while keeping her six year old grandson the Friday night before. Since he didn't know the Lord's Prayer, she decided to teach it to him. He wasn't too impressed. He repeated some of it back to her, but she finally quit.

About an hour later the wind picked up and thunder rolled in the distance. Soon a crack of lightning struck nearby, and the thunder that followed shook the house! Her grandson slid over against her on the divan, and looked up wide-eyed into her face and said, "Grandma, how did that prayer go?"

God alone gives us courage to face the storm. "When you pass through the waters ... through the rivers ... through the fire," God declares, [you will not be harmed], for "I will be with you." Yes, there will be difficulties, but they will "pass," God promises.

Prayer: Thank you, Lord, for your promise, and your risen Presence to back it up. Amen.

Day 285

Acts 1:1-11; 4:8 & 20

Jesus said, "But you will receive power when the Holy Spirit has come upon you, and you will be my witnesses in Jerusalem and in all Judea and Samaria, and to the end of the earth." (Acts 1:8)

Recently I was visiting with a group of laity. I asked them about their understanding of witnessing. They envisioned it as "in your face" talk about your faith. They said they thought that you were just supposed to "live it."

We should not approach our witness through pressure - "in your face" - that gains little! But if you don't name-the-name of Jesus, others will not get the connection to your life of love! They will just think that you are a nice gal or guy, and no more.

The Lord gave us a mandate to be His witnesses. The Greek word here is one who has information about something that they then share with others. That is much more than just "living it." Witnesses is here also a derivative of martyr in Greek. So, at great sacrifice, we should tell others about what the Christ means to us.

Back in the 1950s Harry Denman, who headed up the evangelistic arm of the Methodist Church, was an enthusiastic witness! In his travels across the country, he would ask the hotel clerk, the waitress at his table... if they knew the Lord? Many came to Christ through Harry's efforts.

Why should we be ashamed to name Him - especially to family members, friends, and others who make up our circle of influence? We talk with them about everything, why not Jesus?

We don't have to have an "in your face" approach, but we don't have to deny we even know Him either!

Prayer: Lord grant me the wisdom and courage to be your witness in this day. Lead me to persons who are hungering for your Good News, and give me the words to say to them. Amen

Day 286

II Samuel 24:18-25

Have you ever given someone a white elephant? Usually given in fun, white elephant gifts cost little or nothing. They come from what you would consider as junk.

King David has been forgiven, and thus wanted to offer an offering of thanksgiving to God. A farmer desired to give him his king a plot of ground to use to build his altar on, and offer his sacrifice to God, but David declared: "I will not offer burnt offerings to the Lord my God that cost me nothing."

Have you ever offered a white elephant gift to God? That is why scripture lifts up the importance of the tithe or tenth of our take-home pay as a minimum gift to God. Not to meet some law, but to give us opportunity to make a sacrifice that cost us something!

Consider that as you attend church this Sunday.

Prayer: Lord, how can I show my thanksgiving for sins forgiven and life eternal? I will show it with a sacrificial gift of what you have given me! Amen.

Day 287

Romans 12:1-8

I have referred to this scripture earlier in this book, but there are always scores of insights/revelations in the same passage!

"Present you bodies as a living sacrifice" (v.1b) can be phrased as: "Present yourselves as living martyrs."

Why am I here? Dr. William Marston polled 3000 persons asking this question, and found that 94% said they were enduring the present while they waited for the future. They were waiting for tomorrow to give them something that they don't have today – something that never comes!

Paul gives us the answer we seek by calling us to be living martyrs for Jesus Christ. (Could it be easier to DIE for your faith than to live for it day-after-day?) Yet, our Lord affirms also: "those who lose their life for my sake (i.e. in my cause) will find it (i.e. will find real life!)."

Christ seeks to love the world through us! And the measure to which He is allowed to do that is the measure to which we experience why we are here!

Prayer: Lord, make me a vessel of your love to a lost and dying world, for there is nothing that is so desperately needed in our time. Amen.

Day 288

II Corinthians 2:14-17

"You are the aroma of Christ (v.15a)."

My mother liked to bake homemade bread and cinnamon rolls when I was a youngster, and she was good at it! When one of these delicacies was in the oven, there was nothing like the aroma! The smell would permeate the whole house. It would draw you to it! I could hardly wait for it to be ready to eat!

Think of the aromas from your childhood: a rose freshly cut... cookies right out of the oven... coffee brewing... Thanksgiving dinner just made ready on the table. All of these radiate a fragrance that draws you to the source.

So when Paul writes: "You are the aroma of Christ" he was thinking of how Christ living in us in Love – draws others to the Source.

Prayer: Lord, in a world of hatred, division, and despair, we need your Presence! So fill me with your Love that others will be drawn to you. Help me to name the Name that is Life and Hope and Peace. Amen.

Day 289

Psalm 46:10

A submarine crew was returning aboard their vessel to the harbor from which they left three months before. They surfaced, then came on in to the pier. Family was there to greet the sailors. One wife asked, "How did that terrible storm affect you yesterday?" "Storm?" her husband queried. "Yes, there was a hurricane that went through!" "We didn't feel it, I guess because we were so deep down."

The Lord says through the psalmist: "Be still, and know that I am God." Yet, it is difficult to be still in a world of tumult, busyness, and sounds constantly bombarding our ears! That is why it is so important to probe the deeps of prayer... study of the Word... and quiet meditation, so that the storms don't overwhelm us. The sea of life can be churning, but we are at peace, because we are safe in those things that abide!

When was the last time you spent some quiet time with the Lord?

Prayer: (Relax your body.... Center your mind upon the Lord by repeating His name...... Spend some time thanking Him for your blessings.... Now lift up to Him the concerns of your heart.... Then, holding your hands in cupped fashion envision that all of these concerns are there in your hands... Now turn your hands over -- allowing all of these burdens to pour into the Hands of the Almighty... Amen)

Day 290

Acts 2:1-21; Proverbs 17:22

After the apostles had experienced Pentecost, they were accused of being drunk. Yes they were drunk -- on the Holy Spirit, and their ecstatic joy was proof!

Paul's letters speak volumes concerning Christian joy. He even lists joy as one of the fruits of the Spirit (Galatians 5:22).

While serving in Kansas City, I was guest preacher at a downtown church. I was preaching on the raising of Lazarus. At a climatic point I shouted: "Lazarus! Lazarus! Come out!" Suddenly from the basement stairs came a voice: "I'm coming! I'm coming!" How was I to know that the custodian was named Lazarus?

Laughter is good medicine, Proverbs declares. It is good for your physical and mental health -- it is good for your soul!

Yes, laughter is part of being a Christian. Is that not why we Christians are uniquely known for our hymns of joy?!

Prayer: Thank you Lord for the joy you bring to life. I praise you, O risen Christ, for giving me something to sing about! May my life sing your praises this day. Amen

Day 291

Luke 17:11-19

In our lesson Jesus heals the ten lepers. Only one returns to thank the Lord. Jesus' plaintive query is: "Where are the nine?" Why did the Lord care whether He was thanked or not? Not because it is the polite thing to do. No, thanksgiving is important for OUR sakes! For there is no joy where there is no thanksgiving! Thus, Jesus wanted the nine to share in something that was better than a healed body: a grateful heart!

I had an aunt who taught me the most about the value of a grateful heart. Aunt Mary Holman Grimes was single. Her husband left her after they had been married a short time. She lived in a three-roomed home on an artist's income. She also sold baked goods. Along with the modest amount she got for her paintings she eked out an existence. Yet, Mary was quick to give thanks for the robin in her nest, the rabbit eating grass in her yard, and the ingathering of her nieces and nephews to sing and laugh. She was grateful for life's blessings that are often taken for granted. She taught me that you don't have to have much to be happy, and that joy rests in appreciating the little things that most persons overlook.

Prayer: Lord, make me, like the one leper who was not only healed of his leprosy, but also of self-pity and the ungrateful heart. Amen.

Day 292

Romans 6:23

Sin pays! The wage sin pays is death! Think of it: Sin (big "S") is a broken relationship with God that results in sins (little "s"). A broken relationship with the Author of life means death.

Yet, Paul answers with: "But the free gift of God is eternal life in Christ Jesus our Lord."

Back in the 1840s the organist at the cathedral in Fribourg, Switzerland was practicing for the Sunday service. A stranger came in and stood by listening to the famous pipe organ. Finally, the stranger asked if he could play the instrument. The organist laughed at the gall of the young man, and kept playing. Again he asked. And finally, reluctantly, the organist slid off the bench and let the stranger have his keyboard. Then it was that Felix Mendelssohn sat down, and began to make music – such as had rarely been heard. With tears streaming down his face, the organist said: "To think I almost refused the master my instrument!"

Need I write more?

Prayer: Lord, may I surrender my heart to you, that my life may sing your praise. Amen.

Day 293

Luke 10:25-37

"What must I do to inherit eternal life?" he asked. Jesus answered, as He often did, with a story that contained the answer.

He tells the story of the Good Samaritan. The Samaritan was a half-breed, an outcast in Jewish circles. Yet, Jesus lifts him up as the one who is to be emulated!

"This guy doesn't believe like we believe!" But Jesus is saying: "He loves like we should love!"

"By this everyone will know you are my disciples, if you have love for one another." John 13:35

"If I have all faith, so as to remove mountains, but do not have love, I am nothing."

I Corinthians 13:26

Again: "We know we have passed from death to life because we love the brethren."

I John 3:14

Jesus concludes: "Do this and you will live." (Luke 10:28)

If it sounds like works salvation – it is certainly at least faith that works!

Prayer: Lord, help me to be true in love and deed to the example you have given me. Amen.

Day 294

II Chronicles 15:7

What is the greatest weapon in Satan's arsenal? I believe it would have to be discouragement!

For discouragement precedes resignation -- giving up! Think of the discouragement faced by Christians on a daily basis.

- Take the doctor or nurse who cares so much for his/her patients. Compassion fatigue leads to discouragement to the point that the caregiver can be tempted to quit!

- Teachers who see little immediate results from their labors, can get discouraged, and be ready to go find a job that pays more.

- Parents and other occupations get discouraged!

- As Christians we can get discouraged because our prayer life is not what we would like, or some other aspect of our Christian walk.

Yet we must not give up, for God's Word promises that what we do for Him will not be in vain (I Corinthians 15:58)!

So the answer is for us, whatever our vocation, to labor for the Lord in all that we do, and though we will have disappointments, we know that our labor will is worthwhile, and will reap a harvest if we do not give up. For Paul writes: "Let us not grow weary in doing good, for in due season we will reap, if we do not give up (Galatians 6:9)."

Prayer: Lord it is so easy to get discouraged. That is why it is so important for me to pray, and study your Word, for in so doing I am reminded of your promises of a harvest if I but persist. Grant me the persistence I need for today. Amen

Day 295

John 14:1-7

Abraham Lincoln enjoyed telling about a group of friends that were given a tour of a prison in Illinois. But one of them got separated from the rest. He roamed the corridors, becoming more-and-more panic stricken by the moment! Finally he met an inmate. He ran to him, and grabbing him by the shoulders, he cried, "How do you get out of this place?!"

Jesus says, "I am the way ..." That is, the way out of this prison created by our mortal bodies... out of meaningless existence... out of guilt ridden lives -- out of joyless living... and free to live this life eternally! As John writes: "So if the Son sets you free, you will be free indeed (John 8:36)."

Then we can cry with the late Dr. Martin Luther King, Jr: "Free at last -- free at last -- praise God Almighty I am free at last!"

Prayer: Lord how can we ever thank you for providing the way out for us? We will thank you with our lives this day. Amen

Day 296

I Thessalonians 5:12-18

Paul often speaks of praying without ceasing: verse 17 of our Lesson for today; Romans 1:9; Ephesians 1:16; Philippians 4:4 - to list a few.

Unceasing prayer is not done with lips, or on your knees - however some of my best praying was when I was flat on my back! It is done with the heart on axis with the Almighty. It is perpetual dependence on the Lord, and thanksgiving to Him.

Quaker Thomas Kelley writes in his "Testament of Devotion:" "There is a way of ordering our mental life on more than one level at once. On one level we can be thinking and discussing... But deep within... we may be also be in prayer and adoration... and receptive to divine breathings."

Such prayer is like breathing: exhaling our sin, grief, and needs while inhaling the Spirit of God.

Unceasing prayer is communion with God. It is a yearning for God's blessing upon all those we meet. It is unconscious seeking of guidance for the journey. It is joy in the little things of life.

It does not replace verbalized prayer, but takes our prayer life to deeper level. It is not part of the Christian life - it is ALL of it!

Scottish Pastor William Still wrote that unceasing prayer is "two people, the Lord and you, married and living together. At times you speak, not just with words, but with glances." It is not all talking, nor listening, but the most special times are the wordless ones when we are just together.

Prayer: Lord, grant that I may grow in my unceasing prayer with you. Amen

Day 297

Acts 8:1b-8

Jesus commands His followers that after they had received the Holy Spirit, they were to witness in Jerusalem, Judea, Samaria, and to the ends of the earth (Acts 1:8). But after Pentecost, when the Spirit was poured out upon them, they remained in Jerusalem! Only when persecution broke out there did they scatter (Acts 8:1b).

Sometime it takes suffering to get the will of the Lord done.

Paul was planning on taking the message concerning the risen Christ to Asia, but the Lord prevented him. (Scholars believe that he was prevented because of a physical malady.) He ends up down at Troas where Luke, the physician, lived, and only then did Paul hear the call to go over to Macedonia and take the Gospel to Europe (Acts 16:6-10).

It took pain and disappointment for Paul to come to hear the call of God to go where the Lord wanted him to go.

Fanny Crosby credited her blindness to being instrumental in her becoming the famous hymn writer, and an inspiration to thousands!

What roadblocks are in your path that the Lord is preparing to use to do important work for Him?

Prayer: Lord, we like the familiar, the commonplace. Sometimes you have to shake us out of our nests to get us to fly. Use me this day as you see fit. Amen

Day 298

Ephesians 2:19-22; 3:14-21

Back in the 1960's Richard Avery wrote a hymn which had a chorus:

> "My heart's the Church,
>
> My head's the steeple,
>
> Shut the door and I'm the people
>
> I can be a Christian by myself!"

But Avery was dead wrong! For it takes a Family to be a Christian! Just as it takes a family for a newborn to survive, so it takes the Church for the reborn to survive! You can't be a Christian by yourself!

The Church alone preserved the scriptures and passed them down to us through the generations. The Church brings the faith to us, and helps rightly interpret the Word. The Church surrounds us with support. We couldn't survive long without her!

Thank God for the Church!

Prayer: Lord, it is a privilege to be a part of your Church, and give ourselves and our money to strengthen her for generations to come. Make us faithful in all things. Amen.

Day 299

John 10:11-15

My father herded sheep in Wyoming back in the 1920s. He used to tell how a mother ewe would come each morning at sun up, and tap her hoof on the tongue of his sheepherder's wagon. Dad would wake up, and be on guard as the sheep got up, and began feeding out from the wagon.

The old ewe knew from experience that the flock needed the shepherd to protect them from predators, lead them to greener pastures, and nurse them back to health when parasites irritated their hide. The mother ewe realized she could trust the shepherd, and so wanted him to be on guard for the day.

We need a Shepherd to see us through the hazards of life. Thank God we have such in Jesus Christ (John 10:14). He has proven down through the ages to be up to the task. He is on guard today for you!

Prayer: Thank you, Lord, for being our Abba – Protector – Shepherd. Help us to lean on you, and know that all is well. Amen.

Day 300

I Corinthians 10:1-13

Temptation is something we all share in common. The source of the lure differs from person-to-person, but we are all tempted. "No temptation has overtaken you that is not common to humanity (I Corinthians 10:13)."

Temptation is also conditioned. "God is faithful, and will not let you be tempted beyond your strength (v.13b)." Jesse Duplantis would add: "Don't water and fertilize your temptations ... or they will grow up ... and whip you!"

Finally, temptation is conquerable! "... with the temptation [God] will provide a way out, so that you may be able to endure it (v.13c)." Our weaker side looks for a way into temptation – to dabble in it – but God offers a way out through prayer and through Christian friends in whom we can confide.

Billy Graham once summarized this by saying: "There is nothing wrong with being tempted. It is like: there is nothing wrong with having birds fly over your head. The trouble starts when we let the temptations make their home with us, like letting the birds build their nest in your hair!"

Prayer: Lord, save me from myself. Help me to lean on you, that I may know the Power of your resurrection. Amen.

Day 301

Romans 8:28-30

Can anything good come out of this trial? If someone tells you it will, you can be very turned off! Who are they to tell me – when I'm the one in the trench?!

But Paul is speaking. He who had on five different occasions been beaten with 39 lashes with a whip made of leather thongs with metal tips on each thong. Once he was stoned. Three times shipwrecked – once floating in the sea for 24 hours. He faced daily threats against his life – threats from robbers. He was hungry and cold. He suffered an ailment that left him at times too debilitated to work (II Corinthians 11:28-29).

Yet – yet he wrote: "We know that in EVERYTHING God works for GOOD with those who love Him, who are called according to His purpose." Sometimes we are given a crown – other times a cross, but always God uses our sufferings – as long as we keep on loving Him, and seeking His purposes!

Prayer: Lord, it is easy to feel sorry for myself. Help me to use my cross like your Cross – to draw all unto you. Amen.

Day 302

John 11:1-44

Lazarus died! Lazarus arose! Imagine how his view of life changed!

What once he valued – he valued no more.

In July of 1980 my father died. We decided to have him buried in a family cemetery south of Lebanon, Missouri. It was up to me to mark the grave for the grave digger. I drove to the cemetery, taking with me a hammer, some wooden stakes, and an old t-shirt. I hammered the stakes in the corners of what would be my father's grave. Then I tore strips of the shirt to tie around each stake, so that the grave digger could readily see the site.

Suddenly, things that moments before meant a lot to me, now meant little or nothing. Like in G.K. Chesterton's poem, "The Convert:" "We store the sand, and let the gold go free: and all these things are less than dust to me, because my name is Lazarus, and I live!"

What once Lazarus feared – he feared no more!

Prayer: Lord, thank you that we serve a Risen Savior! Thank you for the confident hope that is ours in you. Thank you for the Power of the Resurrection made available to us now. Amen.

Day 303

Acts 17:1-9

When I was a teenager someone quoted to me the words of the late missionary, C.T. Studd: "Only one life 'twill soon be past, only what's done for Christ will last."

Something deep within me was stirred by those words, and my soul cried: "I want to not just exist, but live for Him, so that my life will have eternal significance!" So I began in earnest to seek God's will, and at eighteen years of age God called me into the ministry.

You do not have to join the ranks of the clergy for your life to have an eternal purpose! For God needs Christian parents, teachers, doctors, nurses, farmers.... We must seek His purposes in prayer, and then do His deeds of love and mercy.

Each day we receive a fresh call... with new tasks... with new deeds of love. Each day we are asked by God to see where He is working and join in.

It is possible for us to "turn the world upside down," in our corner, like the Apostle Paul, when we determine to know nothing save Jesus Christ! (I Corinthians 2:2)

Prayer: Lord, grant me wisdom and courage to be your faithful disciple. Help me to let the world see you through me. Amen.

Day 304

Matthew 16:13-20

The sergeant had had it with the new recruits. So as they finished their last round of drills for the day, he barked: "O.K. you idiots, fall out!" The soldiers all fell out, but one. As the sergeant glared at him, he responded: "Sarge, sure were a lot of them weren't there!"

Call a person a name, and they'll play the game! Persons tend to become the names we call them. Call them good names, and they will strive to live up to the name. Call them a bad name, and they will be prone to live down to that name. Children are especially vulnerable.

Our children need to hear us say, "You are special! God has an important plan for your life. You are lovable...."

Jesus called Peter: "the Rock" – long before he was anything resembling a rock. He was shifting sand at the time, and would be for some time! But he would never forget that Jesus believed in him! He would have to live UP to the name he was called.

Prayer: Lord, enable me to name those around me today the good names that you would have them called. Make me more like you, I pray. Amen

Day 305

Mark 6:31-32

Henry David Thoreau, philosopher, journalist, and poet enjoyed being alone. He built a cabin on Walden Pond, where he would live for a little over two years. While there he wrote: "I find it wholesome to be alone the greater part of the time... I love to be alone. I never found the companion that was so companionable as solitude."

This sounds very strange to us who want people around us most of the time, and when they are away, we are busy texting them our latest thoughts and actions. We feel uncomfortable with stillness, so when we are alone we feel we must turn on some source of noise.

"[Jesus] said to them, 'Come away by yourselves to a quiet place (Phillips Translation), to a lonely place (Revised Standard Version), and rest a while.' For many were coming and going, and they had no leisure even to eat."

Our Lord believed in finding quiet places to refresh the soul, and sought these out on numerous occasions.

We are not more aware of God, because we neglect the quiet places. "Be still, and know that I am God," said the Lord to the psalmist (Psalm 46:10).

Prayer: (Do the following slowly, thoughtfully. Take your time. Find a quiet place.... Now quiet your mind.... Focus on Him who has called you to come away, Jesus Christ.... Repeat His name over in your mind to keep you centered on Him.... Thank Him for being your God! Amen)

Day 306

Genesis 50:20; Romans 12:1

God is taking all the experiences of your past and present, kneading them all together, both good and bad, and preparing you for service with Him in the future!

- Joseph was sold into slavery by his brothers, and imprisoned in Egypt, all to make it possible for the salvation of his family back home when famine struck there.
- Moses fled from Egypt to the Sinai desert. There he herded sheep, in the same region that he would shepherd the Hebrew people through toward the Promised Land.
- Even young Jesus was prepared for His ministry through working with His father in the carpenter's shop in Nazareth, and by growing up under the tutelage of His devout mother!

Good and bad experiences redeemed by the Lord, and used in His service!

The Lord is taking your grief, and preparing you to use it to minister to others in their grief. And/or He is taking your low self-esteem and preparing to use that to give glory to Him when your service is rendered. Or, like Issac Newton, who authored "Amazing Grace" after years in the slave trade, He may be preparing you to use your sinful past, forgiven by His grace, to offer praise and glory to His name.

Joseph said of the awful things that happened to him, all because his brothers sold him into slavery, "You meant it for evil, God meant it for good!" Never underestimate what God is able to use... to redeem... for the building of His Kingdom!

Prayer: Lord, it is amazing what you are able to do with our experiences when we offer them up to you as a living sacrifice! I offer all my past.... and present up to you right now. Use it all to your glory. Amen

Day 307

Revelation 3:4-22

In this lesson the Lord declares: "Behold I stand at the door and knock; if anyone hears my voice and opens the door, I will come in to him and eat with him, and he with me." (v.20 RSV)

Note: the Lord not only knocks, but calls out! Further, he wants to eat with us – Holy Communion – table fellowship – a heavenly banquet!

How far He has come: from Heaven to a manger stall! How near He has drawn – like Francis Thompson's "Hound of Heaven" – on our trail! How long He has waited!

Back in 1992 when we were in London, and had the opportunity to visit St. Paul's Cathedral, we saw Holman Hunt's famous painting of Jesus standing knocking at the door. Shortly after it was put on display back in the 19th century, someone commented: "Mr. Hunt! You made a mistake! You put no latch on the outside of the door." Hunt replied: "That was no mistake, for the door can only be opened from the inside!"

Prayer: Lord, enable me to open the door to my heart afresh to you. Come in to me, Lord Jesus. Amen.

Day 308

Romans 7:21-25

Giovanni de Barnardone was born in 1182. As a young man he rebelled against his parents. At one point he stole some money from his father. Beside himself, his father had him hauled into court. There young Giovanni stripped off his clothes and ran naked from the courtroom!

One day he began to realize his life was at a dead end. Riding past a leper, he amazingly had a wave of compassion sweep over him. He leapt from his horse, ran to the wretched soul, and embraced the astounded man! He gave the leper all the money he had.

From that moment St. Francis of Assisi, as he would be called, went on to found the Franciscan Order, and give his life to a ministry to the poor.

"Wretched man that I am! Who will deliver me from this body of death? Thanks be to God through Jesus Christ our lord!"

Prayer: O God, thank you that you never give up on us – even when we give up on ourselves. Help me to serve you in Thanksgiving – never underestimating what you are able to do through me. Amen.

Day 309

Luke 11:1-4; Romans 8:26-27

Jesus taught by word and deed that prayer should involve honest conversation with God. (Luke 11:4 and Mark 15:34) Further, prayer is often wordless communion with God (Romans 8:26-27).

Dan Rather was interviewing Mother Teresa. He asked her what she said when she prayed. She replied, "Nothing." "You mean you don't say anything?" "That's right, I just listen!" "Well, what does God say?" "Nothing. He just listens too."

Rather than giving God His to-do list, prayer is – in its depths – communing Spirit-to-spirit with God.

Around 3,500 years ago, the Psalmist wrote: "Be still and know that I am God" (Psalm 46:10).

We can create quiet places in our souls where we go to sense the Presence, and get renewed throughout the day in the Power of His resurrection.

Prayer: Help me Lord, to spend some moments in quiet today that I may be renewed and refreshed in your Spirit. Speak to me now I pray.... Amen.

Day 310

Philippians 2:5-13

The greatest lacking for the vast majority of us is humility. Paul speaks of it in II Corinthians 12:7. He believed that the physical malady that he suffered from that he called his "thorn in the flesh," was given him to make him humble. Why is it important to be humble? Isn't it the proud, the self-confident that take the day in our time?

Humility is vital for our prayer life, for only the humble really see their need for God and therefore for prayer. Further, God gives grace to the humble (See II Chronicle 7:14 & James 4:6). Finally, humility is vital for love to be genuine – Christ-like. Without humility, our "love" is condescending, paternalistic.

How do we get more humility? By pausing often before the Cross. By praying often - seeking humility. By walking through the valley of suffering. By spending time in thanksgiving, for the more we express our gratitude to God, the more we have to give God, not ourselves, credit for the good things in our lives.

Prayer: Lord, I pray make me humble, but then give me grace to endure what comes in answer to that prayer. (Spend several minutes in thanksgiving to God). Amen.

Day 311

II Timothy 1:8-12

The Apostle Paul could affirm: "I know whom I have believed in (v.12b)!" On the road to Damascus, when he was knocked to the ground, and blinded by the Light, and heard the Lord speaking to him (Acts 9:1-9), he came to not only believe, but to know the Lord!

Is it possible to actually know the Lord, as we would know a dear friend? Yes it is! He who made voices, can He not speak? He who made ears, can He not hear? He who made legs, can He not walk with us? Of course He can!

It's not about what I believe, but knowing Who I believe in that makes all the difference! Many know what they believe, but far fewer know the One in whom they have believed. In that is peace for uncertain days! Thus, we can be sure that He is able to keep what we have entrusted to Him (II Timothy 1:12c).

In the dark days when he was called before the church authorities with a price on his head, Martin Luther wrote: "A Mighty Fortress is Our God, a bulwark never failing!" Once he had simply believed, now more was demanded, and thank God he KNEW!

How do we get to know the Lord? Through prayer.

Prayer: Lord, give me that assurance for the uncertainties I face. Give me a personal knowledge of you that calms the storms, and gives me peace. Amen.

Day 312

Isaiah 55:1-5; John 7:37-39

We have neglected our souls while playing it safe – while living in the shallows.

A window washer working on the 12th floor slipped and fell. When he passed the 6th floor he was heard to say: "So far – so good!"

Fortunately there are times when we can stop and take inventory, and see where our lives are headed and get serious about the Lord!

In 700 B.C. Isaiah wrote: "Everyone who thirsts come to the waters" (55:1). Centuries later Jesus declared: "Everyone who is thirsty come to me…" (John 7:37b)

Our Lord also said: "Whoever drinks of this water that I will give them will never be thirsty. The water that I will give will become a spring of water gushing up unto eternal life." (John 4:14)

Wade out into the deep – trust Him – drink all you can, and you will be blessed!

Prayer: Lord, save me from living my life in the shallows. Help me to dare to risk, to discover your refreshment in the deep places. Amen.

Day 313

Psalm 13

Charles Spurgeon in his "A Treasury of David," has stated that whenever you read the Psalms you will somewhere or other see yourself. "You never get into a corner, but what you find David in that corner too," Spurgeon wrote. Joseph Parker said, "This Psalm begins with winter, and ends in summer; it begins with low muffled tones of sorrow and ends with a rapture of praise."

At the heart of this psalm is what we have often seen in these pages: the answer to our dilemma is prayer! Casting his burdens on the Lord, brought David out of his perplexity, and took him up the mountain of praise.

Steven Lawson aptly outlines this Psalm with: David's sorrow... (vs. 1-2) David's supplication... (vs. 3-4) David's singing! (vs. 5-6)

Prayer: My soul cries to you, O God, hear my plea. Lift me out of the pit, to sit at your side, my Strength and my Redeemer. Amen

Day 314

John 15:12-17

Jesus calls His disciples "friends." The word "friend" is not to be used lightly, for it was used of Abraham and Moses saying they were considered friends of God. (Isaiah 41:8; Exodus 33:11; James 2:23)

Here the Lord is saying to us: "You are my friends if you do what I command you (v.14)." He had called them (us) "branches" (of the vine), and "servants," but now friends!

In the world of Bible times, friendship was not something that was entered into superficially. It was rather a relationship known for its intimacy, deepest of trust, with no secrets kept from each other. This friendship was not some sentimental: "I'll be your buddy." It was summarized in verse 13: "No one has a greater love than this, to lay down one's life for one's friends." Then He went on to give Himself on the Cross for us!

You have a Friend in high places! You have someone to confide in, who will always be there for you no matter what, who possesses the power to get things done on you behalf!

Prayer: Thank you for calling me your friend, O God. Help me to live up to that in some measure by the life a live for you. Help me to be a true friend in return. Amen

Day 315

Acts 9:10-22

Ananias had some very good reasons for not wanting anything to do with Saul. Saul had committed some terrible crimes against the Church. He had sought to kill Christians, and destroy the Church using all means at his disposal!

But God called Ananias to go find Paul on Straight Street in Damascus, for "he is a chosen instrument of mine to carry my name to the Gentiles." (v.15b)

Ananias went, took Paul under his wing, and Paul became the greatest missionary/evangelist in the history of Christendom!

It is so very easy to prejudge persons - to out of fear avoid them, or to fail to see the potential that God has placed in them. But praise God, the Lord doesn't give up on us, and we shouldn't give up on others, for God made them for special purposes too!

Prayer: Lord, help me to avoid prejudging the persons I meet today. Help me to see in them the potential that you see – the potential you have placed in the most unlikely persons! Amen.

Day 316

I Corinthians 11:23-26

Holy Communion can be experienced with God in nature. You can sense the Presence of God in the beauty of a glorious sunset, or in a fast rushing mountain stream, but the most blessed communion is found at the Lord's Supper! Our Lord set this aside saying, "As often as you do it, do it in remembrance of me (Luke 22:19)."

Hopefully all readers of these devotions are a part of a congregation where Holy Communion is made available often.

Is it simply a remembrance: "Do this in remembrance of me?" Yes it is that, but more! For the One we remember is ALIVE, and present! Thus, the Lord's Supper is a time of glorious communion with our risen Lord. As at no other time – no other place – "Here O my Lord I see thee face to face, here would I touch and handle things unseen... (Hymn: "Here, O My Lord, I See Thee")."

We see Him in the snowcapped mountains grandeur, in the waterfall, and in the child at play, but join with me in knowing His Presence especially in Holy Communion!

Prayer: Lord, we praise your name for giving yourself to us in the incarnation – the cross – and the resurrection! But we also praise you for coming to us again-and-again at your table in Holy Communion. Amen.

Day 317

Matthew 24:35

I remember as a youngster hearing a radio preacher begin his broadcast with these words of the Lord: "Heaven and earth will pass away, but my words will not pass away!" I was always inspired by that statement, but later would learn that such has not been an easy journey for such a beloved Book!

In 303 A.D. Emporer Diocletian ordered Bibles rounded up and burned, and some feared that this could well be the end of the scriptures. But within twenty-five years there was a new emperor, who commissioned the preparation of fifty copies of the Bible at the expense of the government.

No other book has been so attacked and despised. Yet, it is still the best seller as far as books go, with billions of copies in print!

Yes, truly, "heaven and earth will pass away, but [God's] words will not pass away!"

May you treasure this Book, not with warm feelings, but with a hunger to read from its pages the truth about God's action in human history.

Prayer: Make me, with Ezekiel of old, hungry enough to "eat"* your Word, O Lord. Help me to digest its truths, and embody them as part of my very being. Through Christ my Lord. Amen

(See Ezekiel 3:3)

Day 318

Romans 14:13-15:2

In his book "The Wright Brothers," David McCullough tells the amazing story of Wilbur and Orville Wrights' venture in flying. Early on the brothers were criticized for trying something that persons on every hand considered absurd! Even our own government officials failed to see the merits of their invention. Only after the Wrights were received in France, and were able to demonstrate their primitive airplane's ability to fly, were they received back home.

Life has an abundance of critics and skeptics, and far too few encouragers. Our teachers in our public schools are a case in point. They receive criticism on every hand, and little remuneration or praise for their labors. Your pastor is no stranger to critics either, and the list goes on. All the company of Faith need, especially in these days, words of praise for their labors of love - words of encouragement.

Think of someone you can offer honest encouragement to today, and then go out of your way to give the compliment you know they deserve. In so doing you will serve to strengthen a fellow Christian (Roman 15:2).

Prayer: Lord put before me someone I can strengthen today by an encouraging word. Help me to know who that person is, as I pause in silence before you.... Amen

Day 319

Deuteronomy 8:1-10

"...Remember all the way the Lord has led you these _____ years (v.2a)." (Spend five minutes drawing a graph of your life noting the highs and lows. Remember a first job... maybe your marriage... a child or children... Remember significant persons God sent your way, who helped to bring out the good in you... Think of your first home..., and other things that are significant in your journey... At each high, and each low point note what it was that was the key factor in that.)

Most of us can think back on an exodus from bondage in our lives. All of us can think of how God has fed us – maybe not with manna, but in other ways – with literal food, but also with love, and hope, and peace, and strength, and ... In hindsight we can see that there was a Hand that led us, that undergirded us, that was there for us through it all!

Thus, we remember all the way the Lord has led us, and give thanks!

Prayer: Lord, how beautiful are your footprints going before us into the uncertainties of tomorrow! How wondrous are your footprints going beside us - even beneath us - carrying us! Because of this we fear no evil. Grant us your peace this day as we consider all the way you have brought us, and undergirded us. Amen.

Day 320

Romans 15:5-13

Hope is difficult to muster! In fact it is impossible to create on your own. No matter how much you grit your teeth, and strain, hope eludes you!

Norman Vincent Peale, who was born in 1898, authored "The Power of Positive Thinking." In his book, Peale proposes that we should think positively, and good things will come our way. There is something to be said for that, but such thinking soon runs into the brick wall of our own limits, for it is difficult being our own God!

When you are up to your neck in a swamp full of alligators, positive thinking is not the way out! You need One who can come to the rescue and provide a way out!

We need "the God of hope [to] fill [us] with all joy and peace, so that by the power of the Holy Spirit [we] may abound in hope (Romans 15:13)!" THEN we can think positively.

On our own all we have to look forward to is a plot in the local cemetery. But oh the hope that comes in the risen Christ! Therein I can abound in hope and confidence even in the face of death and the grave!

Prayer: Lord, thank you for the hope and peace that comes through your Holy Spirit. Help me this day to abound in that hope. Amen.

Day 321

Matthew 11:2-11

John was in prison, and would literally lose his head there! Thus, he wanted to be sure concerning this One named Jesus: is He the Savior, or shall I look for another?

Court is in session! You are a part of the jury that must decide. Is Jesus guilty of being the Messiah, or must we go on looking for the "guilty" party.

Jesus answered: "Go and tell John what you hear and see (vs. 4-5). i.e. Look up what Isaiah said of the Messiah: 'the blind will receive their sight (Isaiah 29:18b); the lame will walk (35:6); lepers will be cleansed (29:19); the deaf hear (29:18); the dead are raised (26:19); and the good news is preached to the poor (61:1)!'"

Further, who else can give meaning to life (John 10:10); forgive sins (Matthew 9:6); bring hope (Colossians 1:27b); and answer the problem of death (John 11:25)?

Someone has said: "If you see a turtle on a fencepost, you know it didn't get there by itself." AND if you consider the tens of millions of lives redeemed by this Christ, you know they couldn't have gotten there by themselves!

Prayer: Lord, thank you for saving my soul! Thank you for giving me hope and peace and the promise of a glorious reunion beyond death's door. Amen.

Day 322

Luke 2:1-20

You and I are the Inn Keeper. Will you find room for the Christ in your inn - your life?

James Harnish once pastored a United Methodist Church in Tampa, Florida. Behind his desk was a picture of the U.S. Supreme Court – signed by each justice. The story goes back to Christmas Eve 1989.

After the service, a woman, who was a member of the church, introduced Harry and Dottie Blackmun. Justice Blackmun and his wife were active United Methodists. Susie, their daughter, had rebelled back during the Vietnam War. Later she married. After their first child was born, Susie reconciled with her parents, and eventually with their faith – now her faith! That is what made that Christmas Eve Service so special! After Justice Blackmun and Susie had received Holy Communion, they remained at the chancel railing to give the justice time to dry his tears before returning to his seat.

Is there room for Him in your inn?

Prayer: Lord, thank you for the grace you have shown us in Christ Jesus. When our love failed – your love remained constant. Help us to live in such a way that we show the world our thanksgiving. Amen.

Day 323

John 14:1-14

Jesus' death would shake His disciples to the core! They would be like sheep without a shepherd!

Concerned for them, the Lord said: "Let not your hearts be troubled. You believe in God, believe also in me." (v.1) He goes on to speak of His dying as going away to the "Father's House." (v.2) Further, when their time would come to follow, He will come again to take His them to where He is. (v.3)

Thomas interjects a question: "Lord, we do not know where you are going, how can we know the way?" (v.5) Jesus says: "I am the way!" (v.6)

The "way" is not a road that you can find on your GPS. Rather, it is a Person who is the way.

Back in Vermont a couple was lost on a lonely road, when they saw a farmer coming out of his field. The man rolled his window down, and called to the farmer: "We are trying to get to Hancock, can you tell us how to get there?" "Better than telling you, I will take you to Hancock. I need to go myself. It is about ten miles from here." Better than directions is the One who says I will come and get you, and take you!

It is as simple as Jesus - HE is the way!

Prayer: Thank you Lord, for being willing to come and take us to our heavenly home. O Risen Christ, we praise your name, for you are better than a known way. Amen

Day 324

Judges 6:36-40

How do we receive guidance through prayer?

First, we have to be willing to do God's will. God is not a magician who performs tricks for us, but is willing to speak and direct our path if we are truly willing to do His bidding.

Second, God gives us guidance through His Word. The Psalmist wrote: "Thy Word is a lamp unto my feet and a light unto my path (Psalm 119:105)." If the guidance you get is not in keeping with the overall revelation of God's Word, then it is not of God!

Third, sometimes God just opens doors, as He did in Acts 12:6-11 – opening the prison door and setting Peter free. Occasionally He closes a door, but opens a window. Either way, the path is opened to you.

Finally, in the stillness of prayer, God gives guidance. Many times God has guided me back on the path He had for me as I paused to "be still."

Prayer: Lord, guide me in the way you would have me to go, and when I get off track nudge me back again. Through Jesus Christ I pray. Amen.

Day 325

II Corinthians 1:18-22

Have you ever felt that you have toiled in vain? You are not alone! (See Isaiah 49:4a)

Have you ever felt your life was over – you were too old to be of any good. See Exodus 7:7 where it tells that Moses was eighty, and Aaron was eighty-three as they prepared to do their greatest work for God – lead the Hebrew people from bondage!

One of the greatest Methodist missionary/evangelists, Dr. E. Stanley Jones, spoke to my seminary class in 1969 when he was 84. He told us: "When I turned 60, God said to me: 'Now begins the decade of your greatest contribution'. And it was! I wrote more and spoke to greater numbers of persons than I ever had. As I reached 70, God told me I was going to be even more effective – and I was! Then when I reached 80 God said to me one morning: 'Now begins the era of your greatest contribution!'" He said it was "beautifully indefinite." "An era can be five years, or more." "Now that I am 84, I can't believe it! These past four years have been the greatest yet!" At 85 he started a book: "On Tip Toe for Tomorrow." At 87 he had a stroke and had to dictate the rest of the book to his daughter. He died in his 89th year.

Never underestimate what God is able to do regardless of your state or age! Yes, we all can live "on tip toe for tomorrow!"

Prayer: Lord, thank you for going before me, and beside me in the journey of life. Help me to realize the best is yet to be! Amen.

Day 326

Matthew 28:1-10, and 27:22

Pilate asked: "Then what shall I do with Jesus who is called Christ?" That is the question of the ages!

- Give Him lip service!
- Announce: "I believe in Him!"
- Declare: "I am a follower!"
- Or let Him be truly Lord of all my life!

In the movie "City Slickers" two middle-aged men go to a ranch out west to work out their stress. Jack Palance, playing the weathered old cowboy, says to Billy Crystal, the city slicker, "You fellas come out here with the same problems. You spend fifty weeks a year getting knots in your rope, then you think two weeks up here will untie them for you. (long pause) Do you know what the secret of life is?" Crystal answers: "No, what?" Palance holds up his index finger and says: "This." "Your finger?" "No, one thing, just one thing, you stick to that and everything else doesn't mean a thing!" "But what's the one thing?" "That's what you've got to figure out".

The "one thing," friend, is Jesus Christ! You can do without wealth ... you can do without health, you can even do without family, but you cannot do without Jesus!

Prayer: Lord help me to realize what the one thing is that is the secret to life, and that eternal. Help me to make you Lord over ALL! Amen.

Day 327

Psalm 34:1-8

Over a century ago Northwestern University, located on Lake Michigan, had its own volunteer life-saving crew among its student body. On September 8, 1860 the Lady Elgin, loaded with passengers sunk just off shore. Edward Spencer, a young man preparing for the ministry, was one of the students that formed into teams, and swam out to rescue those that they could.

Seventeen times he and his mate dove into the waters, and went and rescued stranded passengers - clinging to pieces of the ship's wreckage. Then Spencer collapsed, and had to be taken back to his room. He never completely recovered from the exposure he endured. Unable to enter the ministry, he spent his life in relative seclusion.

Many years later, Spencer was in the congregation when the pastor was telling about the heroism of the young man, when someone said: "Spencer is here! He is in the audience!" The pastor paused, and called him up front. Then he asked him if anything stood out in his memory of that day. He replied simply: "Only this, sir, of the seventeen people I rescued not one ever thanked me."

David wrote Psalm 34 so that he would not fall into ingratitude. How about us?

Prayer: You have rescued me time-after-time, O Lord. Help me to praise you all my days with my very life! Amen

Day 328

John 18:4-9

The scene is the Garden of Gethsemane, Judas, the betrayer is at hand. When the mob that came with him ask Jesus if He is Jesus of Nazareth, He replies: "I AM." (i.e. Original Greek translation) Jesus repeats this on three occasions: verses 5, 6, and 8. What is the significance of this? GOD calls Himself the great I AM. In Exodus 3:13-14 Moses asks God what he is to call Him. God answers: "I AM WHO I AM." A little later He says simply: "[Moses] tell the people that I AM has sent you." Thus, in the Garden, Jesus is subtly saying: "I AM" [God!]! His hearers immediately fall back on the ground! (John 18:6)

Are we splitting hairs, or is the Greatest Good News? It is the latter, for GOD has come in Christ! (II Corinthians 5:19) In Christ GOD has drawn near! Christ is the incarnate GOD! Therefore, as I have said earlier, God is not the great child abuser - sending His Boy to the Cross - He came HIMSELF! That, my friends, is the greatest news of the entire Bible, and at the heart of our lesson for today!

To know Christ, is to know God, is to know the Holy Spirit -- ONE God! On the night when He was betrayed, Christ revealed who He was and IS: the great I AM!

Prayer: Thanks be to God for you O Lord are the great I AM! Glorious is your Name in all the earth! I praise you for your Sacrifice for me. Make me eternally grateful, and help me to serve you all my days. Amen

Day 329

Zephaniah 4:1-6

In 1665 the Great Plague swept across London leaving in its wake 69,000 persons dead! The following year, 1666, fire swept through that same city – probably stopping the onslaught of the plague – but destroying four-fifths of the city – including 87 churches!

Samuel Pepys, an agnostic of the day, wrote in his diary: "I do not believe that we shall ever recover from this double tragedy!"

But, out of the ashes rose the great Evangelical Revival of the 1700s in which Methodism was born.

In 1741 John Wesley, key leader in this revival, declared: "Give me 100 [persons] who fear nothing but sin, and desire nothing but God, and I care not one straw whether they be lay or clergy, such alone will shake the gates of Hell, and set up the kingdom of God on earth." And they did!

"Not by might, nor by power, but by the Spirit, says the Lord of hosts (v.6b)."

Prayer: Lord, to you all power belongs! By you our story is written! How glorious it is to be flung into the hands of the Mighty God! Amen.

Day 330

I Samuel 17:1-51

For 40 days the Philistine Army taunted the Army of Israel! One of the Philistine soldiers was 8 feet tall, Goliath. We might say he was over 300 pounds of muscle and wore size 19 sandals! In full body armor, he was a Sherman Tank!

One day the boy, David, came to the battlefield with sandwiches for his older, soldier brothers. He heard the giant, Goliath, hurl a challenge across no-mans-land that he would fight any soldier in the Army of Israel, and whoever won that would decide the victor of the battlefield.

David, all of 5'2" and 110 lbs,, said he would like to take Goliath on! His brothers told him to go home to his mother, but he insisted!

You know the rest of the story recorded in our lesson for today: i.e. he took the giant on, and killed him!

How often life tells you, "You can't!" -- but God says, "You can!"

Prayer: Help us, Lord, to never underestimate your power. Thank you for opening the way for us to do great things to your glory! Amen.

Day 331

Psalm 54

Martyn Lloyd-Jones wrote: "I sometimes think that the very essence of the whole Christian position and secret of a successful spiritual life is just to realize two things: I must have complete, absolute confidence in God, and no confidence in myself." I like that!

Life's trials have a way of taking care of the second of the two. The experience of prayer takes care of the former. This is all summed up in our lesson out of Psalm 54, climaxing in David's testimony: "He has delivered me from every trouble (v.7a)."

Japanese Christian, Kagawa, stated: "If you are prepared to die for a cause, there is nothing that you and God cannot accomplish." Or to put it in today's context: When, in prayer, you develop complete confidence in God, there is no trial too great - no mountain too high - but what God will deliver you, and no task too large for you and the Almighty to accomplish!

Ponder these truths throughout the day...

Prayer: Increase my courage, Lord! Help me not to rely upon my own resources today, but upon yours. You hold me in the palm of your hand. Cause me to realize that. Amen

Day 332

I Corinthians 15:12-20

"If for this life only we have hoped in Christ, we are of all persons most to be pitied" (v.19)

I once had a man tell me: "Death is a very natural thing, a tree must lose its leaves to make room for growth in the spring, so we must die to make room for younger generations that will follow. Death doesn't bother me!"

And I thought how sweet! So rational, and so very naïve! For death is the ultimate enemy! It brings the destruction of all we hold dear. It separates us from all we love. If it is so "natural" and "friendly," then why all the efforts to stay alive? Why all the grief when one near-and-dear dies?!

I have officiated at about 500 funerals during my ministry. Around 10% were "unchurched" – non-believers. Those funerals were by far the toughest, because you cannot give a crash course in hope in a few hours. Their grief is always the most unbearable there is!

Paul writes: "But in fact Christ has been raised!..." (v.20) Hope has come!

Prayer: Thank you, Lord, for coming to bring us hope by conquering death and the grave! Save me from doubt, and give me confidence in you in all circumstances. Amen.

Day 333

John 18:10-11

After Jesus announced that He was the great I AM, and the men who had come to arrest Him fall to the ground (John 18:6), Peter steps forward, pulls out his sword, and cuts off the ear of Malchus, the high priest's slave. It is a bizarre scene! They are all lying on the ground, sapped of all their power! While the One with all the power is speaking peace! Jesus scolds Peter for his action, and steps over and heals Malchus (Luke 22:51). Then He reminds them that He must suffer these things.

Wars and violence do not "win the peace" - only the love of Christ loosed in the world can do that!

I visited the Garden of Gethsemane in 1996 where all of this took place. Some of the olive trees are believed to date back to the first century. Today Franciscan friars tend to the grove. It is a peaceful place of unusual beauty. It struck me that it was a living memorial to the power of love amidst a world of hate!

I hope you have a garden - a quiet place - where you can be alone with God, and sense His power and love. We all need that!

Prayer: In a world of violence - you speak peace. In a world of hatred - you speak love. Come Holy Spirit my soul inspire, and fill me in this hour. Amen

Day 334

Read again Philippians 3:12-16

"Forgetting what lies behind and straining for what lies ahead, I press on toward the goal … of the upward call of God in Christ Jesus."

Laying aside all guilt and shame - I press on! Laying aside the burdens of yesteryears – I press on! Laying aside grudges nourished in my soul – I press on! Laying aside all doubts and fears - I press on!

After the disaster at Dunkirk in World War II, the British Army narrowly escaped capture by retreating back across the English Channel. Winston Churchill called an emergency session of his Cabinet officers. Pacing before them, the famous Prime Minister painted a very gloomy picture of the prospects for the country. Then, after a long pause, he said, "Gentlemen! I find it rather inspiring!"

Inspiring? Yes! For "when I am weak, then I am strong (II Corinthians 12:10)!" When I have run out of my own resources, I am left with the resources of God!

Press on, dear Christian!

Prayer: Lord, thank you for my weaknesses – those doorways to your heart. Inspire me in my time of need to see the possibilities you bring to life and living. Amen.

Day 335

Galatians 1:11-24

He was so excited! He said: "My sister is going to have a baby! But as of yet, I don't know whether I'm going to be an uncle or an aunt!"

Births – yours and mine – were not accidents – even if your parents didn't plan to conceive you – God did! You are a special creation -- with an eternal purpose, and an unutterable worth! Never forget that! Never forget that!!

Paul wrote: "[God] set me apart before I was born (v.15b)."

After you were born, you had valleys to traverse, and mountains to climb, dangers to be faced, times of want to be endured. Through it all God was preparing you for such a time as this! God is very frugal, He doesn't waste any thing! He uses good and bad experiences alike. He doesn't throw any of it away. He uses it all. Through it all He is preparing you for ministry now!

Prayer: I thank you Lord that you see untold worth in me, and value in my life's experiences. Reveal to me ways I am to be used at this phase of my life. Amen.

Day 336

John 20:24-29

I think God for doubting Thomas. Thomas reveals that the Biblical writers were not trying to make things look good, but even included Thomas' suspicions that things might not be the way they were being portrayed. After all how could someone, whose funeral you attended on Friday, be alive on Sunday?!

Yet, as soon as the witnesses to the risen Christ could find Thomas, they cried: "We have seen the Lord!" Well the doubter would have to be convinced. However, you could not have kept him from Church the following Sunday! Sure enough, the Lord appears again, and Thomas gasps: "My Lord and my God!"

Thomas had expected the death of the Lord. It says in John 11:16 that he was willing to go with Jesus "that we may die with Him!" He never lacked for courage, but Thomas was a pessimist! So after the death of Jesus, he went off by himself to grieve, and missed the Lord's appearance.

There is an apocryphal book, "The Acts of Thomas," which says that Thomas went as a missionary to India. There he convinced King Gundaphorus that there was a palace beyond death's door for the king through Christ. The king accepted the Lord, and so Thomas brought Christianity to India.

Doubts have their place! They can lead to the evidence, and to the conviction that what was once thought to be an absurdity is true! A faith like Thomas's is better than a glib profession.

Prayer: Thank you Lord for the testimony of Thomas. Help me to work through any doubts I have, to come to full assurance that you live, and thus I can live forevermore. Amen

Day 337

Psalm 64

Erwin G. Tieman once said: "Nothing influences the quality of our life more than how we respond to trouble!" How true those words are!

- Moses, relegated to a life as a shepherd in a foreign land, used his trials to lead the Hebrew people through the same land.
- The Psalmist, always struggling with difficulties, yet could praise God! Leaving us to look to the Psalms for comfort and hope.
- Paul, who faced a life of adversity, would repeatedly call for his readers to "rejoice in the Lord always!"

Think of the persons who have had the greatest influence for good upon your life, then note the sufferings in their lives that they responded to positively.

David, in our lesson for today, is faced with enemies on every hand. He cries out for the Lord to do battle for him. Yet, in the midst of his trials he is able to declare: "Make praise your habit!" (The Message translation.)

Prayer: Sometimes, O Lord, I resort to whining and self-pity in the face of difficulties. Help me to look up to where my help comes from, and find a sense of peace and joy. Let not the sufferings of life overwhelm me, but may I be under-girded with your love and peace. Amen

Day 338

John 15:18-20a; Romans 8:35-38

By the time John wrote these words in the 15th chapter, Christianity was illegal. All a magistrate had to do was to establish that a man or woman before him was a Christian, and if so other crimes did not matter, the convicted could be put to death. Thus John is writing, not of an imaginary situation, but from the realities of life in the last portion of the first century.

Even in our day, though it is not against the law to be a Christian, yet when we walk-the-walk persecution comes! Jesus said: "As they persecuted me, they will persecute you (v.20)." It comes with the job description, for you are after all a follower of the Crucified One!

Further, some persecutors won't change! Thus, Jesus said: "If anyone won't listen to you, shake the dust off your feet as you leave (Matthew 10:14)." Again He said: "Do not throw your pearls before swine lest they trample them under foot and turn to attack you (Matthew 7:6b)."

We will face persecution as we witness for our Lord, but we should know when it is time to speak, and when it is time to walk away!

Prayer: Lord, give me strength today to serve you in spite of the opposition I will face. Grant me courage to be your witness, and wisdom to know when to walk away. Amen.

Day 339

Genesis 50:15-21

Where is God when life hurts?

Joseph was betrayed by his brothers – sold into slavery – leaving his father wondering what happened to him. It looked as though life was over for Joseph! Why go on?!

But in time, God lifts Joseph out of slavery, and he becomes what we would call Secretary of Agriculture in the Pharaoh's cabinet.

Famine strikes in Palestine, and Joseph's brothers come to Egypt looking for food. There they end up before Joseph to plead their case, and face possible death! But Joseph forgives them saying: "You meant it for evil, God meant it for good!" (v.17)

Andrew Murray, author and saint, once wrote some advice for himself in a time of great suffering:

- God has brought me here ... in that I will rest.

- He will keep me here in His love, and give me grace sufficient for this trial.

- He will make this trial a blessing, teaching me lessons He intends me to learn.

- In His good time He will bring me out again. How and when – He knows.

Prayer: Lord, I don't like it when I hurt! It sometimes seems like the end! Grant me trust sufficient to see that you are still in charge, and will bring me out of this in your own good time. Amen.

Day 340

Psalm 136

There is a Hebrew word that is far richer in meaning than the English translations, the word is hesed (HEH-sed). It is often translated as loving kindness, or mercy, but the meaning is more that of an enduring, extravagant, eternal love - without limits. It is at the heart of the acts of God in the Old Testament, as well as the New. It is love demonstrated in the Savior's life, and death on the Cross.

It is an attribute that is seen in the attitude of Ruth for Naomi in the latter's time of trial. (Ruth 1:16-18)

Though we often think of the Old Testament being about a God of vengeance, hesed is found approximately 250 times there - most of these instances in regard to the Almighty. About half of these are found in the Psalms.

When God gave Moses the Ten Commandments, He said: "I am the Lord... the merciful (hesed) and gracious God. I am slow to anger, and rich in unfailing love and faithfulness (hesed) (Exodus 34:6).

In Psalm 136 we find hesed repeated 26 times! For example, in the first three verses it states: "...for His steadfast love (hesed) endures forever."

God's hesed toward you is unshakable!

Prayer: Lord, thank you for your enduring love. Fill me with more hesed toward you and others. Amen

Day 341

II Corinthians 9:6-15; Luke 6:38

Boomerang blessings! It is the law of the harvest. It is the law of love. It is the law of giving.

- Farmers know about it. They sow seeds expecting to receive back accordingly, and much more!

- We experience it in the realm of happiness. When you do acts of kindness to make others happy - it boomerangs back to you, and you experience it too!

- It is true of our Christian walk: we pray, and study God's Word, and we are blessed with growth in the Lord, and other blessings beside.

We have all experienced it, we reap more than we sow!

The Lord taught us: "Give and it will be given to you; good measure, pressed down, shaken together, running over, will be put in your lap (Luke 6:38)!"

I remember her coming up with the other third graders to receive her Bible. Her beaming smile said it all! I gave her a Bible – she gave me something I shall never forget: Joy unspeakable!

Prayer: Thank you Lord teaching us by word and deed the blessings that come our way when we seek to bless others. Amen

Day 342

Lamentation 3:22-26

Two days ago we looked in some depth at the word hesed. Remember it means extravagant, steadfast love, love that never comes to an end! It is the story of God's relationship with the Hebrew people of the Old Testament: i.e. extravagant steadfastness. It is found in the New Testament in the life, death, and resurrection of our Lord: i.e. extravagant love!

In our lesson for today we find the word again: "The steadfast love (hesed) of the Lord never ceases... great is your faithfulness (vs. 22 & 23b)."

Like the manna God provided the Hebrews in the desert, so His hesed is fresh every morning!

In 250 A.D. Felix of Nola, a town near Naples, Italy, was running from the Roman authorities who were persecuting Christians. They sought to take his life! Felix hid in a cave to escape his captors. While praying, he noticed a spider spinning a web across the entrance to the cave. When Felix's pursuers arrived at the cave, they saw the complete spider's web, thinking that no one had entered, they passed on by.

A spider web is as good as an invincible wall, when God is there! Great is His faithfulness!

Prayer: Thank you Lord for you faithfulness to me. (Name a dozen evidences of His faithfulness in your life) Amen.

Day 343

Psalm 68:1-20

Have you heard about Albert? At age twenty-two, in a letter to his sister, he expressed sorrow for having been born! In his growing up years he had been labeled retarded. He was removed from school several times, since the teachers did not know what to do with him. Even the family maid referred to him as the "dopey one." He managed to finish high school, but could not get into college. He couldn't get a job.

Finally, a friend of the family, Fred Haller, felt sorry for him, and gave him a job at the Swiss Federal Patent Office. Inspired by this break, Albert began to show potential. From this humble beginning came forth the genius that we know as Albert Einstein!

In the lesson for today, the Psalmist begins with "God shall arise!" How often has God arose in leading persons from mediocrity, doubt, and/or fear?

Jesus said, "With man it is impossible, but not with God. For all things are possible with God (Mark 10:27)."

Yes, our "God shall arise!" He did so from the grave, and He does so in every life from that which would keep us from being all we can be. Claim His possibilities today!

Prayer: I praise your Name, O God, for the possibilities you bring to life. I celebrate the fact that even in our time we shall see repeatedly "God ... arise!" Give me the faith to believe, and the courage to claim your possibilities today. Amen

Day 344

John 1:6-9; Hebrews 2:1-3a

I had a colleague in Kansas City who was coming back to the city on I-70. He set his car on cruise control. Some time later he fell asleep! He awoke in time to see the backend of a truck fast approaching. He swerved, lost control, crossed the median, and became airborne, lit on his front bumper and began to flip end-over-end! Amazingly no other car was coming, and though his car was totaled, he walked away with only a few scratches.

How often do we place our spiritual lives on cruise control, then wakeup (hopefully!) in the midst of a crisis – having strayed from the God we once loved?

It is possible to "backslide" away from the Lord! (Hebrews 2:1a; 2:3a; John 6:66-71)

On the morning in 1873 when famed missionary, David Livingstone, was found dead beside his bed in Africa, the attendant found his journal in which he had just written: "My Jesus, my Savior, my all, anew I dedicate myself to you." Livingstone knew the importance of daily rededication of his life to the Lord.

Prayer: Lord, this day I dedicate myself anew to you. Save me from laxity in my relationship with you. Fill me with love for you and all persons everywhere. Amen.

Day 345

Matthew 5:1-12

In verse 3 of our lesson for today the Greek rendition would read: "Blessed are those who suffer from abject poverty of spirit, for theirs is the kingdom of heaven."

But I thought that it was those who had it all together spiritually who were the blessed!

Peterson's translation, The Message, helps us understand: "You are blessed when you are at the end of your rope. With less of you, there is more of God..."

John Newton, who was born in England in 1725. As a young man he saw the profits that could be made in the slave trade, and in time became a trader himself. Years later he was convicted of his sin under the preaching of George Whitfield. He repented of his wicked ways. Realizing God's grace, he wrote in 1779 the now famous hymn, "Amazing Grace" - "Amazing grace how sweet the sound that saved a wretch like me..."

A beggar – with an empty cup – filled to the overflowing!

Prayer: Lord, we fall short, but your grace overflows to us! Thank you for saving us from ourselves. Amen.

Day 346

II Chronicles 28:1-15

After the Hebrew people came out of bondage in Egypt, through the Red Sea, and then the forty years in the wilderness -- all as one people. Now at each others' throats, Israel attacks Judah, and kills tens of thousands! The army was about to lead another 200,000 back to Samaria as slaves, when Oded, the prophet, steps in. He announces that the only reason God allowed the defeat of the tribe of Judah was to punish them for their idol worship, but Israel was far more guilty of such!

Devastated by the prophet's rebuke, the leaders of Israel's army take the captives and care for them. They clothe them, and feed them, and bring them to Jericho, the city of palm trees, to their brothers.

Rarely has such compassion been shown toward an enemy in time of war!

Do we really worship Jehovah God, or do we worship the god of materialism? Who is our enemy? Who is God calling us to care for in their hour of need?

Prayer: Lord, it is so easy to strike out at our enemies, and so difficult to show compassion toward them. Help me to love as you have loved me. Amen

Day 347

Luke 23:33-46

The evangelist preached on "Hell and What It is Like." The soloist closed the service with: "Tell Mother I'll Be There."

Wonder of wonders the Cross tells us that the Lord of history would rather go to Hell than to see us die without hope!

On the Cross, He told the thief: "I tell you today you will be with me in paradise (v.43)." Then He breathed His last.

In June 1998 I found a pamphlet that my mother had left in her Bible before her death. It was by Norman Vincent Peale on "The Life to Come." On the cover, Mother had written: "Read this!" It was a wonderful reaffirmation of what she had taught me since I was a boy. I could hear her speaking from the grave words of reassurance to me! It was a powerfully moving moment!

Paradise – Heaven – a Place prepared for you in the Father's House! Think of it, and rejoice!

Prayer: Lord thank you for the wonderful promise you give us in your Word of a Place for us beyond death's door in the Father's House. Amen.

Day 348

Exodus 5:10-23

Prayer is, among other things, honest communication with God.

Throughout the Old Testament, in particular, we find God's people expressing their feelings to God in a very straightforward way. No less so in the lesson for today.

After Moses had failed to get anywhere with the Pharaoh, he prays: "Lord, why have you done evil to this people? Why did you ever send me? For since I came to the Pharaoh to speak in your name, he has done evil to this people, and you have not delivered your people at all (vs. 22-23)!"

We hear similar prayers in David's Psalms, and Job's laments, but it is present in all of scripture.

Even Jesus, the Man/God of Galilee, showed His human side when He prayed: "My God, my God why have you forsaken me (Mark 15:34)?!"

How should we address God? With unflinching honesty! For God knows our feelings anyway, so there is no need to try to hide how we feel. Is it not a part of any good relationship - to be able to be honest?

Prayer: Enable me, O Lord, to be blatantly honest with you concerning my doubts and fears. Help me to have the courage that is necessary for us to have a blessed relationship. Amen

Day 349

Romans 8:12-28

When I went to visit him, his home was dark. It didn't matter to him, because he was blind. He had lost a son ten years before, and then his wife recently. But each time I got ready to go, he would say, "Reverend, before you go, let's sing 'Amazing Grace.'" Then his quivering voice would begin seeking out the tune, as I would join in. -- Friends, I could hear the angels sing!

"The Spirit helps us in our weakness (v.26)." Certainly my blind friend was a living testimony to those words!

"We do not know how to pray as we ought..." Yes, we should pray with honesty (as we covered yesterday), but yet there are times when words just won't come, because we are too overcome with emotions, or are spiritually exhausted. Then we must count on the Spirit praying for us "with sighs to deep for words." (v.26b)

My blind friend had been to the Well, and had drunk of its waters often! I always came away having received far more than I had given!

Prayer: Lord, when I can't pray, pray for me. When I hear the angels singing in the presence of one of your suffering saints - accept my praise! Help me too to drink from the Well often. Amen

Day 350

Job 30:20-31

Two days ago we discussed how prayer, among many things, is honest communication with God. I believe this is important enough for us to look further at today.

In "Fiddler on the Roof" Tevye, after his mule has injured its foot, sighs: "Dear God. Was that necessary? Did you have to make him lame just before the Sabbath? That wasn't nice. It's enough that you pick on me. ... But what have you got against my mule? ... Really, sometimes I think, when things are too quiet up there, you say to yourself, 'Let's see, what kind of mischief can I make for my friend, Tevye?'"

We wonder about such honesty expressed in Tevye's prayer. In spite of his theology which credited God for all the bad things that came to him, at least he was honest. We see a reflection here of the honesty of Job in our lesson for today.

We are prone to tidy up our prayers, for fear God will reject us if we get too honest, but our relationship with Him is in trouble when we aren't honest! God invites bluntness. Remember again Jesus Himself said upon the Cross: "My God, my God, why have you forsaken me (Matthew 27:46)?"

Psalm 145:18 states: "The Lord is near to all who call on Him, to all who call on Him in truth."

Prayer: Lord, let's be honest, for there are times when I am not. Forgive me, Lord. Renew in me a fearless heart that enables me to express my honest feelings. Amen

Day 351

Proverbs 3:5-12

"Trust in the Lord ... and do not rely on your own understanding." (v.3)

A pioneer was traveling through an arid region of the west – dry and thirsty – how he longed for a drink! Finally he came across an abandoned cabin in a valley, and there beside the cabin an old iron pump. The pump had a jug attached, and a note written on the side: "There's just enough water in this here jug to prime the pump. Pour the water in the top of the pump, and pump the handle quickly. You will get water! The well has never run dry. After you have gotten your fill, fill the jug for the next fellar." Signed: Desert Pete.

It can be scary to trust our little to the unseen God. Yet, when we do, we discover a well of blessings pouring forth that we cannot contain! We discover His bounty available to us!

Yes, "trust in the Lord ... and do not rely on your own understanding."

Prayer: Lord, help me to trust, and keep on trusting, so that I may see your bounty in a dry and thirsty land. Amen.

Day 352

Colossians 1:21-28

If Beethoven were in you think of the music you could compose. If Albert Einstein were in you consider the universe you could reveal. And if "Christ is in you" think of the love, hope, joy, and life eternal you could realize!

When I was a lad I planted some watermelon. I plowed the ground, disked the soil, and laid off the rows. Then I mounded up the soil in hills, and placed three or four seeds in each hill. Then I waited. In time the seeds sprouted forth out of the dirt, and produced beautiful watermelon. The water – in the melons – was not dirty, though they were planted in the dirt; because within them was the potential of the bright red watermelon meat.

"Christ in you – the hope of glory!" It is not about you, but about Him! He is what brings your life to fruition.

Prayer: Lord, open my life to receive, as never before, your Presence, that your Life may become incarnate in me. Help me to be a little Christ - to show the world who it is that is in me. Amen.

Day 353

Ephesians 4:17-24

Dr. Paul Brand was training physician candidates in India. One morning he was making rounds at the hospital with some of his students. They came to the bedside of a young patient. The student, who was designated to tend to the woman, knelt down beside the bed, and began to ask questions of her about her condition.

Suddenly, something about the medical student's appearance reminded Dr. Brand of a professor he had studied under in England. Once out of the room, the doctor asked the student if he had ever studied in England. He stated that he had never been to England. "Well," Dr. Brand said, "Your expression reminded me of a professor of mine." The students laughed, and said, "Dr. Brand, that is your expression that he was mimicking."

We were made in the image of God, "created in the likeness of God," Paul writes. (v.24a) Called to be imitators of God - to show forth hesed! (As we examined in devotion #340)

Prayer: Make me like you, O Christ! That others may see your image on my face - your actions lived out in me. May I show forth your hesed to all I meet today. Amen

Day 354

Psalm 95

Occasionally we hear folks say, "I didn't get anything out of worship today." In the Psalmist's day that comment would be laughable! For the Psalmist, and his generation, knew that worship was not something others did for our benefit, but something we do out of love for God! Worship is the giving of our songs, prayers, praise, and offerings to God. It is what we do for God.

In Old Testament times worshippers would bring a dove, a lamb, or some other animal to offer on the altar to God. It was believed that as the smoke rose to the heavens, the sacrifice was being offered up to God - an expression of thanksgiving.

"O come, let us sing to the Lord... the rock of our salvation... O come let us worship and bow down; let us kneel before the Lord, our Maker. For He is God... (vs. 1 & 6)."

What will you offer to God this Sunday?

Prayer: Lord, help me to offer you my worship – not that I may be blessed, but that you may be blessed by my gratitude for all you have done for me. Amen.

Day 355

Luke 21:25-36

We live in uncertain days! Terrorism is knocking at our door. A worldwide financial crisis hovers over us. Threats to us on a personal level by various maladies is ever present. No wonder we are at times anxious and worried!

Jesus said: "When you see these things begin to happen, raise up your heads, because your redemption is drawing near (v.28)."

When I was serving in Warsaw, Missouri, I had a gentleman in the congregation, Richard Anthony, who had served in the army during World War II. One of the things he told me about his experience in Europe, was to never raise up, and look out over the battlefield, for an enemy sniper would be sure to be watching, and you would be killed.

But here Jesus is saying to "raise up your heads." When evil is knocking at your door - raise up your heads! But what Jesus was saying was to lift up your heads to see the Redeemer coming, because He is always drawn to us in our hour of need. Therefore, we can face the enemy with an expectancy of good - for God is drawing nigh!

Prayer: So easily I get mired down in the bog of fear and anxiety, Lord. Thank you for your word of hope that I shall carry with me today. Help me to take my eyes off my worries, and focus on you, my Strength and my Redeemer. Amen

Day 356

John 14:1-6; Revelation 21:2-4

Heaven! Books have been written on the subject.

Where is Heaven?

- It is nearer than you may think! Hebrews 12:1 says: "We are surrounded by so great a cloud of witnesses. Heaven is not off in some distant place, but it surrounds us!

When do we go there?

- Immediately at death. God would not leave us to wait in some grave, but to have immediate and continuing fellowship.
- Jesus told the thief on the cross: "Today you will be with me in Paradise (Luke 23:43)."
- Again Moses and Elijah – long since dead – appeared before the Lord on the mountain. (Matthew 17:3)

What will it be like?

- Like a loving, Father's House! "In my Father's House are many rooms, I go there to prepare a place for you (John 14:2-3)."

Prayer: Lord, how wonderful is the Heavenly Home you have prepared for us! Wean us from things that do not last, and help us to look forward to that place you have prepared for us on Heaven's Shore. Amen.

Day 357

Colossians 2:1-5

Here Paul lifts the veil on his inner feelings. You are able to see the very heart of the apostle. He confides: "I want you to know how great a struggle I am going through for you." People who he had never seen, yet loved!

Remember Paul was in prison in Rome awaiting judgment, and almost certain condemnation from Nero, when he wrote the letter to the Colossian Christians. Thus, Paul could only pray for those at Colossae. But what more could he do if he was able to go to them, for prayer taps the very Spirit of God!

Paul was facing execution for his faith! It would have been easy to give up the cause of Christ, and save his own neck! Thus, he was struggling with the human desire to live, and the fact that so many young Christians were watching: would he falter or not?

We too do well to remember there are many who are watching us. Our actions can either confirm or destroy their faith. Which will it be?

Prayer: We too struggle at times, Lord. We can easily rationalize the selfish way out. Yet, we know that you are counting on us, as well as young Christians. Keep us faithful, O God, for the sake of the Gospel. Amen

Day 358

II Corinthians 4:5-11; II Timothy 3:1-5

There is a sickness in the land more serious than bird flu, or any other malady that can strike our world. It is what Soren Kierkegaard called the "sickness unto death."

Paul writes that in the last days people will be known for their utter self-centeredness, greed, contempt for authority, ingratitude, lack of self-control, love of things more than God, maintaining a façade of being religious without the love, and power. (II Timothy 3:1-5)

Why do we crave the very things that would destroy us? Because we have a sickness that can lead to death.

Friends, it is not up to us to fix this! "You are only the earthenware jar that holds this treasure." (II Corinthians 4:7) That is: we are only the pill bottle that holds the precious cure – which is Christ Jesus the hope of glory!

Broken vessels! Yet out of our brokenness shines the Light that shows the Way (John 14:6)!

Prayer: Lord, I too am broken! I too fall short. Forgive me. Renew me in that faith that opens the door, so the Light can shine out into a world of darkness. Amen.

Day 359

Psalm 91

The Golden Gate Bridge spans 8,981 feet! Located at the beginning of San Francisco Bay, it is the largest suspension bridge in the world. When it was being constructed several workers lost their lives - falling two hundred feet to the water below. Finally, someone came up with the idea of placing a safety net under the workers, so that if one fell he would be caught by the net.

The work proceeded on schedule for the first time, because the workers knew that if they did slip, they would be caught by the net, and their lives would be spared.

The psalmist writes: "I will say to the Lord, 'My refuge and my fortress, my God in whom I trust'. .... Under His wings you will find refuge; His faithfulness is a shield and a buckler (vs.2 & 4b)."

The psalmist is sure of the "net" that God provides to protect him from danger. Like an eagle that swoops down beneath a young eaglet struggling to fly, and catches it upon its back, so the Lord is there for us. Yes, "underneath are the everlasting arms (Deuteronomy 33:27)."

Prayer: Lord, as I launch into this day, keep me mindful of your protective care. Save me from anxiety, and help me to realize that underneath are your everlasting arms - I have nothing to fear! Amen

Day 360

Mark 10:17-23

"What must I do to inherit eternal life?" he asked. (v.17b)

Living a Godly life – wasn't enough – the man was doing that. Rather, Jesus says: "Go sell ... give to the poor ... and come follow me." (v.21b) That is he must surrender his all to the Lord!

Years ago former President Jimmy Carter went with Habitat for Humanity to the Philippines to build houses for the poor. It was hot work. As he labored, President Carter was sweating profusely – his perspiration dripped into the cement with which he was laying the concrete blocks. It literally became part of the wall.

Later, when the new resident was thanking everyone for her new home, she commented on how special it was that the walls of her home contained the sweat of the former President!

This is what Jesus was teaching. Eternal life begins when we give our sacrificial labors to the "least of these" our sisters and brothers -- i.e. when we put our faith into action.

Prayer: Lord, help me to move beyond mere belief to action! Help me to see where you are at work in my world, and join in. Amen.

Day 361

Isaiah 12:2-6

When I was a youngster we would sing the chorus: "I've got the joy, joy, joy, joy down in my heart..." I was thinking of that when I stopped to realize how many times the scriptures refer to joy. It is recorded over 175 times, not counting the 150 times that rejoice is referred to. All this to say that the Lord intended for His people to know joy in their lives!

Note a few of these passages today:

- "Consider it pure joy, my brothers and sisters, whenever you face trials of various kinds, because you know that the testing of your faith produces perseverance. (James 1:2-3)
- "Fill my heart with joy ... In peace I will lie down and sleep, for you alone, Lord, make me dwell in safety." (Psalm 4:7-8)
- "Blessed are you when people hate you, when they exclude you and insult you... because of the Son of Man. Rejoice in that day and leap for joy, for great is your reward in heaven." (Luke 6:22-23)
- "Do not be grieved, for the joy of the Lord is your strength." (Nehemiah 8:10)

How is "the joy of the Lord your strength?" Joy produces thanksgiving, and thanksgiving produces joy, it is a glorious cycle! So as we count our blessings, rather than our adversities, we find strength, for we are drawn closer to Him, who is our strength.

Prayer: Draw me nearer, Lord, for the world is very near! Strengthen me with the grateful heart, so I may sing your praises today. Amen

Day 362

I John 5:1-5

John is affirming that obedience is the only proof of love. If we love the Lord we will do what He asks of us. John adds that these expectations are not difficult either.

Now he is not saying that loving as the Christ loves is easy. For it is never easy to love persons who injure us, do us wrong, insult us... Yet, John is probably remembering that Jesus said, "My yoke is easy and my burden is light." (Matthew 11:30) How can this be?

William Barclay says that a yoke in Bible times was carved by a master craftsman to fit two specific oxen. He would place the fulcrum ring closer to the stronger of the two, so that it would have "the short end of the stick" - it would bear the greater burden. Thus, when Jesus says: "My yoke is easy, and my burden is light," He was saying that He will take the short end of the stick -- and bear the greater load.

The commandment to love, which sums up all the law, is difficult, but never greater than we can handle.

Prayer: Give me more love, Lord, so that the joy of doing what you ask will be with a glad heart. Save me from reluctance to do the loving thing. Make me more like you in love. Amen

Day 363

Isaiah 40:21-31

We have traveled to the Canadian Rockies several times. We love to hike up Johnson Canyon outside of Lake Louise, and see all the waterfalls along the way. It is inspiring!

I once read the story of John Elliott who was making his way through that same area in the dead of winter on foot. At dusk one evening exhaustion and cold began to take its toll, when he came across a vacant mountain cabin. He stumbled inside with his St. Bernard dog at his side. He collapsed in the floor, and, without realizing it, began to give way to the cold. As he was about to enter into a coma, his dog, sensing his plight, sprang into action! He began to paw at his master, and whine, and was finally able to arouse him. Elliott got up, and managed to build a fire. The dog had saved his life!

"They who wait upon the Lord shall renew their strength; the shall mount up with wings like eagles; they shall run and not be weary; they shall walk and not faint (v.31)."

Prayer: Lord, it is easy to fall asleep to the dangers of sin in my life. Then your Spirit nudges me to awaken from my seemingly innocent sleep. Thank you, Lord, for saving me from myself again-and-again. Amen

Day 364

Jude 1-2

Few things tell us more about persons than their attitude toward themselves. Sometimes we want to be known by our titles. Other times by who is related to us in a biological sense, or through business associations... We like to engage in name-dropping. But Jude, in his little letter begins by declaring that he is a "servant of Jesus Christ, and the brother of James."

Jude, Judah in Hebrew, or Judas in Greek, was probably the brother of our Lord. (Matthew 13:55) We know from his introduction, that he was the brother of James - probably the earliest leader of the Church. But rather than elevating himself, he says simply: "Jude, the servant of Jesus Christ, and the brother of James."

Jude was content with second place. The only honor he was willing to take for himself was that of "servant of Jesus Christ." Even here things are not as they seem, for the Greek word translated "servant" was "slave." As a slave of Christ, he would not only do His bidding - whatever that may be - but stake his life in the hands of his Master! (For the master of a slave, we know, held his life and death in his hands.)

As Christians we are to take a backseat to the Lord. We are to be willing to place our all in His hands - to be His servant, yes, even slave!

Prayer: It is tempting, Lord, to flaunt my credentials - seek others praise of me - engage in name-dropping all for my ego's sake. Forgive me, Lord. Humble me that I may know nothing but you as my Master and my Redeemer. Amen

Day 365

Jude 24-25; Psalm 121

Three times in the New Testament praise is given "to the God who is able." (Romans 16:25; Ephesians 3:20; and here in Jude) Here Jude gives a great benediction affirming that truth.

First, Jude writes that God is able to keep us from falling. (See also I Corinthians 10:13) The Greek word here is one that is used of a powerful, sure-footed horse that is able to traverse rugged terrain without faltering. Yes, God is able to keep us from falling to sin.

Second, God is able to present us blameless in the presence of his glory. God's forgiving grace makes this a reality. For we all fall short, and need God's love to cancel every record of the debt (Romans 3:23; & Colossians 2:13b-14).

Third, God is able to bring us into His very Presence with rejoicing!

Go into this day in the reality that you are special! You are forgiven! You are a child of the King! He wants to have fellowship with you! Rejoice, and give thanks!

Prayer: Praise and dominion is yours Almighty God, our Savior and King! You have time and again enabled us to be your people. You have crowned us with your purpose and power. You have brought us into your very Presence rejoicing! Accept our gratitude, honor and praise now and forevermore! Amen and Amen